Playing with My Dog Katie

New Directions in the Human-Animal Bond

Alan M. Beck, series editor

Playing with My Dog Katie

An Ethnomethodological Study
of Dog-Human Interaction

David Goode

Purdue University Press
West Lafayette, Indiana

978-1-55753-420-0 (hardback)
978-1-61249-917-8 (paperback)

Library of Congress Cataloging-in-Publication Data

Goode, David, 1948-
  Playing with my dog Katie : an ethnomethodological study of dog-human interaction / David Goode.
     p. cm. -- (New directions in the human-animal bond)
  Includes bibliographical references and index.
   ISBN-13: 978-1-55753-420-0 (alk. paper)
 1. Dogs--Social aspects--Research--Methodology. 2. Human-animal relationships--Research--Methodology. 3. Ethnomethodology. I. Title. II. Series.

  SF426.G664 2006
  636.7--dc22

                                        2006018367

To Katie,

and to all the dogs that,
from our beginning,
we have played with and loved

Contents

"[T]he dog was created especially for children. He is the god of frolic."

—Henry Ward Beecher

"We can safely assert . . . that human civilization has added no essential feature to the general idea of play. Animals play just like men. We have only to watch young dogs to see that all the essentials of human play are present in their merry gambols. They invite one another to play with a certain ceremoniousness of attitude and gesture. They keep to the rule that you shall not bite, nor not bite hard, your brother's ear. They pretend to get terribly angry. And—what is the most important—in all these things they plainly experience a tremendous amount of fun and enjoyment. Such rompings of young dogs are only one of the simpler forms of animal play. There are other, much more highly developed forms of play: regular contests and beautiful performances in front of an admiring public."

(Johan Huizinga, Homo Ludens, 1950, p. 1)

Acknowledgments

It has taken more than seven years to complete this book, and I want to acknowledge various persons' help and encouragement. Thanks to David Bogen, George Psathas, and Fran Waksler for inviting me to present this research while in progress at the Communication and Culture Seminar at Harvard University. Detailed suggestions by Bogen at that time were quite useful, and the positive reaction of all those attending the lecture was encouraging. Readers of earlier drafts supplied detailed criticism and suggestions, including my colleague Phil Sigler and his wife, Rose Sigler, Eileen Crist, and Eric Laurier. My son Peter and some friends at the Rhode Island School of Design read an early draft of the second chapter and provided positive feedback. Several colleagues at the College of Staten Island, Roslyn Bologh, Bertram Ploog and Sonya Ragir, attended the first public presentation of this work and were helpful with comments and encouragement. Students and colleagues at the Sociology Program of Graduate Center of the City University of New York (CUNY), among others Cynthia Epstein and Jack Levinson, attended presentations of this research given there. Their positive questions and suggestions urged me forward. Long telephone discussions with my friend and teacher Mel Pollner were important in the formation of some of the ideas in the book, as were some lively e-mail exchanges with David Sudnow about ethnomethodology. Robert Emerson's careful reading and comments on an earlier draft were extremely helpful. Paul ten Have's interest in and defense of the announcement of my project on the Ethno Hotline was well timed and eased my way forward. I received some good advice as well from my teacher Robert Edgerton.

I wish also to express particular gratitude to Kenneth Shapiro and Robert Mitchell, both of who carefully read earlier versions of this book and whose suggestions were incorporated into the current version. Professor Mitchell's review was extremely thorough and helpful, as was another by an anonymous reviewer. Kenneth Shapiro's confidence in the project and his continued support made the book possible.

The technical staff of the College of Staten Island was extremely helpful in matters relating to the computer aspects of this research. They included Anita Conte, Mark Lewental, and Tony Gallego. The departmental secretary, Nancy Vega, provided support.

Colin Jerolmack, a doctoral student at the Graduate Program in Sociology at the Graduate Center of C.U.N.Y., worked closely with me on the editing of the book. His substantive and editorial comments were extremely useful in shaping the final text. I also wish to thank Margaret Hunt of Purdue University Press for her careful editing and for guiding me through the final stages of the publication process.

Initial videographic research was partially funded by a grant from the College of Staten Island.

Finally, I want to express appreciation to my wife, who had to put up with all the shenanigans of the past six years; and, of course, my dog Katie, who, as the reader will discover, ultimately benefited little and unfortunately suffered unintentionally as a result of this research.

Foreword
Michael Lynch

Playing with My Dog Katie takes up a pair of rich themes: play, and human-animal communication. The phenomenon of *play* among animals, and between animals and humans, has a rich intellectual history. Gregory Bateson (1972) developed his famous account of contextual "keys" and "keyings" from observations of dogs playing in a park. Bateson marveled at the way dogs were able somehow to communicate that apparently aggressive moves and expressions were aspect of "play" as opposed to serious attack. Erving Goffman later expanded on this example—largely in connection with human encounters—in his *Frame Analysis* (1974). Both Bateson and Goffman treated play among dogs as indicative of a basic theme in human communication, but they did not treat it as a concretely observable phenomenon that routinely occurs between, for example, dogs and their human companions. Vicki Hearne (1987) opened up this phenomenon in her popular book on the "language games" played by humans with domesticated animals. Her vivid account of the routines she developed with her dog "Salty" is highly suggestive for the study that David Goode develops in this book, though it remains at the level of personal recollection and ideal-typical example.

The Wittgensteinian themes that Hearne opened up were deepened in a more recent collaborative study by an animal behavior researcher, a philosopher, and a literary theorist (Savage-Rumbaugh et al. 1998). Savage-Rumbaugh's research group devised an entire environment of daily routines for the Bonobo named Kanzi, who grew up and lived in that environment. The ape's ability to communicate was facilitated, not only by living among humans as well as other chimps, but also by the systematic design of pathways for daily "games" complete with characteristic sites and props for developing performances. Though Kanzi's demonstrable language-use could never fully withstand the withering skepticism of a committed Cartesian behaviorist, it became clear that whatever Kanzi knew and did stood up to such skepticism no worse than the "other mind" of a human-human encounter.

To my knowledge, *Playing with My Dog Katie* is the first truly ethnomethodological study of interactions between human and nonhuman animals.

By "ethnomethodological," I mean a study that delves into the moment-by-moment production of organized, intelligible, concerted actions—actions that are responsible for the recurrent scenes that constitute daily life in a society. To speak of *actions* or *inter-actions* in this context is already to grant that the nonhuman "other" of the encounter is an agent rather than a mechanism that can only react on cue. People who *play* with dogs grant such agency as a matter of course. If we fail to grant it, the concrete details that Goode describes become mere possibilities overshadowed by skepticism. My advice to readers of this book is to put aside general skepticism and to see where the descriptions lead. The key to the descriptions is what they are able to *say* of what the human and nonhuman players are *doing* in the course of a game with sticks, gestures, and vocalizations. If the premise that Katie is a player in the game is denied, are we able to *say* more or less about what goes on?

The phenomenon of human-animal interaction has been of interest for ethnomethodologists for many years, dating back at least to D. Lawrence Wieder's (1980) insightful study of the "chimpers" (handlers and caretakers of the chimpanzees that were used in language-learning experiments). Wieder pointed out that a behaviorist framework was imposed on formal experiments designed to demonstrate animal linguistic ability. It is not so much that the animal researchers were committed to behaviorism, but that they believed that their experiments would be inconclusive unless they withstood the criticisms of behaviorist interlocutors. This constraint severely restricted the interactional repertoires that otherwise took place between humans and chimps as part of daily routines in the laboratory complex. Wieder's phenomenological analysis suggested that chimps and chimpers engaged in routines that presupposed reciprocity and mutual intelligibility, but he did not attempt to convey the kind of detailed analysis that David Goode delivers. Similarly, Eileen Crist's (1996; 2000) explications of naturalists' accounts of insect behavior illuminated the extent to which such accounts relied upon "anthropomorphism" even when they attempted to limit the intelligibility of animal communication to strictly observable behavior. Crist did not deny biology, or biological difference; instead, she elucidated how action is no less animal, and no less biological, than anatomy, physiology, and behavior (also see Hearne, 1987 and Haraway, 2003, on the actual and mythic status of breeds and breeding). However, like Wieder, Crist did not attempt to examine the moment-to-moment unfolding of contemporaneous human-animal interactions. To say this is not to identify a fatal flaw in their studies, but to point to the possibility of an unexploited domain of further investigation.

Goode's (1994) earlier work on communicative practices with severely incapacitated children provided an interpretive basis for his analysis of playing with his dog Katie. As part of his study, Goode spent countless hours observing interactions between adults and children who were diagnosed with severe mental retardation, as well as a combination of other disabilities. Contrary to clinical accounts that reduced the children's functioning to little more than a vegetative state, Goode empathetically observed the routines thorough which, for example, a mother would grasp the child's needs and intentions in fine detail. Less empathetic outsiders were prone to dismiss the mother's sense of the child as mere projections, but Goode took up the task of explicating that sensibility. To apply insight from that study to play with a dog might seem to demean the human subjects of his earlier study, but it would be more accurate to say that both studies elevate the dignity of their subjects.

References

Bateson, Gregory. 1972. A Theory of Play and Fantasy. In G. Bateson, *Steps to an Ecology of Mind.* San Francisco: Chandler Publishing.

Crist, Eileen 1996. Naturalists' Portrayals of Animal Life: Engaging the *Verstehen* Approach. *Social Studies of Science* 26, no. 4: pp. 799–838.

Crist, Eileen. 2000. *Images of Animals: Anthropomorphism and Animal Mind.* Philadelphia: Temple University Press.

Goffman, Erving. 1974. *Frame Analysis.* New York: Harper & Row.

Goode, David. 1994. *A World without Words: The Social Construction of Children Born Deaf and Blind.* Philadelphia: Temple University Press.

Haraway, Donna. 2003. *The Companion Species Manifesto. Dogs, Species, and Significant Otherness.* Chicago: Prickly Paradigm Press.

Hearne, Vicki. 1987. *Calling Animals by Name.* New York: Knopf.

Savage-Rumbaugh, Sue, Stuart G. Shanker and Talbot J. Taylor. 1998. *Apes, Language, and the Human Mind.* New York and Oxford: Oxford University Press.

Wieder, D.L. 1980. Behavioristic Operationalism and the Life-World: Chimpanzees and Chimpanzee Researchers in Face-to-Face Interaction. *Sociological Inquiry* 50, nos. 3–4: pp. 75–103.

Foreword

Robert W. Mitchell

For many of us who live with nonhuman animals, whether in the home, on the farm, or in the field, their ways are a source of enjoyment, frustration, and perhaps fascination. Yet we often don't take the time to look at and think about them, or our interactions with them, with any concentration. They are part of our everyday world that happens to us. One of my cats may wake me at 4 A.M. with cries for sociality, and I may pet her happily purring body wishing she hadn't woken me, but I don't videotape it or write it down—I just go back to bed until it is time to get up.

In this book, participant observer *par excellence* David Goode has focused his (and our) attention on a common, everyday event—a man playing with his dog. At the heart of this book is the exuberant play relationship between David and Katie who seemed to do the same kinds of things over and over again, for fun. One must admit that, when reading this material, one gets the sense that humans and dogs are strange creatures—and made for each other. Could play between other species be any better coordinated? Could players of other species respond as well to each other as these players do? In fact, both humans and dogs are great players, and can develop games with other tamed or domesticated animals with ease. Whether we play better with each other is still an open question.

By focusing on the development of play of a unique social unit, Goode shows that the play transforms as each player gets to know the other player. The players can then turn that knowledge into variations on a theme for fun. Goode's interpretations of Katie's experiences are enjoyable to ponder with him, as our psychological interpretations of animals (and of other humans as well) continue to be vexing to comparative psychologists.

Goode might be viewed as pursuing a relatively new field of study here— developmental ethology. Whereas early ethologists such as Konrad Lorenz offered descriptions of the behavior and psychology of animals in nature and tamed, most tended not to provide extensive study of the same animal throughout its life. Some more recent ethological and evolutionary studies, mostly of primates, have tended to focus on the life histories of animals, for scientific purposes. Goode says, let's just look at and understand this remarkable phenomenon for its own sake (and to elucidate ethnomethodology, which seems to be the same thing). Here we humans spend our time doing something that we don't think much about, and it's quite interesting in and of itself. Why do we humans—adult humans—engage in something so ridiculous as playing with a dog? My suspicion from my own observations and reading Goode's book is this: in a world where most everyday things are under our control, it is enjoyable for us to feel out of control (especially in a situation over which we think we have ultimate control, of course!).

Goode makes clear that his and our interactions with dogs do not occur in a philosophical vacuum. Along with descriptions of his play with Katie, Goode informs us of the conceptual backgrounds behind our notions of dogs (and corgis in particular), animals, play, psychology, anthropomorphism, science, ethnomethodology, and videotaping. He also examines similarities and disparities between his own work and that of others. These sections might be viewed as "intrusions" on the presentation of his playing with Katie, but for Goode (and for others with a philosophical or thoughtful bent) they show that even our everyday actions are packaged with numerous ideas and knowledge that we should attend to for fuller understanding of the everyday. Such intellectual concerns elucidate our understanding of what I suspect most readers are drawn to: the descriptions and images of the play itself. I hope Goode's presentation of Katie-David play produces as many smiles of recognition—of the joy of play and the sheer silliness of it—for most readers as it did for me.

1

An Introduction in Three Parts

As the title of this book states, this is a study of playing with Katie, who is my companion dog. The research addresses concerns of two separate readerships: those from a variety of academic disciplines who study animal-human interaction and animal studies on the one hand, and sociologists interested in ethnomethodology (EM) on the other. While there are some commonalities of method and findings in their respective literatures, these two schools of researchers for the most part have not informed one another's work. The first two sections of this introduction overview some basic concerns of each group in relation to the current inquiry. Highlighted are certain continuities and discontinuities between animal studies and ethnomethodological research. Many of the issues raised in this introduction will be focused upon in more detail in later chapters. The third part of the introduction is a brief background to the study.

Part I. Introduction for Students of Animal-Human Interaction

One way to think about this study is as a contribution to animal-human interaction research. Scholars from a wide variety of academic disciplines study animal-human interaction, including dog-human play. While data for this study was collected without knowledge of their writings, that literature was consulted a posteriori to the data collection in order to make clear implications of this current research for animal studies. The following will introduce the reader to some of the important themes that will emerge in the course of the writing.

It is a curious but notable fact of science that it often produces the opposite of what scientists seek. Most scientists do science in order to clarify and come to a better understanding of some state of affairs, and at least in their own eyes they often do. In pursuing this particular work they produce controversy and competing viewpoints about what can and cannot be established "scientifically" and how. Thus it was not terribly surprising to find that animal studies researchers interested in animal-human play did not agree about what play was or how it should be studied (Mitchell, 1990, p. 197). Mitchell notes that many attempts to come up with a general definition of animal-human play have failed and that the current literature is left with, simplifying a bit, three approaches to the topic.

One view is that play is understandable, intentionally motivated, intrinsically organized and social. This is the approach that the reader will find in the current study's data, but it is important to iterate that the data were not constructed in satisfaction of a previous belief in this approach. Another view sees animal-human play as dysfunctional, perhaps not enjoyable, or at least without function. A third construes animal-human play as practice for real life, i.e., as functional and adaptive in this evolutionary sense. Each approach has theoretical and empirical bases for its position.

Disagreements abound about how to proceed methodologically. Researchers utilize different methodologies to study play and animal-human interaction, from phenomenological to experimental. Mitchell (1990, p. 197), in characterizing the overall animal studies literature, notes a general bias against intentional interpretations of animal behavior. This is a product of the dominance of behaviorism in animal, and to a somewhat lesser degree human, sciences for the past century. This is a big issue for the literature about animal-human interaction: whether intentional descriptions—that is, descriptions of interaction that portray actors as having intentions and inner mental states—are appropriate in studies of animal-human play (or for that matter human-human play). The topic will be taken up in various ways throughout the text. For purposes of introduction, suffice it to say that the descriptive data about our play is thoroughly infused with intentional descriptions. This is the way our playing was "naturally available" to me, without reference to theories or scientific studies of dog-human play (see also the discussion at the end of part 2 of this introduction).

The presentation of the data is without reference to positions found in scientific publications. They were produced without respect to any paradigm or theory about dog-human play. The data were attempts to retrieve the "lived order" (see part 2 of this introduction) of the everyday practices involved in playing with Katie. The interpretation of the play in field notes and of videotaped play reveals heavily teleological (perhaps better "teleonomic"; see below) inferences about Katie's and my play. We are both portrayed as trying to "bring something off" (to use Huizinga's [1950, p. 193] language)—as engaging in play that is clearly directed to some end or that has some comprehensible point to it. Play behavior is not "just behavior," but behavior directed intentionally to some ends. Moreover, it is, I will maintain, primarily social behavior, not the result of atomistic additions of individual behavior and psychological repertoires.

Robert Mitchell and his colleagues have studied dog-human play extensively. Their work will be used to explicate the current data's relationship to the extant literature on dog-human play. Of all the viewpoints represented in the animal studies literature, Mitchell's most closely approaches that found in my data. We both conclude that dogs and humans have intentions in play. We do not claim that dogs, or in many cases humans, are necessarily conscious of or have control over these intentions. We do not argue that dogs and humans have the same intentions or share the same understandings in play. Plus, we share a critique of non-intentional, behavioral approaches to understanding play as "fundamentally misconstrued" (Mitchell, 1990, p. 200)—leaving the scientist unable to account for observable instances of play.

My naive description of play with Katie allowed for language that would imply a certain sharing of intentions and possibly even of mental states associated with play. An important idea that will be taken up in reflections on these data will be to what degree such language implies "actual" sharing of mental states and perceptions of things. The answer will be complicated because dogs and humans can share many aspects of reality, while at the same time the experience of each other's mental lives can never be understood directly. The reader will see that there were aspects of reality that Katie and I shared, intersubjectively, without reference to interior, internal states or experience. In addition, there were "lively inner states" associated with our play, observably the case, but about which no description could establish sameness or commonality. I will refer in the explication of these materials to the idea of dogs' having "dog motivations," "dog reactions," and "dog emotions" that share certain commonalities in expression with those of humans. While dogs and humans can recognize lively inner states in each other, neither can directly know the other's experience of these.

There may not be agreement about the nature of animal-human play, but there have been some useful characterizations of it. With respect to the functionality of play, three types of play have been suggested: (1) play is autotelic, i.e., has no end outside of its own enactment (that is, as "fun"); (2) play is devoid of goal or means; and (3) play is activity whose "real" end is different from its apparent end (Mitchell, 1990, p. 201).

As the reader will see, repetition is often an indicator of autotelic play, and much of my play with Katie can be seen in these terms. To say that play is autotelic is to invoke "an intentionalistic framework" in which actors pursue ends that are distinct from normal, everyday action.

> . . . [W]hen actions have no end other than their own production, these actions are often called autotelic . . . because they are or seem to be performed for their own sake—that is, the activity itself is its own end, rather than some end other than the activity. (Mitchell, 1990, p. 202)

The exuberant and repetitive play described in my field notes is autotelic play. The notes perspicuously lack examples of play that was frivolous or play whose end was different from its apparent end (for example, play fighting). Many of Katie's and my play forms were extremely repetitive—for example, various forms of ball chasing. This suggests that the reenactments were not done solely to achieve the end (capture of ball), but that the throwing and kicking (on my part) and the chasing and capture (on her part) were done for their own enjoyment and as a contest to measure prowess in play.

Not all play consists of the same kinds of things, and different kinds or types of interactions are properly construed as play. As a result, there have been typologies of play proposed. For example, in addition to autotelic play there is play that simulates some other "real" activity, pretend play, which can be done in various ways, consciously or without reflection. There is a developmental hierarchy of play in which each subsequent form is based upon one's having mastered the previous one. At each level, the design process required to engage in the play becomes more complex. It is a typology that moves from perceptual and motor-based play to learned play, to intentionally simulated play, and to what is called communicative pretend play, where the animal produces signals indicating to the other that pretend play is being intentionally simulated. Mitchell and his colleague Thompson (1986) also propose a specific paradigm to understand dog-human play based upon videographic analysis. It is possible to explicate play with Katie in terms of their typology, and this will be done after presentation of the data.

Given the growth of animal studies and books about dogs, the literature predictably contains many descriptions and typologies of animal-human play. Most of these are based upon a theory about how to understand animals and their relation to humans, which is then "applied" to the topic of animal-human play. Strict behaviorists have no room for inner life, intentions, or interpretation with regard to their view of animals and humans. Those of Darwinian persuasion who believe in evolutionary theory are willing to entertain the idea that animals and humans can have similar, or even the same, inner states because of evolved phylogenetic similarities among different species. One position about the different theories and approaches is that there is no one right viewpoint and that methodological triangulation, viewing animal-human play with multiple methods and theories, is the most sensible scientific strategy.

One frequently advanced theory about play is that it is adaptive to animal development, as some of it consists of actions that simulate real, i.e., non-play, activities. We can call this the "play as practice" theory. This would be true of what are called simulative play activities such as play fighting, play chasing and sexual play, but also true of play in *general* in its *outcomes* for sensory, bodily and cognitive development. The proposition that Katie and I played as practice will be taken up after presentation of the data.

Virtually all research and analysis about animal-human play is based upon a theoretical understanding of play. Even the most empirical researchers, such as Mitchell and his colleagues, in whose work theory is highly informed by detailed, direct observation, theory appears to drive the researchers' investigation and explication of play. Science generally, and animal science particularly, are theory-driven. The data presented about my play with Katie and their explications are not theory-driven in this same sense. In the second part of this introduction the reader will see that EM, or a praxiological approach to understanding everyday life, eschews formal theories as the basis for describing or explicating observable everyday events. In essence, this view extends the logic employed by Mitchell (1990, p. 201), who criticized animal researchers for basing analyses of play on evolutionary theory on the grounds that play as a behavioral category appeared well before the invention of evolutionary theory. The current data and their explication from an ethnomethodological perspective take this observation to the extreme. *Play appeared before the invention of any theory and is carried out by players in complete ignorance of any theory about it. A praxiological account of play is thus not concerned with play from the perspective of an academic theory, but instead with describing the mundane knowledge and practices, reflexive and tacit, that actual players display in producing observable instances of it.* It is this main ethnomethodological insight that is explored with regard to playing with Katie.

The data were not collected from a preconceived theoretical perspective, and what the data are after, the embodied practices and experiences of actual instances of play in vivo, are non-theoretical objects achieved without knowledge, or even cognizance, of any theory of play or dog-human interaction. This view characterizes EM and distinguishes this study from others in the animal studies literature.

There is another set of issues related to those discussed above that will be of interest to readers who are considering this text from the viewpoint of animal studies. These issues have to do with the anthropomorphic and anthropocentric use of language to describe animals and animal-human interaction. There is much written about this topic, especially recently, and despite a long history of criticism from behaviorists and biologists, there has been a recent renaissance of anthropomorphism in animal studies.

Again, data were not constructed with issues of anthropomorphism in mind, but they can be brought to bear upon the current discussion. The discussion is contentious, with various groups taking principled positions about anthropomorphism: what it is, how to study it and how it is to be viewed as a methodology in animal studies.

Generally, anthropomorphism refers to the extrapolation of human characteristics to nonhumans. Usually, but not exclusively, it is animals that are anthropomorphically described. Usually anthropomorphic portrayals of animal behavior occur within a story-like format, what Mitchell refers to as "anecdotalism." Taken together "anthropomorphism and anecdotalism create a method of interpretation" (Mitchell, 1997a, p. 151), an appropriate characterization of the written data in this study, which are comprised largely of stories about Katie and me that employ anthropomorphic language. As with other scientific topics, examinations of anthropomorphism have led to differing conceptions of it. Mitchell writes about three "kinds" of anthropomorphism. "Global anthropomorphism (which includes the other two forms) is an expectation (perceptual and theoretical) that things in the world are like human beings or are caused by human beings or humanlike entities. Inaccurate anthropomorphism is an erroneous depiction of animals as having (uniquely) human characteristics (usually psychological). Lastly, subjective anthropomorphism is attribution of mental states or other psychological characteristics to animals (whether accurate or not)" (Mitchell, 1997b, pp. 407–408).

It is the third kind of anthropomorphism that will be of concern in interpreting the data on my play with Katie. The assignation of mental states to Katie is naively present in many of the descriptions of our play, and I knew that any explication of these texts would have to come to grips with their anthropomorphic character.

Because of the general bias against subjective anthropomorphism that has dominated the field of animal studies for so long, there is an explicit concern with the accuracy or inaccuracy of mental state attribution. One can be "wrong" or "inaccurate" in assigning mental states in two basic kinds of ways. One way is "categorical," that is, assigning "uniquely human" mental or psychological abilities to animals. A second way is "situational," in which inaccurate interpretations are made about an animal's behavior in a particular situation. In reading and viewing the data, readers will likely ask questions like, "How does the author know that is what Katie is doing?" or "How does the author conclude that Katie is 'morally offended' at unfair play?" These are legitimate questions about the anthropomorphic nature of the data. While they may be legitimate, they are not easily answerable, or, I admit, even "ask-able."

One has to accept that any description of anything is globally anthropomorphic and anthropocentric. This is simply the nature of human thought and its expression in language and not a matter of which particular vocabulary or language one uses to describe something. Since there is no perspective that one can take outside of human thought and language to describe something, it is difficult to conceive of how one could "establish" the rightness or wrongness of anthropomorphism. Yet such arguments are commonly advanced with regard to categorical or situational anthropomorphism in which the possibility of being in error or correct exists, even if such error or correctness is difficult to establish. For example, the idea of assigning "uniquely human" characteristics to animals presumes that we have a grasp of what are uniquely human characteristics and that we have sufficient understanding of animals to be able to say that they can have these or not. These are two difficult proposals to back up. Similarly, situational error can only be established against a competing description or narration of the behavior. That description usually comes from a "non-anthropomorphizer" who proceeds from different assumptions and beliefs about what is being observed. Given the lack of what one writer calls "an amorphic description," i.e., a description untainted by any point of view, all questions of accuracy or error are matters of competing descriptions based on different belief systems and values, and their differences may be difficult, if not impossible, to resolve.[1]

My own position about subjective anthropomorphism is very similar to that of scientists such as Robert Mitchell, who argues for a new, critical anthropomorphism. Mitchell advances the position that the use of psychological terms to describe animal or human behavior is an "appropriate use of language" (Mitchell, 1997b, p. 416). The question is on what bases such terms are assigned and what such assignation entails. *Previewing the discussion*, in his view, and in EM's, one does not need to inspect another's inner experience in order to say that she or it is angry. One does not project one's inner mental state onto the person or animal in order to make the description that she or it is happy. Instead, it is proposed that subjective anthropomorphism is a form of conventional interpretation of animal behavior that sensibly emerges within concrete situations of action.

> Naïve psychological interpretations of animals depend upon what animals do in particular contexts, such that the criteria for psychological terms can be satisfied if an animal performs a specific type of behavior in a specific context. The same criteria are used for people (about whom the psychological descriptions are presumed accurate) as for nonhumans (about whom they may or may not be accurate). Because naïve interpreters view the criteria for psychological terms as satisfied by specific behaviors-in-context, they feel no need to examine animals further to decide if they actually have the psychological experiences or abilities that often go with the use of psychological terms when they are applied toward people; they simply assume that the animals have similar experiences and abilities. (Mitchell & Hamm, 1997, p. 198)

This describes the basic interpretive process, which other than the presumption of accuracy in attributing human psychological states does not differ between humans and animals. Humans regularly attribute psychological states to other humans that are assumed to be accurate unless found otherwise. The psychological state that is attributed may or may not be "actually" accurate, just as with animals, but it is assumed to be unless proven otherwise, i.e., the attribution is "practical" in ethnomethodology's terms. I think the same is true for animals. One proceeds assuming that one's experience of the animal-other is a correct one until that assumption is violated. Whether animals or humans, we presume our psychological interpretations are correct-unless-proven-otherwise.[2] Our method consists of "utilizing behavior-in-context for psychological evaluation . . . such that . . . behavior-in-context determines . . . or is identical to . . . the animal's psychological characterization" (Mitchell & Hamm, 1997, p. 199). Ethnomethodologists observe that we do this with humans as well.

What does it mean to say that humans interpret animal behavior within context? Arguing in parallel with Mitchell, it means that they rely upon the animal's global bodily movements and expressions of "lively inner states" (this phrase will be explained below) *as they are embedded into some here-and-now interactional structure* to interpret what the animal is observably doing. People read the bodily movements of the animal as indicating what a human might do in that situation, taking into consideration the obvious fact that animals and humans have naturally different bodies and expressive and behavioral potentials. The similarity of actions and expression allows humans to conclude that the animal is doing *x* or *y* or showing emotion *a* or *b*, where *x, y, a* and *b* are all "the same as" or "similar to" a human action or emotion. These readings of expression and action in context are based on a natural ability or empathy. The importance of this kind of ability and empathy for understanding animals can be found in the work of early animal researchers such as Jacob von Uexkull (1934), and is consciously utilized by researchers like Kenneth Shapiro, whose work we will examine.

Mitchell notes that observations of animals produce narratives or anecdotes. Using studies of legal testimony, he properly concludes that narratives have features that exert influence over their believability and the believability of those features, and that they are independent of what may have "actually" happened. Further, he notes that in the same way testimony can be found to be false in a courtroom, anecdotes about animals can be found to be wrong in science. In a courtroom it is known that two different stories can fit the facts, that presumptions made within stories can go unchallenged, and that narrative elements of the stories affect their "truth value." For researchers interested in animal-human interaction, the lesson to be drawn is that anecdotes about animal behaviors cannot be used naively. They must be "triangulated" with other bodies of knowledge and approaches to understanding animals.[3]

That said, this research relies heavily on the constructed narratives of my play with Katie, both direct observations of that play and literary reconstructions of its practices and features. The stories are constructed so as to capture observable features of play and how the players enacted play under particular circumstances. In producing the data, the concerns were indifferent to theoretical matters.

This is a study of a companion dog and her guardian in play, and its findings pertain to that form of social relationship. As it is a single case study, many in the field of animal studies would point out its limitations, especially in terms of the lack of generalizability, even with regard to companion dog-guardian play. While this is a limitation, in actuality the situation is a bit more complex.

Much of my own empirical research has been composed of in-depth single case studies. I am familiar with this form of inquiry, due in large measure to my training in EM, with its focus upon the documentation of the detailed practices involved in the achievement of everyday life. Single in-depth case studies examine social praxis microscopically. Through this lens one comes upon phenomena that are not otherwise observable, phenomena that require the in-depth, long-term commitment and punctilious documentation often associated with single case studies.

For example, in one study (Goode, 1994a) I spent a year observing the Smiths, a family with a deaf-blind daughter. I wrote a thousand pages of field notes about them, some of which later appeared as data in academic books and articles. When I would give presentations about this family to parent groups of multiply disabled children, many parents recognized what I had discovered observing the Smiths and how what I was talking about worked in their own cases. Many would come up to me after the lecture and point out the differences and continuities between their own family and the one I had described. This experience helped me to reach the conclusion that by focusing in great depth on one case, one comes upon organizational features of ordinary life that may be otherwise hidden, but may indeed be general. It is my hope this is true of *Playing with My Dog Katie*.

Part II. Introduction for Students of Ethnomethodology[4]

> The specific aim [of sociological analysis] is, in the first instance, to see whether actual single events are studiable and how they might be studiable, and then what an explanation of them would look like.
> —Harvey Sacks, lecture, fall 1967, introduction

In part 3 of this introduction the reader will find a brief narrative about how the idea to study playing with Katie came about. It will be clear in that description that this research was initially undertaken as a contribution to the ethnomethodological literature. Before presenting the data and analyzing play with Katie, I want to introduce the reader to some of the ethnomethodological themes that will emerge in the course of the text.

Ethnomethodology is a subfield of academic sociology that was invented by a group of California sociologists in the 1960s. The group included its founder, Harold Garfinkel, and Harvey Sacks, Aaron Cicourel, Emanuel Schegloff, David Sudnow, and, somewhat tangentially, Erving Goffman. EM was (and still is) a form of sociology that rejected on the one hand the formal theorizing characteristic of mainstream sociology and the empiricist "measurement madness" of that same discipline on the other. Instead, EM was concerned with naturalistically displaying and analyzing what societal members do in the most ordinary events of everyday life—having a conversation, lining up at the store, giving directions, dying in a hospital, taking a test in fourth grade, crossing the street and so on. It was concerned with, as indicated in the epigraph of this section, how to study these everyday events, how to display them and how to analyze them. In the almost forty years of its formal existence, this way of describing EM's work has not changed.

It is not the purpose of this introduction to overview EM and all the nuances of the various groups that practice it. Suffice it to say that there are many different members of the EM family and that they do not share the same interpretation of Sacks's statement or how to go about implementing it. In this introduction I am going to summarize only some of the basic tenets found in EM that are pertinent to the current research.

With risk of oversimplification, it is possible to say that EM has a particular view of social order. EM sees a world that is composed of ongoing, here-and-now, "lived orders."[5] Lived orders are concrete, actual, and observable events, such as those described above. By "lived," Garfinkel means to say that they occur at a specific time and place with particular interactants. There are no general solutions as to how to organize these everyday events. While members of society have been taught general solutions (consciously or unreflexively), such as how to have a conversation with one another or how to line up at a supermarket, in any real occasion the general social logic needs to be fit to the circumstances, with just these people, at just this location, at just this time, with just these problems, etc. Nowhere in this world can one find a conversation, a supermarket line, or a person playing with a dog *in general*, only particular instances of persons doing these things. EM is interested in accounting for how societal members *achieve* these instances.[6] The term "lived order" reminds us that what we see when we observe an instance of anything reflects both a general aspect and a particular one.

For the most part, EM is concerned with describing what it is that persons are doing when they concertedly create a lived order. EM wants to be able to describe in as much detail as possible the practices that members utilize in conversing, in lining up, in playing with companion dogs, in deciding between a discovery and artifact in electron microscopy, or what have you. Garfinkel (personal communication, 1978) once considered describing his interests as "neopraxiology," and though he did not, the idea is that EM is a praxiological science; it seeks to discover, display and analyze the practices and accounts social members employ in creating the most ordinary things. Detail is thus important in our work, and virtually all forms of EM are characterized by extreme detail in description and displays of phenomena. Ordinary events are only done in detail; they must be displayed and analyzed in their detail.

EM confronted mainstream sociology with the fact that sociologists had by and large not studied ordinary and mundane realities of society in a naturalistic fashion. Instead, sociology employed what Garfinkel and others referred to as "constructive analysis." Constructive analysis means that the scientist uses a predecided theory about social reality and applies that theory to (uses that theory to "parse") individual themes or events. This is called "representational theorizing" by Garfinkel. Or one applies a predecided methodology, usually based upon a theory about social reality, to each topic or instance. This is termed "formal analysis." Almost all of sociology in the 1960s employed these analytic devices. EM specifically eschewed, and still eschews, these forms of analysis as much as possible. Instead, it conducts research under a policy called "ethnomethodological indifference," by which is meant "to pay no ontical judgmental attention to the established corpus of social science. Not to decide in advance what the phenomenon consists of on the basis of prior formal analytic studies" (Garfinkel, 2002, p. 171).

EM is not theory-driven in the sense that its view of social reality requires the analyst to account for it in strictly "local" terms. That does not mean it is ignorant of theory. But EM is not an interrelated set of propositions that allows the social scientist to derive testable hypotheses. It is, instead, a way of looking at social order through everyday practices—functioning as a paradigm rather than as a theory. As noted above, EM takes to its logical conclusion Robert Mitchell's (1990, p. 201) critique of scientists who use evolutionary theory to derive what dog-human play is. He notes that play as a "behavior" appeared before the invention of evolutionary theory, and therefore utilizing evolutionary theory to derive a definition of play is oddly ahistorical. In EM, we would see play as having come into existence before any theories. This is why describing play in its own terms, i.e., terms naturally available to the players as a matter of their praxis of playing together, cannot be based upon any theory of play. Approaching play this way makes this current analysis of dog-human play unique.

More than that, everyday activities are performed without reference or understanding of theories, however many such theories exist and wherever they appear. The practices EM seeks to document and analyze are not theoretical objects and cannot be collected by using a theory. Garfinkel has a phrase about understanding lived order: "nothing needs to be introduced" (2002, p. 191). That is, the collection, display and analysis of the practices of everyday life should be done, at least in the first instance, in a way that holds itself strictly responsible to what is known (consciously or without reflection) and observably done by those engaged in the thing studied.[7] This is what I have attempted to do in chapter 2.

In *Meaning of a Disability*, Britt Robillard, a student of Garfinkel who became a person with quadriplegia, notes that no other sociology could have prepared him better to explain the experience and social construction of his disability. EM's concern for the embodied doing of social life is one of its strongest features and has enabled students to engage in analyses of topics that required sensitivity to embodied practices of mundane life. This same strength makes it a particularly useful tool for analyzing interaction between individuals with very different bodies and bodily potentialities. This was true for my research about children born deaf-blind, and it is also true in this current research.

In addition to the above features of EM, the following points summarize central ethnomethodological initiatives present in many of its studies of everyday life and that emerge in this writing (adapted from Pollner & Goode, 1990, pp. 204–209).

1. *a concern for the enacted nature of social settings*—by respecting but "bracketing" ontological claims made by members and instead observing and reporting upon their everyday, embodied practices, EM constructs a version of reality that is not based on pre-existing theories or empirical research based upon constructive analysis;

2. *a respect for the indigenous*—an ethnomethodological stance generally precludes simple acceptance of extrinsic characterizations of members as deficient, moral or immoral, pathological, or irrational (or superior, rational, etc.). Such phenomena are of interest only as unfolding features of the setting. Rather, EM is concerned with the accomplishments of members in settings, and this often leads to *a concern with the displayed competences of members;*

3. *a method involving immersion and distancing*—all social phenomena can be understood from "within" or "without." Further, there are a host of different intrinsic and extrinsic perspectives one can take about a person, event, institution or topic. At least some expressions of EM, particularly those concerned with specialized, technical settings (scientific for example), or with populations whose life experiences are either unknown or difficult to characterize (persons with profound mental retardation or animals, for example), require the researcher to become familiar with the various intrinsic perspectives/practices encountered in a setting. The workings of these, of the skilled ways members make sense of, manage, and constitute the places they inhabit, are the objects of ethnomethodological analyses. To know them, they require the analyst to be engaged directly with the "object in itself" (to borrow from phenomenological language), i.e., to immerse him or herself in them. *These perspectives and practices can then be articulated with respect to any number of extrinsic logics and practices. EM as practiced thus often involves a series of immersions into and distancings from the phenomenon;*[8]

4. *the individual as an enacted feature of the social setting*—because EM treats the individual or person as any other feature of a setting—i.e., as an indigenously produced, accountable feature of the event—EM advances a version of the situation in which the individual is not taken as given, and social facts are not the additive result of individual action. Further, a lived order is not accounted for through the presence of individuals, but rather individuals are understood as "staffing" lived orders in ways required by them.

This latter point is particularly critical for our current study. It represents one way in which EM construes play a bit differently than most researchers in animal studies. Garfinkel writes about lived orders as providing for the appearance of individuals rather than the reverse. This is significant because much of animal research is psychological and often embraces a psychological or social-psychological view. EM advances a radical sociological conception in which events are not additively composed of individuals with their own "projects" (see my discussion of the work of Mitchell and associates in chapter 3) who come together and are able to achieve coordinated action together to the degree that their individual projects coincide or are coordinated with one another. While driving on the freeway, for example, it is not that individual drivers have come to the freeway with pre-existing individual driving projects in mind and then decide in the course of the driving to cooperate with one another or not. Instead, the actual doing of the driving together, just then and there, provides for what it is that any one of the drivers could be doing. The driving creates the drivers' practices in this sense; the occasion of the conversation creates what it is that a conversationalist could be doing; and in the current case, the actual playing creates its players.[9]

Another central observation of EM is that coordinated action between human beings does not require shared meanings or a shared understanding of each other's inner mental states. The reader will recognize this same theme in the writings of scientists studying animal-human interaction. Even within sociology, EM is often associated with other "qualitative" or "interpretive" sociologies, such as symbolic interactionism, which is an approach to human social order that explains everyday order based upon shared, internalized meanings. EM does not advance the idea that shared meanings are required to organize human social interaction. In fact, in a classic EM study, Garfinkel (1967, chapter 1) demonstrated that the meaning one finds in interaction does not rest on an understanding of the intended meanings of the other, and that the requirement of clarity of understanding inhibits communication (see also the discussion of the work of Clinton Sanders in chapter 6).[10]

A similar argument can be made with regard to the inner mental states of actors. In EM there is no requirement and little observation to substantiate that coordinated social action requires actors to understand each other's "lively inner states." While such states are witnessable features of lived orders, their observability does not mean that they are comprehended in the way they are experienced or intended by the other. This observation is similar to that found in animal studies research, except that in EM it has referred specifically to human-human, not animal-human, interaction. As mentioned in the first part of this introduction, humans, whether interpreting animals or other humans, function as if their interpretation of the other is correct until something occurs to disturb that belief. They go about the world interpreting it while assuming that what they see and hear is what they think it is, unless proven otherwise. Their understanding of the meanings, motives, intentions, and emotions of others is interested and practical, not objective or scientific.

Finally, EM's understanding of method must be appreciated in order to read and watch the data in the way they are intended. This has to do with the idea that methods create results and do not reflect pre-existing, given, objective realities. This theme was also discussed in part 1 of this introduction when we examined the idea that all methods are based upon certain beliefs and values and that there is no amorphic or transcendental perspective from which we can claim objectivity or truth.

For this and other reasons, EM is concerned with being reflexive about the ways it uses methods to construct the object of research. It is explicit in its requirement to utilize methods without naïveté by critically examining suppositions and practices that are involved in their actual employment. As stated above, EM is predicated on direct and close looking at the world, but it would be misleading to think that close looking is a simple or programmatic affair. Its basic requirement, that of being in the presence of the object-in-itself, can take many forms and result in many kinds of analyses. Importantly, the relationship of the data (in whatever form) produced by the analyst to observable features of the lived social order is never simple or isomorphic. The key word here is "produced." Features of social order always require the use of an analytic device (or devices) whose concrete application results in production of data. For the social scientist engaged in analysis, data in written accounts or recorded videotapes (or what have you) represent or stand on behalf of actual features of the observed event. The nature of any research process requires that data, not the events themselves, become the analyst's objects of interest. It is the data's features that are taken advantage of by the researcher and used as the basis for claims of truth. This is true for all forms and instances of research.

Garfinkel's device (see Garfinkel, 2002; Garfinkel & Wieder, 1992; Goode, 1994, pp. 127–146 for a fuller explanation) is a way to clarify epistemological aspects of the methodology of social research.[11] It is a generic device that can be used to describe virtually any research. Its use makes clearer the relationship between mundane, observable, everyday actions and analytic procedures employed to record/describe/display and explicate them. By displaying research as mundane practice embedded in equally mundane social realities, Garfinkel's device clarifies the procedures upon which researcher's claims rest. Figure 1 applies Garfinkel's device to the current analysis.

Figure 1. Garfinkel's Analytic Device as Applied to the Current Analysis

(Lived Order) (Lived Orderliness)	Methodic Procedure	Data/ Rendering Description	Scheme of Detail Techniques of Analysis
(DPBWK)*1	reflecting on play and writing about it as it is naturally available	reflection style textual data (data type 1)	content analyze/use as grounds for examining analytic and methodological issues
(DPBWK)*	ethnography of actual instances of play	ethnographic data (data type 2)	same as above
(DPBWK)*	videotaping actual play using tripod-mounted camera	videotapes of actual play (data type 3)	repeated viewings of tapes—examine tapes for examples of textually defined phenomena
			examine tapes for unnoticed aspects of play
(DPBWK)*	capturing video image in computer to produce still video images and sequencing them	image sequences (data type 4)	utilize images to illustrate textually defined phenomena

1 - (DPBWK)*, the nomenclature in the first column refers to David Playing Ball With Katie as a lived order.

The figure names the methodologies used, the logics of the empirical inquiry, in making play with Katie a researchable object. The reader will note that four "types" of empirical data were produced and analyzed in different ways in order to "collectively represent" (for want of a better phrase) the observable details of our play. The data were produced through "methodic procedures," i.e., any systematic, rationally conceived set of data-gathering activities that are reasoned to encode, record, capture or reflect real features of phenomena under investigation. Through their actual administration, such procedures produce "data," i.e., concrete results of the methodic procedures in the form of *accounts*, measurements, descriptions, representations, etc. In the research process, the data come to "stand for" or "stand on behalf of" the lived orderliness, and the data's competent manipulation becomes the basis for defensible claims about what can or cannot be claimed as having been established, i.e., as really being the case. Data are typically subject to techniques of analysis, by which Garfinkel means the cleaning and graphical representation of data, diagramming, sequencing, modeling, statistical manipulation, content analysis, and so on. Scientific conclusions are based upon what is demonstrable through competently performed, discipline-based, carefully described, professionally sanctioned analytic techniques.

Garfinkel's device illustrates the constructed relationship between data produced by methodical procedures and the details of the organization of everyday orderliness. The relationship is not isomorphic or "objectively" determinable. That is to say, no matter how many methods or kinds of data, or the particular capability of these methods to recover this or that feature of the punctilious organization of everyday life, there will always be an interpretive dimension to scientific data, both in its construction and subsequent explication. There is no way out of this, no objective space, and no amorphic perspective that allows researchers to write as if they had direct access to transcendental knowledge. Yet this should not be taken to mean that all analyses are equally useful or hopelessly interpretive.[12]

One clear implication of Garfinkel's deconstruction of sociological methodology is that its findings must be appreciated as constructed matters. All data and their analyses are constructed for a purpose. Methods, in a sense, capture aspects of the thing being researched selectively according to the purpose(s) of its utilization. Acknowledging and detailing this in my own work is not an attempt to weaken its claims. I am not trying to be equivocal about the value of the current analysis of dog-human play to the sociological or animal studies literature. One of its contributions is in making problematic the assumed and unrecognized epistemological commitments of previous research studies.

It is important to appreciate that EM is a form of research that does not escape its own logic. In presenting this case study as a piece of EM work I am saying that I tried, as much as possible, to observe the goal, procedures and sensitivities associated with this form of research. I believe that in attempting to abide by EM's understanding of social research, I have been able to document and explicate dog-human play in a way that is somewhat different from has been done before. Yet it must be explicitly stated that many of the initiatives within EM are ideals that researchers attempt to observe to the greatest degree possible. They are practical guidelines. Thus, in line with the policy of ethnomethodological indifference, I tried to display and analyze play in terms intrinsic to actual instances of it and not to import theory into my analysis. Of course I have failed in this because such a thing is not possible, particularly for an ethnomethodologist with a Ph.D. What is gained is in the attempt.

Separating what a researcher knows professionally from what he or she knows personally is not easy. What is naively and naturally available to me as a player with Katie is partly a reflection of what I have personally incorporated from EM about how to see the world and myself in it. These beliefs are clearly part of the way I think about playing with Katie, and therefore represent forms of thinking that are not strictly speaking extrinsic to the playing. Yet this begs the question of whether they are forms of theorizing that find their way into the collection, organization and analysis of data. Despite EM's policy of indifference to formal theorizing, including its own and mine, all attempts to account for play between dogs and humans are based upon ideas and language whose origin is extrinsic to the playing itself.[13] While this does not mean that EM is wrong in what it is trying to display and analyze about everyday life, it does mean that portraying lived orders in concepts and language that are strictly intrinsic to them is a research maxim, what Blumer called a "sensitizing device," a way of looking, and not an actual, achievable goal.

In seminars, Garfinkel often said that the structures of everyday life are "only witnessable, not imaginable" (personal communication, UCLA., fall 1975). This proposal highlighted the claim of EM that the social practices of everyday existence are not theoretical objects. They are only discoverable through direct participation with and observation of the scene, process, event, or individual(s) being analyzed.

In light of this, here are two exercises the reader may wish to do before reading the next chapter. While it is not likely that many readers will actually undertake either of them, I intend the suggestions seriously. They are meant to provide the reader with access to some of the details of what it means to display and analyze (DPBWK).

Exercise 1. With "pen and paper at hand," imagine an instance of Katie and me playing ball. Write it down. It can be as long and detailed as your imagination permits. Put it away and do not look at it again until you finish reading the book and have examined the data. In the last chapter you will be asked to take out and read your imagined description again. That reading should powerfully demonstrate that the social order of things is "only witnessable, not imaginable."

Exercise 2. If you own a dog, or if you can otherwise arrange to play with one, do so. Take notes and some videotape if it is not too hard to do. You do not need a lot of notes or video. Ten minutes of play is fine. Watch the video. Try and write an ethnographic description of what you are doing with the dog. You can include problems and issues that occur to you as you try to write the stuff down or analyze it based upon the video. This exercise will provide the reader access to the production of the current work in some comparative respects. The reader will be able to bring to mind the embodied work of the exercises. His or her experiences can be consulted as he or she reads along and looks at the data. The reader may thereby be able to attach to the words/video a sense of the embodied details of structures that they attempt to display. By having done the second exercise, the reader will have provided him-/herself with real, observational access to the lived details about which I am writing.

Part III. Why I Studied Playing with Katie

In 1996, after delivering a paper at an international conference on the education of persons born deaf-blind, I decided to step back from twenty-five years of research and writing about persons with this or other multiple disabilities. Some publications had achieved sociological and practical importance (see Goode, 1994a, 1994b), but the exclusive disability focus had resulted in a felt narrowness in my work. I had "burned out" doing research about disabilities and wanted to turn my attention elsewhere.

Having concentrated on disabilities for so long, selection of a new topic of research was not a simple or obvious matter. The choice occupied me for some time. Inspiration came, unexpectedly, in a flash during a walk in the park with my companion dog, Katie.[14] Standing in a large grassy field with some other guardians watching our dogs frolic and play, I asked, "I wonder how many other people are standing together right now and watching their dogs play together?" The woman to whom I had addressed the remark responded, "Oh, I bet you a lot of people are doing that. So many people own dogs, and dogs love to play." The proverbial lightbulb lit up. Illuminating it was the idea of studying playing with Katie.

Understanding that the following language appears contradictory to the idea of analyzing play in terms that are naturally available to the players (I will deal with this a bit below), what I wanted to study was the "lived order" or "lived orderliness" of playing with my dog. As discussed above, Garfinkel uses the term "lived order" as a reformulation of the Durkheimian notion of "social fact" (Durkheim, 1938). Lived order is intended as a convenient way to summarize the ethnomethodological conception of social order, while linking it to and distinguishing it from Durkheim. As described above, "lived order" refers to any observable social arrangement in a society. In this sense, any everyday event is a lived order. The term is a generic descriptor intending to convey that observable social events are structured through preexisting knowledge/practice (i.e., are orderly), but that in every instance such knowledge/practice must be put into play by particular people, at a particular time and place, under such and such circumstances and for this or that purpose (i.e., are lived). Thus, there can be no general solution of how social order gets put together, only instances of persons employing the society's social machinery (ideas and practices) to mutually put together events of everyday life. In order to understand how observable instances of social reality get put together by real people, one needs to get a handle on both socially structured, general features as well as unique, contingent features of their accomplishment. It was these socially structured and contingent features of playing with Katie that I wanted to make observable and explicate.

This prospect was immediately appealing for several reasons. These are what Schutz (1974) would have referred to as my "in order to" motives for engaging in this study. First, it was something I knew intimately and enjoyed, having played with my dog often during the four years she had been with us. I was, in these ways, what EM describes as "uniquely adequate" to the research (see below). Second, the phenomenon of playing ball with Katie seemed entirely mundane and most unremarkable, and these elements were attractive in making it a candidate for analysis. The topic had an immediate blush of "what could be said, and even if anything could be said, why would anyone want to say it?" It seemed specifically unremarkable and uninteresting.[15] Yet I had a suspicion, using a conventional logic, that playing with dogs was something massively socially distributed in American society and probably in most others. As such, it represented a significant kind and amount of human/animal "work" (here recalling Schutz's usage of the term "work" as mutual effort). It was observable work that made up the events of ordinary society.

Indeed, traditional forms of sociological research—survey, observation and interview studies of human/dog play—bear out the suspicion that a lot goes on. As reported in Hart (1995), Stallones et al. (1988) found that 95% of companion dog guardians regard their companion dogs as friends, with a similar proportion of dog guardians reporting "playing often" with their dogs. In Sweden, 80% of dog guardians responded positively to the statement "the dog gives me an outlet for playing" (Adell-Bath et al., 1979). Observational studies (Messent, 1983) reported a rate of 36% spontaneous play on walks with dogs. Through interviews, Turner (1985) found that Swiss dog guardians spent an average of 17.5 hours per week interacting with their animal. However, in a study of Californian pet guardians, Angus (personal communication as cited in Hart, 1995) reported an average of 35.3 hours per week of interaction with their dogs, with 44% of that time estimated to be in play. If these figures are at all indicative, the amount of time spent playing with our dogs is a significant part of our everyday lives. With 65 million dogs owned in the United States and 39% of households owning at least one dog (The Humane Society of the United States, 2004), playing with them is a massively "seen but unnoticed" part of everyday society.

Yet, while studies about dog-human play indicate its regularity as an occurrence, and while there have been many studies of dog-human play, I was specifically indifferent to them at the time when I formulated the idea to study playing with Katie. I did not allow myself to read the literature until the collection of data had been completed. I expected that the data would be relevant to the topics and discussions in previous research, but for methodological reasons allowed these relevancies to emerge after leaving the field. As the reader will discover, many of the phenomena described and discussed regarding my play with Katie are consistent with features of dog-human play described in previous research.

Following the recommendation of ethnographers and ethnomethodologists under whom I studied, to avoid what Garfinkel calls "programmed observations" and to carry out observation under a practical policy of ethnomethodological indifference (i.e., to not produce observations in satisfaction of programmatic definitions or constructive-analytic theories), no literature or secondary analyses were consulted before or during the collection of ethnographic and video data. In the data's production I tried to display "play events" and "matters relevant to play" as they were "naturally available" to players, apparently and observably (what Huizinga [1950] would have called play in its primary quality).

Because of my own professional training, play's events were naturally available to me as sociological, specifically ethnomethodological, phenomena. This is evident in the way I thought about the project as a display of the "lived order" of playing with Katie. This is not an idea that would occur to a non-ethnomethodologist, and I guess one of the complicating factors about "naturally available to players" in this case was that one of the players happened to be an ethnomethodologist. This is also evident in the various theoretical discussions within, or amended to, the written data. That is, even with an explicit research focus on trying to display endogenous, emic knowledge and practice, it is not being proposed that I brought no intellectual baggage to the task. I did not (and could not) pretend to be ignorant as either a player or a sociologist. Thus the research is phenomenological in one sense, in that it satisfies that discipline's requirement that knowledge about anything be produced in the presence of the object-in-itself. Yet it is not consistent with another of phenomenology's basic tenets—being able to suspend one's presuppositions (called by Husserl the eidetic reduction) in order to produce knowledge that is transcendental to the individual and circumstance.

Thus, without trying to maintain that the research was "completely inductive," it is methodologically important that it was "procedurally inductive" as much as possible, and that no readings or consultation of literature on dogs or animal-human relationships were undertaken until the collection of ethnographic and video data was completed.

Studying play with Katie accomplished several things. It allowed me to examine a very common and massively distributed social phenomenon. It permitted me to analyze something that I found intrinsically enjoyable and that I "knew" already from the inside as a practitioner, although the nature of this knowledge up until the decision to do research was *praktognosic*.[16] Also, it let me distance myself from something in which I was naturally immersed. As stated above, this possibility of deep immersion in a phenomenon, followed by a radical distancing from it—in this case through ethnography, autoethnography and videotape analysis—is part of the practice of EM. Through these procedures I hoped to produce a work that would be of value to its students as well as those interested in dog-human interaction.

2

Playing with Katie

"Ethnomethodology is applied Ethnomethodology."
—Harold Garfinkel (2002, p. 114)

The analysis will display the observable details of play with a companion dog in a particular case. The animal in question has a breed and biography. Information about breed and biography bears upon our understanding of play and interpretation of play. Before proceeding with a detailed display and analysis of playing with Katie, it is important that the reader have some appreciation of these factors.

Personal History

The following are notes (made 8/30/96) about meeting and purchasing Katie.

Katie is a Welsh Pembroke corgi female who was whelped on September 9, 1992 at Tracey's K&J Kennels in Fair Grove, Missouri. Her mother, Rippee's Amanda Jane, and her father, L-S Monty Montana, were bred from English champion dogs. Katie is thus fairly representative of her breed, both in form and temperament.

Tracey's K&J Kennels turned out to be a large supplier of puppies to pet shops around the country—in other words, a "puppy mill." My family had researched buying dogs and we decided that if we were to buy a dog, one bought directly from a breeder was what we were interested in. Buying from a pet shop was consistently not recommended by books on dog guardianship, guardians to whom we talked, or by the Pembroke Welsh Corgi Club of America. In fact, the club publishes a newsletter in which I found a request to notify the club of any corgis found in pet stores so that they could be rescued. We had seen one or two in pet shops in New York, but they were not yet common in 1992.

On January 24, 1993 we found ourselves walking with friends in New

York City. We all decided that we would go and visit a pet store to see the animals; our friends were interested in cats. When I walked in, I immediately spotted a corgi sharing a cage with another dog whose breed I did not recognize. My wife and son wanted to see the corgi, and I also, since this was the first I had seen that looked "right" according to the breed standard.

The dogs were shown in an elevated pen, and when the corgi pup was let loose in this pen she was full of energy, completely out of control, absolutely unfocused and unresponsive to us. Apparently she was just very happy to be out of her cage. It took a good ten minutes for her to calm down enough to even interact with us or with Vivian, the handler from the shop. The dog was a cute but not overly friendly pup that apparently wanted to escape the pen and run away. She was really a handful. The handler explained that the dog had arrived in early November and had been in the shop since. Like other herding group dogs, she had a lot of energy and was very tired of being in her cage. (In retrospect, I can comment that this is an almost inhumane thing to do to a corgi.) Vivian told us that she would give us a great price if we wanted her, so that she could get her out of the shop and into a good home.

While I had misgivings about even considering such a wound-up animal, my wife and son wanted her. My son was on the verge of tears when I told Vivian to put her back in the cage. My wife looked at Peter and then at me with a clearly disapproving expression, and I told Vivian to bring the animal back. My wife and I, realizing the seriousness of the purchase, conferred for some time. In the end I conceded and we bought the dog, whose gender, I must confess, we did not even remember at the time of our decision (I had to check after we had left the shop). We had violated virtually every rule and procedure I had learned about buying dogs, but luckily have never suffered any consequences for our lack of judgment. Katie turned out to be a basically well-behaved lady and a wonderful house pet. Admittedly she can be a bit ill-tempered, and occasionally she displays unusual behaviors, probably resulting from her early breeding and confinement; but all in all she is a devoted and loyal family pet. Much of this is due, I think, to the strength of her breed.

The Welsh Pembroke Corgi

As one observer of dogs put it,

> so far as I know no one has yet been accused of "breedism" when speaking ill of a Black Lab or a German shepherd. We expect dogs to live up to their reputation and to express their identity. Commenting on a dog's behavior in relation to its breed is understood within the paradigm of identity/reputation, whereas commenting on a person's behavior in terms of ethnicity is understood within the paradigm of stereotyping. (Michalko, 1999, p. 133)

While the exact history of any particular breed may be uncertain, most dog trainers and many companion dog guardians take the notion of breed completely seriously. Their dogs are often described in terms of how their behaviors compare with that of the standards and expectations for that breed (see chapter 5 for a discussion of the Victorian origin of many modern breeds).

A prevailing account of the origin of the Pembroke Corgi holds that it arrived in Wales in 1107 with Flemish weavers (see note 17 for two newer stories). These dogs interbred with local goose herding dogs, and hence the origin of the breed. The word "corgi" is derived from the Welsh "corcci," meaning "dwarf dog."[1] The breed's ancestry may include spitz, schipperke, keeshond, and chow chow. They were bred to be working dogs (as all breeds would have been in the twelfth century), and in the American Kennel Club groups they are classified in the herding group. In Wales they worked on farms as guard dogs, "reverse goose herders" and "ratters." Two related types of corgis emerged— the Pembroke and the Cardigan, each referring to different parts of Wales and to slightly different anatomical and psychological characteristics. Eventually, with the introduction of sheep and cattle, corgis were used to herd these species as well. They were renowned for their stamina, speed and strength, given their small size. The average female corgi is about 25 pounds and 10–12" at the withers, about Katie's size.

Corgis were introduced in the United States as working and show dogs in the middle of the twentieth century. They are still used today in both of these capacities. Within the past ten years, they have become quite popular as house companion dogs. In New York City one sees the breed on the street increasingly. There are many reasons for this, marketplace and otherwise.

Knowing Katie as well as I do, I believe it is important to appreciate that she is an example of a breed of dogs created to work. Corgis continue to be used as working dogs on farms and ranches. The following excerpts from Harper (1994) indicate their capacity for, and intensity during, work. She cites a description, provided to her by Lynn Brooks, of how corgis were used in the 1970s at her Wisconsin Angus cattle farm. It illustrates the kind of work of which this breed is capable. Dogs in groups of three to six were used. Brooks writes,

> If we want a particular animal or animals put somewhere, the dogs when sent will usually rush the cow or cows to get them moving. They will circle at a run with what seems like wild, uncontrolled foolishness and drive the cow where it's supposed to go. Often one or another of the dogs will lead the cattle, cavorting and teasing, which entices the lead cow to chase it. Often cows with calves or bulls will get in a fence corner or against a building and turn to face the dogs, lower its head and refuse to move. This is about the only time the Corgis do bite and then they will occasionally draw blood.

As for ducking flat [the theory that corgis avoid being hit by cattle hooves by ducking flat to the ground], I have yet to see one do it. Animals do not kick that high and they are fairly accurate in hitting what they kick at. I'm sure that a dog that practiced this method would be in a constant state of injury. Our dogs depend upon their quickness and agility to keep out of flying hooves' way. They dash and dart around, always on the move and barking. They are absolutely fearless, taking on the biggest of bulls, if asked. (Brooks as cited by Harper, 1994, p. 141)

Another example, a champion corgi who "retired" from dog show competition to farm life, will help me make an important point about the breed generally, and Katie particularly. An amazing description of the working nature of the Pembroke corgi breed, and perhaps of their "reputational character," can be found in a letter from Thelma Gray to the British Gazette *Pure Bred Dogs* in 1952, in which she tells of the exploits of her Pembroke, Chateau Rozavel Golden Corn.

It will amuse you to know that since we started the farm, Golden Corn has become a super farm dog. She fetches all of the cows daily as if she had done it all her life, and is so crazy to do so that we can't keep her in; she scales a five and six foot wall to get out when she knows milking time is near. When we were threshing out a few Ricks of corn she killed over 200 rats and mice, and was so worn out by the end of the day that she quite literally could not stand, but by 8 A.M. next morning was chewing at her kennel door to get out and be on the job again. Nothing remarkable in this, of course, excepting that for a bitch that has lived in a kennel and show life until eight years of age, to take to farming in such a big way, is a tribute to the inborn abilities of the breed and sock in the jaw for the people who say that show dogs have no brains. She is still one of the leading Chs. [sic] With her eight Challenge Certificates. (Harper, 1994, p. 143)

There are many similar examples in Harper's book. The descriptions of working corgis convey their utter seriousness and intensity while so engaged. They point to "work" as having particular and powerful significance to these animals. Both accounts show the agility, intelligence and courage of the working corgi. The same willingness to take on large animals, even head on, is something I have noted about Katie. There was a particular incident in the park in which she charged a very large male deer that had become agitated, felt cornered, and was about to charge back at Katie. Although ill-advised from the point of view of personal safety, this kind of behavior indicates what Vicki Hearne calls "responsibility of a high order." Many authors characterize corgis as incredibly fearless and performing physically well beyond what one might expect based upon size and build. As the reader will see, the working nature of the corgi bears upon the description and analysis of playing with Katie.

Today most corgis are companion dogs. The breed is probably most well known as Queen Elizabeth's companion dogs. She was always very fond of corgis, was often seen traveling with them, had them in her children's nursery as companion dogs, and continues her association with them to this day. Corgis love children, children love them, and as long as the dogs are trained not to nip, they make very fine family companion dogs. Corgis have a reputation of being playful, insistent (strong-willed, they are considered generally "hard dogs" rather than "soft dogs") and with a penchant for showing off. Katie has the above attributes. She is in this sense representative of her breed. She is an exemplar of a working breed living in the situation of a household companion dog.

The details of her history and breed are reflected in how I understand Katie. She was fifteen weeks old when we bought her, the product of puppy mill and pet store life. As with many such dogs, it is doubtful she was handled and socialized by humans much before we got her. She was never really affectionate, never our baby, and did not bond with us perhaps as she would have if we had gotten her when she was a very little pup. Without direct and ongoing observation, it is difficult to determine the origin of her temperament or to attribute it to age or any other factor. Whatever its origin, she is not oriented to petting or cuddling, perhaps with the exception of our son Peter, with whom she will occasionally sleep and snuggle. She rarely sits on our laps, or next to us so we can stroke her. In fact, when she was younger she appeared to tolerate our strokes, rather than enjoy them. We know other corgis that are not at all like this, and at age ten she has begun to seek affection a bit more than in the past.

With all one can know about a dog's breed and history, it is still the case that every dog is a unique being that cannot be fully explained by breed or life experiences.

> Somewhere in this web of nature, breed, and training lurks the feature of personality. Behind the idea of "just a dog" exists the particular, individual personality—a dog like no other dog. (Michalko, 1999, p. 135)

This is of course true for Katie and, just as for people, so it is hard to know what to attribute to what (see also Shapiro, 1990, p. 189).

A final matter germane to introducing the reader to Katie as my ball-playing partner has to do with how she learned to play retrieve with a ball, something that occurred before we got her. From the first time I threw the ball for her I could see that this was not a new experience. Because Katie was such an avid ball player, my wife Diane and I wondered why and where she learned to play ball (see Appendix B-II: Peter's Picture of Katie for an artistic impression of Katie's intensity). Katie was from the outset a ballplayer of a certain type, compulsive and completely serious about her play. This was so much the case that before I had begun to research our play I had thought about these matters.[2]

However, the consequence of not knowing the details of her play history means that the current analysis cannot address how play was originally learned or generated, or how such learning may have affected our play.

Locating the Phenomena of Play: Structures, Orders, and Motifs

There are two types of text that are included in this section. The autoethnographic text, written at home, reflects on occasions of play with Katie (data type 1). These reflections are detailed, sometimes based upon observations of play that had occurred earlier that day, and sometimes just based upon what I generally knew about the aspect of play about which I was writing. I went back to these descriptions over and over again, adding details and reflections when I felt it made the account of play more coherent and comprehensive. This procedure resulted in a "general production account" of play with Katie—a description based upon the accumulated observations of our history of playing, but divorced from an attempt to display any actual specific occasion of play or to analyze such an instance. That is, the historical particulars of our mutual play were constructed through ethnographic observation and recall data. I refer to this kind of data as "autoethnographic." Because autoethnographic data were produced in this way, through multiple occasions of writing, and occasionally about no particular occasion of play, notes are not dated.

The other type of text, linked specifically by date to a particular occasion of observation, is also presented (data type 2). This type of text is dated and presented as an ethnographic field note, which means that the writing took place immediately after a particular occasion of play and was an attempt to represent some aspect of that actual play, as in the fashion of an ethnographer.

As stated above, in partial fulfillment of the requirement of ethnomethodological indifference, no analysis of videotaped data was undertaken during the writing of the autoethnographic text. After completing the data collection phase of the study, I began to view tapes. Part of the methodological reflections include notes dealing with the use of videotaping in documenting our play together.

At times, the text references visual data in the form of sequenced captured images taken from videotaped play (data type 4). The reader is invited to inspect the sequenced images and watch the videotape sequences as a way to directly inspect recorded visual features of our play together.[3]

Locating Playing Ball with Katie

[H]istory informs the experience of a particular animal whether or not it can tell that history. Events in the life of an animal shape and even constitute him or her. . . [My dog] is an individual in that he is not constituted

through and I do not live toward him as a species-specific behavioral repertoire or developmental sequence. More positively, he is an individual in that
he is both subject to and subject of "true historical particulars"... I cannot
replace him ... for he is a unique being. (Shapiro, 1990, p. 9)

As a practical matter, playing ball with Katie can be described as an endlessly
elaborated-upon theme of everyday life, these elaborations being a mutually
constructed affair between her and me. Katie, as a matter of her own displayed
preference, makes playing ball the primary activity of interaction with me, Diane,
or whoever else will "listen" to her requests for play. Strictly speaking, Katie's
interest in ball playing, and specifically the throw-and-retrieve activities associated with ball playing, is not confined to spherical objects; although she does
evidence a preference for these, she will also participate in fetch games with
other objects, such as rolled-up socks, plastic bones, sticks, and plastic play toys.
While much of this writing is primarily concerned with playing ball (or "bally," as
we use the word with Katie), it may also make reference to similar forms of play
with other objects. As described in the epigraph to this section, any occasion or
instance of play can be said to have a history for us, since I have owned Katie
for over three years and we have built up quite a repertoire of play activities.
Each instance can also be said to consist of elaboration of "here and now"
possibilities of play with just this object (i.e., how plastic bones tumble, while
tennis balls roll), under just such weather conditions, in just this space, but also
reflecting the ongoing and cumulative nature of our mutual play biography, i.e.,
"true historical particulars."

Thus, for example, it has been possible to find ourselves in what we both
would regard as very poor play conditions with very meager possibilities for
Katie, but to nonetheless find her highly motivated to play because we have
been unable to do so for some time. This kind of situation occurs in the winter
or summer when weather may make outdoors play problematic. After such a
spell of bad weather, the first day I take her to the neighborhood park to walk
and play will often result in poor play conditions but with a highly motivated
player. Katie is still a young and vigorous animal, and I can remember many a
similar occasion in my own youth, playing basketball in the early spring and
coming in with frozen fingers. Under whatever conditions, any instance of play
with Katie will reflect our specific individual biographies as well as our mutual
biography as co-players. We, as many ballplayers who play with each other
regularly, have gotten to know each other's moves well over time and developed strategies in response to each other's new moves. The specific organization of any occasion of play will reflect what we have brought individually to
the game as well as this progressive, mutually shared history of our play together, its "event biography" so to speak, in the long term and immediate senses.

The Routines of Play

Normally Katie will sleep on the end of our huge California king-sized bed. In the morning she waits for me to wake, pick her off the bed, take her downstairs and let her out the front door to do her morning business. This she will do while I make my coffee. When I open the front door the second time, there is the expectation on her part that I will have a ball with me to play our games (when I come out without a ball then an alternative routine involving play with a stick is suggested by Katie). From this time on, so long as I am at home, Katie expects me to play with her regularly and shows me this by either presenting me with balls that have been left around the house, or by staring, barking and sometimes whimpering at the drawer in the kitchen where the balls are kept. From the moment I open the front door for the second time in the morning, I am an available playmate to her, at least by her reckoning. Although this availability is not constant, she will sleep away much of the day while my wife and I work in our rooms. When we are not working, she is often demanding that Diane or I play ball with her. She is so incessant that a friend of mine, with whom I left Katie while I went on a trip, said he would need shoulder surgery from throwing "the bally" for two weeks. When I let her out at night to do her nighttime business before bed and she happens to find a ball, she will wait for me with ball in mouth, no matter how late. Next to eating, Katie lives for ball.

Play orders/structures/motifs[4]
The following is a "production account" of our play as displayed in autoethnographic texts, ethnographic data, videotapes and sequenced video-captured images.

As a routine matter, the play with Katie consists of variations on the theme of fetch, coupled with the additional theme of getting the ball past Katie, as in the human games of football, basketball, or soccer.

Getting the ball past Katie
In one common variation, Katie will present the ball to me by releasing it at my feet and getting into a "ready to play" position. I try to roll or kick it past her, to get it by her so that she has to chase after it, and she tries to stop me from rolling it by her. When I use my feet to get the ball past her I call the game "doggie soccer," having made up that variant of play one day to make things more interesting for Katie. (See sequences 2 and 3 on the CD; SOCCER A contains JPGS SOCCERA-1–15 and SOCCERA.AVI; SOCCER B has SOCCERB-1–13 and SOCCER B.AVI. Both sequences are further described on page 161, and images of SOCCERA are printed on pages 167–171.)

If the reader views the video sequences he or she will see instances of the kind of play to which I am referring. The videos are offered as recorded exemplars of the matters described in the text. They are meant to link the text to concrete, particular instances of play. At the same time, these segments have limited value to the reader. For example, there is sometimes insufficient detail and context for the reader to employ them as empirical data to analyze. Even interpretation and analysis of the original videotapes, with their relative good quality, long duration (some sessions would last a half an hour) and intact audio track, would still be difficult for the reader. I will explore some of the reasons for this below.

In the sequence recorded as SOCCER A, Katie and I are standing in front of my house on the driveway, which is the play surface for all the recorded instances of play in this study. At this time the play surface is covered with leaves fallen from surrounding trees (see below on field of play and conditions of play). The fourteen-second sequence begins with me standing with both hands in my pockets, a demeanor indicating a relaxed attitude of play. Katie comes from left of screen and energetically presents the ball to me for play by trying to place it between my knees. This is a common form for Katie to use to present the ball for play, and she tries several times to insert the ball between my knees in this instance. I fail to hold the ball and it drops from between my legs. I walk toward the ball and control it with my feet, Katie moving along with me and apparently monitoring my bodily positioning. Using my feet I bring the ball back "soccer style" to approximately the same spot at which Katie initially presented it for play. Then there is a series of quick and mutually coordinated bodily movement on my part and hers. Observably, I am attempting to fake her out of position, and she is following my movements carefully by monitoring my torso and waist. It is noteworthy that she does not look at my feet or the ball during the time I am attempting to misdirect her; she watches the direction of my waist. This is a common feature in much of the forms of play that involve the use of my legs/feet to strike the ball. It is an important, defining and easily witnessable matter in this sequence and in the next that each player is, to again utilize Huizinga's (1950) formulation, "trying to bring something off." My attempts to put Katie out of position are vigorous, including jumping off the ground, turning my torso deceptively and feigning kicks with my legs and feet. Katie's moves, made to defeat my efforts, are equally energetic. Katie does not fall for my feints and deceptions, releasing for pursuit only after she sees the ball has left my foot.

In SOCCER B we see another simple example of doggie soccer. The play is midstream. Katie enters the frame from the right, having already retrieved a previous kick. She is panting. She approaches between my legs, hesitates for a couple of seconds and then drops the ball between my legs. This invitation for play, with Katie waiting a bit before dropping the ball, is common in situations when she has already exerted herself strenuously in her pursuit and captures. I gain control of the ball and Katie "shadows" my movements as I do so. I begin a series of feints and positional changes that resemble those of the previous sequence except that I advance forward up the driveway as I make them, like an offensive soccer player moving the ball upfield against a defender. There is "witnessable intent" within these movements, intent to get Katie out of place and to pass her with the ball when I kick it. During this sequence Katie is intensely shadowing my movements. She watches my waist carefully and moves and shifts her body in response to the direction of my waist (unless you are an accomplished soccer player you cannot kick a ball in a direction you do not face; at least I cannot). She maintains her position in front of me, thwarting my efforts to fake her out. She begins to lean her weight backwards as she anticipates my kick. It is evident in her movements that she is making game moves in anticipation of the kick. Once the ball is kicked, her objective is, judging from what she does, to pursue the ball with the most efficient and efficacious movements possible.

In both sequences, the movements of the players resemble those of offensive and defensive soccer players. Of course, that way of describing them and labeling them is metaphoric, not literal. While the basic project or motif is the same, i.e., for the one player getting the ball past the other, the rules and game of soccer have nothing to do with our play. "Doggie soccer" is a convenient gloss to summarize the familiar look of the play to me, given my awareness of the sport soccer. Another part of doggie soccer that I describe below is where Katie shifts from the role of field defender to that of goalie. Again, the naming of that form of play with the word "soccer" is not meant literally.

In the following variations, Katie and I play this same motif of "get the ball past me" that we saw in the two previous segments (see on the CD sequence 10: SHADOWINGA-1–10 (also printed on pages 174–177) and SHADOWINGA.AVI; and sequence 11: SHADOWINGB-1–17 and SHADOWINGB.AVI).

In SHADOWINGA, a short sequence picked up midplay, Katie has already dropped the ball between my legs and is waiting for me to respond. I am standing and Katie is clearly focusing on my body during this sequence, and not looking directly at the ball. As the sequence progresses we see several attempts on my part to "fake out" Katie. While only eleven seconds long, the sequence illustrates well the intensity of our play, with very many "offensive" feints on my part and extremely quick and intense defensive reactions on Katie's. At around six seconds into the sequence I try to kick the ball and miss-strike it. This is an example of a missed or bad kick. While Katie notices the miss she does not react, maintaining her concentration on the orientation of my body to the ball. She focuses on my bodily orientation throughout the sequence and adjusts to that orientation with her own body until her release to pursue the ball at the end of the sequence.

SHADOWINGB begins with a clear presentation of the ball for play by Katie. She does this in the opening sequence by running up to me and dropping the ball between my legs. She proceeds to shadow my movements in a manner similar to SHADOWINGA, perhaps even more focused in this sequence on my bodily orientation. She rarely looks down at the ball at all during this sequence of play. In this particular instance of play I am less energetic and do not make as many fast feints as I do in the other sequences I have asked the reader to examine. I am less committed with my bodily orientation and Katie appears to maintain a similar orientation, staying close to my midline and leaning neither to one side or the other. Towards the end of the sequence, just before striking the ball, I place the ball under my foot and control it there, moving my foot back and forth. This is a particularly problematic move for Katie to react to because the possibility exists that I could kick it any direction from that position. There is no way for her to anticipate my next move. The particular kick I use employs the knowledge that "ball under the foot" is a game move to which Katie orients, and finds problematic. After feinting with the ball under foot, I quickly take that foot off the ball and I kick it with the opposite one.

In "doggie soccer" one can see in Katie's movements that she is cued to the prospective game event of my kick. It is evident in the look of things. Her bodily positioning in these sequences is aimed at achieving, of pulling off, the capture of the assumed-to-be-kicked ball as quickly and efficiently as possible, preferably before it requires a lengthy pursuit. In each sequence she releases from the bodily shadowing and vigorously pursues the ball almost instantaneously at the moment of its being kicked. She is both quick (reacts quickly) and fast (accelerates quickly) in her bodily efforts to thwart the thing that I am trying to "bring off" in the game. The actions of these sequences clearly display the basic object of the game, a most common motif of almost all ball sports. Getting the ball past one another is a way of organizing what can be done with a ball by one player with/to/against another. In these cases of play, because of my standing position and electing to use my feet as the bodily part to strike the ball, the way of organizing this motif resembles, in detail, the human-human interaction between soccer players. However, as the further variations on this motif indicates, there are many ways for humans and dogs to play around with this basic theme.

For example, a non-soccer version of this "getting the ball by Katie" theme occurs when I am sitting on the stoop. From this position I cannot use my feet to control or strike the ball. It is a game in which I use my hands, arms and body to again try and fake her out, misdirect her, put her out of position, etc. Katie's role as field defender is somewhat similar during this form of play, except that the event to which she is oriented is not a kick but a throw. Her object is that she does not want to get faked out by a fake throw, and she wants to pursue the throw in such a way that indicates she is on top of the game, i.e., with maximum efficiency and efficacy of action. Because kicks are along the ground and throws are in the air, I have much greater latitude in determining the specific conditions of her pursuit and capture. The exact thing that I am "trying to bring off" is different than when kicking the ball. This is accepted as part of the game (see sequence 13: THROWINGA-01–06, also printed on pages 178–179, and THROWINGA.AVI; sequence 14: THROWINGB-01–16 and THROWINGB.AVI).[5] There are many different specific game events that are collected by the gloss "throwing the ball" for Katie.

In THROWINGA, a nine-second sequence, we see a very typical kind of play. Beginning with my sipping coffee while seated on the steps, Katie comes from left of screen and energetically presents the ball to me for play. I accept the ball and begin play by hand feinting while holding the ball in between my legs. During this part of the sequence Katie intensely concentrates on the ball and my manipulations of it. In this and other sequences of play Katie's extreme focus on the ball is a remarkable phenomenon. Play proceeds behind my legs. I transfer the ball quickly from one hand to the other, and Katie approaches and watches that move intently. This, like putting the ball beneath my foot, is a particularly problematic move for Katie. I could flick the ball with either hand in either direction. When I actually do throw the ball I use my left leg as a visual barrier out from behind which I could manage a deceptive throw. Katie understands and adjusts to this as a matter of course. I throw the ball from underneath me in an underhanded flick, outside my left leg. Without hesitation Katie turns and pursues the ball in a seamless flow that almost suggests a premonition of its release. Some ball players might refer to this as "being in the flow" of the game. As described above, another version of this seated throwing game is that the ball is simply thrown without expectation on my part or Katie's about the particular nature of the throw. It is thrown just to be chased down and captured. However it is thrown, the object is the same, to capture it in the most efficient, exacting fashion possible.

This is not the case in THROWINGB. Here we see a short sequence in which I am seated on the steps and throwing the ball. In this sequence Katie presents the ball and wags her tail in anticipation of play until exactly that moment I pick it up (this is a common occurrence). What is notable about this particular instance of play is that while the motif is in some way the same, that is, use of my body to project the ball past Katie and cause her to pursue it, there are remarkable differences in the way this project is achieved compared to the previously illustrated sequence. First is the way in which Katie "automatically knows" (praktognosically) that she must watch my hand and the ball in this configuration of play, and not my waist as in the "soccer" forms. In this sequence even the throw is substantially different from the previous sequence. Other than the defining characteristic that the ball is projected with the hand and arm, the throws in THROWINGA and THROWINGB are notably different occurrences when witnessed in their real time, embodied form. In THROWINGB the ball is taken from the space of presentation (not so in THROWINGA) and presented to Katie, right to her nose. She follows the ball as I bring it up from between my legs smoothly. Her intense concentration on the ball is a remarkable feature. (She is the ultimately accomplished player at being able to "keep your eye on the ball.") At around thirteen seconds I feint very slightly that I may throw, but Katie does not take the feint. She waits for the ball to be thrown before releasing to chase it.

Katie's object in play is related to my object of play, to what I am trying to do. I can be trying to fake her out and get her to pursue the ball when I really do not throw it (a rare occurrence). Or I may be trying to get her out of position at the point of release so that she must pursue the thrown ball a long distance, this latter occurrence being a minor victory on my part. Katie feels victorious in this form of play when she does not fall for my feints, as well as when she captures the ball quickly and in stride, clearly evidencing her being "on top of" the game events, that is, on top of my attempts to bring game actions off, all along.

During this type of play I also use the stoop and the rock wall as objects to bounce the ball off, as when I used to play "stoop ball" as a child. When the ball bounces off the stoop or wall, Katie's job is to pursue and capture as quickly as possible (see sequence 15: WALL-01–9 and WALL.AVI). In the forms of play such as those illustrated in this sequence, play boundaries become incorporated alternatively as features of the playing field.

This segment begins with me seated on the steps and Katie presenting the ball between my legs. I accept with one hand while stroking her neck with the other. She is typically indifferent and does not react to my affection. Play continues. I hold the ball in front of her and she concentrates on it. She does not "fall for" a quick feint. Then, holding the ball in an ambiguous position and not indicating clear intention, I flick the ball under my right leg in a way that projects it at a ninety-degree angle to our face-to-face play. The move is "cute" and designed to keep Katie on her toes (i.e., to be ready to move in any direction). The ball leaves the formal field of play and bounces on top of the wall. Katie follows without hesitation its path onto the wall. A normal boundary of play, the wall, becomes part of the playing field. This is an infrequent but unremarkable play event. In play there are all combinations of frequency and felt importance, as in the classic four-fold table in sociology.

Pursuit and capture

In many of our play forms, as Katie pursues the ball she accelerates to the chase and rears up slightly to "pounce" on the ball at the moment of capture. She appears very much like she is pursuing small prey, as if she were hunting a rat. She energetically pursues the ball with absolute abandon and lowers her ears at the moment of capture.

Such pursuits are her responses to my trying to "get the ball by Katie."

This recognizably is what this part of playing ball is, recognizable to each of the participants. Players know they have to approach it with qualities of effortfulness, preciseness, and even courage or daring (as, for example, when she went off the edge of a trail in pursuit of a misthrown stick). She *appears* proud of particularly effortful performances, as if she is showing off.[6] Pursuit-of-the-ball-by-Katie consists of and results in various outcomes as contingent accomplishments of a course of bodily actions in play. These include the ideal run and capture (see sequence 9: PURSUIT-01–19 and PURSUIT.AVI), missed attempts wherein she fails to capture the ball in stride (see sequence 8: MISSED-01–08 and MISSED.AVI), occasionally "dribbling" the ball with her mouth as she attempts to capture while on the run, or jumping up in the air to capture a ball that is bouncing high.

The sequence PURSUIT contains two examples of successful and graceful captures of the ball by Katie, the first in the middle right of the screen and the second on the left. These are instances when Katie pursues a ball that I throw from standing position (I am off screen behind the field of the camera lens). What makes the pursuits successful examples is that the balls are captured in stride without hesitation or fumbling. The reader can watch as the ball bounces up the driveway (in the first pursuit twice and in the second four times) and as Katie times her run with precision, capturing both throws without any hesitation or breaking of her stride.

After the first pursuit and capture Katie energetically brings the ball back to me for another throw. There is nothing remarkable about these two captures of the ball in the sense that they are ordinary, regularly occurring events in our play. They are not to be monumentalized, i.e., made more of than they are, which is a dog running after and capturing a thrown ball. On the other hand, the displayed events can be, and for purposes of understanding should be, seen for exactly what they are to the participants. The throwing and capturing in good form is part of our history of play together. When the throwing and capturing are synchronous, as they are in this video excerpt, they are events of *specific moral value* for both Katie and me. That is, such events are appreciated by players as examples of "good" throws and captures. Further, players understand that the successful completion of the throw and pursuit and capture is the responsibility of both. Mine is to throw a ball that enables Katie to time her pursuit and capture in such a way that an in-stride, efficient capture of the ball is possible. Katie's project in these affairs is to watch and take advantage of my throw in just this fashion.

Sometimes, when she is really into it, I compliment her by saying, "Good catch!" or "What a fast dog." If she does something really remarkable, like catch a ball on the fly, I might say, "That was really great!" or "What a dog!" These are verbal summaries and assessments of her pursuit and capture performances.

For an example, see sequence 10: SHADOWINGA, frame 10 (also printed on page 177). In that frame I am clearly watching her capturing of the ball in an admiring and appreciative way. Two other possibilities for Katie to vary this motif during this part of our playing are for her to begin to pursue the ball and stop or to not pursue the ball at all. These aspects of play are rare, very difficult to capture and have not been recorded.

Another common play occurrence, Katie's mistiming and missing a pursued ball, is illustrated in MISSED.AVI. I am seated in the lower-left screen playing with Katie by feigning throwing the ball. As I stand up Katie maintains her concentration on the ball. She releases to pursue only after I have thrown. Her pursuit is vigorous, and perhaps because of this, she outruns the ball and has to turn back to grab it. This is a particular, typical way of failing to retrieve the ball in the desired fashion. Yet another common variation is when she misses the ball entirely and becomes completely disoriented about its whereabouts, sometimes spinning and turning confusedly as she tries to figure out where the ball has gone. She can also fail to grab the ball in her mouth by running along in what appears to be dribbling the ball (she is actually trying to grab it repeatedly but failing to do so). Finally, she may miss the ball because it bounces too high or too irregularly. Such game events are all "less" or "different" than what is being aimed at by players. Assembled collectively as a category, the above phenomena are "misses."

Simple throw and retrieve and a variation
In another variant of fetch, also mutually comprehended, accepted and produced by each of us, I throw the ball along the ground and she simply chases it; there is no attempt at trying to block my getting it past her. The game is really one of straightforward chase and capture. She chases after the ball and is again most intense and effortful in her actions. In terms of successful or unsuccessful play, we react to these chases as described above. I sometimes cuddle her and praise her for her good performance, but she appears to take the game much more seriously and often resents pats and verbal encouragements. When I say, "Good girl," her demeanor and bodily comportment is as if to say back, "of course I am a 'good girl,' this is what I am supposed to be doing and I need no praise for it." Her playing has this serious, "worklike" character to it. I comment about this at length in a field note (August 27, below).

A variation of this simple structure is when I use the command "Go" while poised to throw the ball. When I say, "Go," she turns to run without monitoring my actions any further. Upon her turn, my responsibility is throwing the ball as a quarterback to his/her receiver. I try to time the throw so that she can catch it in stride (on my end), purposefully mimicking the passer-receiver relationship in football (see sequence 6: FOOTBALL-01–11 and FOOTBALL.AVI.)

In the FOOTBALL.AVI sequence, we begin with Katie presenting the ball to me for play while I am seated on the steps (similar to THROWINGA/B.AVI). She releases the ball to my hands while they are between my legs, and I accept while petting her neck. Katie is again indifferent to the affection. She concentrates intensely on the ball as I bring it slowly upwards. At a couple of points I feign a throw and Katie reacts but does not release to pursue the ball. At the end of the second feint Katie has transferred her weight backwards and is preparing to release to pursue the ball, but does not. Some time after the second feint she clearly turns and pursues the ball well *before* it is thrown. In the original video sequence one can hear the word "go" at the point she turns and runs. This is a common vocal "game prompt" said by me and understood by Katie as a signal that she should turn and pursue the ball even though it has not yet been thrown. The word communicates to her that she should no longer be involved with monitoring the ball or my bodily placement, and that she should run, understanding that I will be throwing the ball "as if a quarterback." We are in a situation like that of a football quarterback and a receiver. In that game the receiver will often run a pattern to receive a pass without ever looking at the passer. It is an understood matter between the two players that the ball will be thrown in a prearranged way to a prearranged time and spot. Similarly, when Katie hears "go," she hears it not only as an indication that she should turn and pursue the as-yet unthrown ball, but also that "go" means that I will be trying to throw the ball in a way that will allow her to catch it without breaking stride, in an efficient and seamless manner. This sets up a kind of bodily judgmental *frame of reference* for both of us within which we can judge play's outcomes—that is, the successful or unsuccessful attempt to throw the ball in a fashion that allows her to catch it in perfect stride. For both players, there is an *aesthetic appreciation* associated with successful attempts. Further, there is a *definite moral element* set up by the verbal prompt. Katie expects that I will throw the ball. She turns and runs, trusting that I will do so. That trust is something that can be violated, and her disapproving reactions to such violation are observable. Play is thus a moral matter for players.

It should be understood that naming this sequence FOOTBALL is to acknowledge the similarity in this particular game motif in our playing with one that occurs in football. As with the previous naming of recorded sequences of our play, there is no implication that somehow we are playing the game football in any organized way. It is, rather, that in the course of our play we produce one of the kinds of game events that a passer and receiver of a thrown ball can.

Free kicker–goalie

Katie sometimes sits at the top of the hill, uses the hill's slope to roll the ball to me, and crouches in a "ready" position, waiting for me to kick the ball and try to get it past her. This is a highly ritualized form of playing ball that often occurs after she has become tired playing the other two forms of ball play (see sequence 7: FREEKICK, two single images showing Katie in ready position waiting for a free kick, and FREEKICK.AVI).

FREEKICK lasts fourteen seconds and begins with Katie already at the top of the driveway in a crouching position, staring intensely at me. This is a position frequently observed in many dog breeds and especially those involved with herding (highly characteristic of border collies). She is carefully monitoring my actions, awaiting my retrieval of the ball she has rolled down the driveway. Her tensed-crouched position indicates her anticipation of my kicking it back to her. I feign kicks and Katie initially maintains her crouch. At about eight seconds into the sequence she rises up, evidently anticipating my kicking the ball. She reacts to some feints but does not release, i.e., she is not fooled by them. She watches me as I kick the ball and runs in the kicked ball's direction, pursuing it with abandon into the dog run to the right of the driveway. Kicking the ball into this area is similar to kicking a ball out of bounds; it is intersubjectively understood by us as a poor kick. The pejorative evaluation is part of the general understanding that I am not to either kick or throw the ball into the dog run area on purpose.[7] On the other hand, Katie (and my Labrador, Jack) will chase the ball without hesitation into that area when the exigencies of play, or my poor skills, require it. While they do not appear to like to do it, they do it without hesitation, perhaps as a way to indicate that they are doing their part, their duty. When it comes to kicking, the general idea is for me to kick the ball on the asphalted area, and for Katie to prevent it from passing the plane of her body, or at least minimize the distance beyond the plane of her body that she has to chase. This is what provides the sport of it: I can produce kicks that can get by her and Katie can make game moves that are particularly notable in preventing my attempts to do so.

When she gives up the ball—and that time can be highly variable in duration depending on many factors—she normally assumes a crouching position again with her paws out in front of her, intently watching the ball and me, with her body tensed in readiness for the sprint. My job in this variant of playing ball is somewhat similar to a soccer player with a free kick at the goal, and Katie's job is to be the goalie and prevent me from getting the ball by her. What I do is use my body and my legs to try to "fake her out"—i.e., to get her to run in the wrong direction and get the ball past her. Both getting her to run in the wrong direction and getting the ball past her are known to me as specific orders of detail; there are several variations on this motif that I recognize and try to produce. One is to try to get her to run to the right and then kick the ball behind her. Or I can try to get her to "think" left (not actually run left) and kick right. Yet another variation is to simply kick the ball so hard and fast to the right that she simply cannot pursue and capture, and thus it gets by her. What actually happens in any instance of this style play is quite contingent on the actual doing of the play. I rarely do get the ball past her, partly due to my own ineptness as a kicker. I am perhaps successful in two of ten tries, but the game is obviously enjoyable to her, and is a relatively low-effort way for her to continue play. My memory is that this form of ball playing, which is also part of what I sometimes call "doggie soccer," was made up by both of us when she had tired of the "field defense person" role and had retreated up the hill looking for a less aerobically demanding play motif.

If Katie captures the ball before it gets by, or if she has to chase the ball because it got by her, she will normally return to the top of the driveway and hold the ball in her mouth. She gets into a crouch with the ball in her mouth. If we have been playing for a while she is usually panting heavily. Often she sits with the ball in her mouth and does not release it for further play. When this happens I coax her to "give me the ball," which she will do eventually, usually after several attempts, by pushing the ball out of her mouth with her tongue and throwing her head forward. Because of the slope of the driveway the ball will roll down towards me; thus, despite the distance we are from one another, her action effectively presents the ball to me for further play. In this case, because of the distance between our bodies, the further play would consist of the free kick motif described above. Katie controls how long she wants to rest between kicks. The period she rests can vary and is sometimes so long that play is effectively ended. An example of this aspect of our play is in the video sequence CONTROL.AVI.

The sequence is approximately 30 seconds long, during which Katie neither moves nor releases the ball. She is standing at the top of the driveway controlling the ball in the fashion mentioned above. What occurs visually during the sequence is my approach and attempt to get her to release the ball to me, occurring on the left hand side of the screen. Absent from the visual images is the repeated verbal coaxing that I am providing her, "Give poppy the bally . . . Don't you want to play with poppy?" (see below on vocalizations during play). In the original video one can hear my coaxing her to release the ball throughout the segment. I walk toward her, escalating my requests that she release the ball and play. Just as I begin to walk toward her Katie looks away to her left. As I approach her ears flatten and then become erect. She otherwise does not react. When I retreat, and despite my urgings, Katie sits still at the top of the driveway, ball in mouth.

All these motifs are mutually doable ball-playing moves in which man-dog ball game players could engage, given their respective bodily, cognitive and sensory characteristics. At the same time it is the possibilities of these mutual doings that creates the players and playing. That is, it is in the doing of game moves that "players" are constituted, rather than the reverse.

Occasions of play as mutually chosen mixing of motifs

Actual occasions of play consist of a mixing of these motifs, with the switching of play motifs initiated by either player.

Katie clearly has choices about the way different forms of play are initiated and/or terminated. The observability of her choice-making consists of recognizable bodily movements and positions that either create/offer or negate/deny the possibilities of various motifs of play. For example, she may change from the free kick style play to another one simply by approaching me with the ball and staying close, or she may do the reverse, initiating the free kick style play by taking the ball and moving up the hill away from me, then releasing it and assuming the crouching position. These bodily expressed preferences for play motifs are things to which I am held accountable, since they are "apparent" and cannot really be misinterpreted by me without recognizably ignoring just what is happening in our play. That is, the way she presents me with the ball and her position relative to me when she drops the ball indicate her willingness to engage in certain motifs of play.

Katie's presentation of the ball, whether from afar by letting it roll down the driveway, or up close by dropping the ball near me or placing it between my knees, can be done with various nuances that also communicate her attitude in play. Katie can "throw" the ball in a limited way by building up some speed and then projecting her head forward as she comes to a halt. This is a very energetic and almost challenging way to present the ball, as if saying "let's do it!"[8] She can insistently and purposively place the ball between my knees to indicate a similar attitude. At other times she is far less energetic and presents the ball by simply dropping it and then assuming a ready position for play. Less frequently, she will present the ball very casually, simply dropping it at my feet and not even assuming a play position, indicating a casual attitude towards play.

Another regular choice observable in our play is when Katie chooses a play stick rather than a ball. She does this simply by not chasing the ball, running up to a stick, sitting, looking at me, and waiting by the stick. If I do not respond by walking toward the stick within a few seconds, she will begin to bark loudly until I do. Stick playing is discussed further below.

Katie's game move of controlling play by sitting with the ball in her mouth was described above. A lot of playtime is spent waiting for her to give me the ball and coaxing her to do so.

She can also choose to not chase the ball while engaged in any motif, thereby abruptly ending play, at least for the moment. Often this choice appears to me to be due to her feeling too hot or tired to pursue, but this is not always the case. On occasion she ends play abruptly by running toward the front door and waiting for me to let her in, even when play conditions are ideal. However, on a very hot and humid day I interpret these abrupt terminations as indications of her wanting to get into the air-conditioned house, that interpretation being grounded in her commonly collapsing next to an a/c vent when I let her in.

My own choices of motifs in play occur in different ways and for different game reasons when compared to those of Katie. Like Katie, I make my own determination as to whether there actually will or will not be play on any occasion. I often provide for the physical possibilities of play, including the ball and her presence on the playing surface, in the routine way described above. Once on the playing field, we each have a series of reciprocal choices that affect the other's play. Here is where clear differences can be seen. I very much initiate the changes in the motifs of play by standing or sitting, using my feet or my hands, and throwing or feinting with the ball with my hands along the ground; and I switch freely between these motifs, often without Katie's indicating to me her preference one way or the other. In many of the recorded sequences of play it appears that my mixing of motifs occurs frequently at the beginning of play when she is usually very energetic and probably does not care one way or the other which form of play we do. Then, as the play continues, Katie begins to exercise her choices more by bodily placement and positioning.

One can see the change in game motifs by watching my bodily posturing, for example in the sequence SWITCHING (see sequence 12: SWITCHING-01–29 and SWITCHING.AVI).

This sequence begins with Katie coming from the left of the screen and presenting the ball to me by dropping it between my legs. I am in standing position and gain control of the ball with my feet. I feign a kick, and Katie quickly reacts by shifting her weight to the rear in readiness to pursue the ball. After a fake kick with my left leg, I kick the ball with my right. The feint and the kick are not quick and not done with intensity on my part. They are casual game moves and produce a chase that is not difficult for Katie. She maintains concentration on the ball and pursues it out of frame. She enters frame from the left and drops the ball at my feet for further play. I begin another round of doggie soccer, and Katie is clearly treating the play as soccer (i.e., she has shifted her weight back and tensed in anticipation of the kick). However, at around 22 seconds I back away from the ball, then lean forward and slowly grasp it in my hand, profoundly shifting the motif of play and the orientation of both players to the possible next move. During the previous part of the sequence, Katie was monitoring my bodily position in the fashion described above in the SHADOW-ING sequences. As soon as I shift the play from my feet to my hands, Katie without hesitation follows my lead and shifts her attention from my torso to my hands. In replay one can readily follow that shift in her attention. In the latter part of the sequence she is intently concentrating upon my hands and the ball. She reacts to feints but is not fooled by them. I keep the ball back, between my legs, using my legs as visual barriers to hide my movements from her. Katie reacts slightly to a couple of feigned throws from behind my legs. With my right hand I flick it behind my legs to the left in what is an attempt at a deceptive move (it looks all too obvious in replay). Katie releases to pursue only while watching the ball being released. My feints and "flick" were not effective. Her pursuit is short and efficient; she "successfully" captures the ball in stride.

What we see in this sequence are the orderly micro-events involved in choosing to initiate different modes of play. While it is I who bodily initiates a new mode of play in this instance, both Katie and I have a kind of existential parity in being able to simply stop play, initiate new play or not cooperate with the other's choices in play. We regularly exercise these choices, and each of us knows that we require the good will and cooperation of the other in the choices we make during play.

The orderlinesses of stick playing at the park
Playing Stick at the Park: Generally Speaking (May 7, 1997) — This set of notes has been too long put off. Their inspiration comes from this past Sunday (it is now Thursday) and the visit we made with Katie to the pet fair. This is an event held yearly at the local park where we usually walk Katie. There are always fifty or more dogs around, of all breeds and mixtures, with various events, information and product booths.

Katie was on unusually good behavior on Sunday. We were a little worried, since she has developed the habit of snarling and barking at some of the dogs we meet along the trail during our walks (especially young males who want to play with her—she "puts 'em in their place," as one of the guardians commented). But she was really very well-behaved at the pet fair, even sniffing and interacting with larger males without incident.

We were with Gail, Jeff and Chester, the latter being a male corgi about Katie's age. Katie is completely comfortable with Chester and so familiar with him at this point that she takes him for granted. (A lot more actually can be written about Katie's relationship with Chester but not in the present context.) One thing that was common but remarkable about Katie's behavior was her desire to play stick throughout the whole visit. This is typical of our walks together, when, in addition to the special stick play that is described below under the notes titled "The Subjective Meaning Attached by Players to a Field of Play: Playing Sticky at Madison Square Garden," we play stick all along the way as we walk. The fact that I play with Katie in this way, which slows down our walking considerably, is what made my wife object to stick-throwing during our walks. On pet fair day Katie also had Jeff, Chester's guardian, to present her stick to, and to the extent he will cooperate, she does so regularly throughout the walk. Luckily Chester is not into sticks, just Frisbees.

By playing stick all along the walk I mean the following practices: on walks when Katie and I are together she and I will engage in a form of stick tossing along the trail as we walk along. Katie will approach a stick alongside the trail, bark and pause, intently staring at it in "play position." This is a request that I throw it for her. Some of these sticks are so large they are literally trees, far too heavy to even budge, let alone throw. I sometimes can't help but laugh at Katie's appetite for these impossible sticks. Others who witness her behavior likewise find it amusing—the actual visual image of such a small animal trying to take on such an overwhelmingly large tree. Other sticks she picks are smaller (although she definitely shows a preference for unmanageably large sticks).[9]

The stick having been selected, I throw it for her. This means something specific to the trail walking. That is, we do [throwing-the-stick-as-we-walk-along-the-trail-together], where the brackets refer to the following specific practices—that I pick up the "stick" (whatever size it may be) and "throw it" (whatever that physical action might consist of, given the size of the stick and position on the trail), either forward or backward on the trail depending on several factors, but never purposefully off the trail, as most of the trails in the park have precipitous drop-offs. There is a clear preference from Katie's point of view that I throw forward. This she expresses by repeatedly failing to chase and retrieve sticks thrown backward and by barking vocalizations indicating displeasure. I attribute this reluctance to her having "figured out" that throwing backward is a more effortful form of play, requiring her to cover the same distance twice to carry the stick back to me in order for me to continue play. This contrasts with the relative ease of forward throwing.

When thrown forward the practice is that Katie will chase the stick and wait for me to catch up to her, either gnawing at it or standing next to it until I arrive. Then I am expected to repeat the action, to throw the stick forward. She again pursues it, waits by it or gnaws on it until I catch up to her, and so on. This sequence is repeated until either she or I have had enough. Katie indicates this by simply not running after the thrown stick, or she runs after it but shows no interest in it once she arrives at its location. When I do not want to repeat the sequence I walk past the stick and do not repeat the throwing. Sometimes Katie will pick the stick up and repeatedly "present" it to me for throwing. I can either acknowledge these requests or not. Sometimes, after several such ignored presentations, she will leave the stick on the trail, ending that particular sequence of play.

Obviously, this form of play is somewhat different from that at my home or in the field. At the park, the playing surface is constantly changing; it is literally wherever we happen to find ourselves on the trail. In fact, the play spreads itself over the entire geography of the walk, including, for example, the streams that we walk along or cross. At such times, water conditions permitting, Katie very much enjoys chasing the stick into the water. At certain locations, where conditions are conducive to such activity, we have developed a routine that I will often throw sticks into the water for her to fetch. Generally I do not send Katie into the water unless the temperature is over 50° F. In the winter, water fetching is not practiced.

By "water fetching," I mean that Katie will run into the water and try to retrieve the stick I threw. Her success at doing so—indeed her willingness to actually proceed into the water and retrieve the stick—is dependent on water conditions. Katie will not swim. She has repeatedly demonstrated that she is afraid of her paws' losing contact with the rocks and soil on the bottom of streams. I am fairly confident she could swim but I have not forced the issue. Yet she loves to be courageous to the extent of her limitation and will forge across streams two-thirds submerged. When she has confronted nasty, deep-water conditions she appears to be proud of herself and requests recognition. Her actual success at retrieving the stick is secondary to her mastery of the immediate water conditions. She will often go in after the stick, but by the time she has negotiated the water it has floated downstream beyond retrieval. She will then often try to find another stick to play with or may bark at me vigorously, trying to get me to find another stick and throw it to her, having done her duty as she sees it.[10]

Another part of her behavior on pet fair day was her showing off (see my discussion below). She is absolutely and virtually compulsive in her desire to show strangers, dogs and humans what she can do with retrieving sticks. Even during the dog obedience trials, her response to the event was to try to retrieve sticks to attract attention. She likes to show you what she can do. Later in the walk we met a third corgi and his guardian. Again, Katie was beside herself to show the new guardian and her dog how she retrieved big sticks. She found a large one and presented it to me. Not wanting to interrupt the group greeting, I ignored her at first, until she barked vigorously at me to throw the stick. I showed the new guardian Katie's routine and, sure enough, when she returned the stick she dropped it at the new corgi guardian's feet, apparently asking if she were a potential playmate or not. I warned her about the consequences of her response—if she threw the stick she might be bugged for the rest of her life by Katie, the compulsive stick player. The lady actually threw the stick once and said as she did it (it was a heavy one), "Ooh that's enough I think." Katie of course fetched the stick back but I picked it up and threw it, saying to the new guardian, "See what I mean?"

One thing is apparent about Katie's behavior, whatever generative arguments one uses to account for its presence. She displays her conviction that presenting and retrieving the ball (or stick) for humans is something they would like her to do, will appreciate when she does it, and will praise her for having completed her mission. The more difficult and daring the retrieve, the more she likes it, I think because she is "showing them what I can do." Again the remark of a trainer who trains corgis to herd sheep comes to mind, his love of training animals like Katie.

Huizinga (1950) also wrote that play is characterized by a "setoffness" from everyday life—it is temporally and physically defined, distinct from non-play activities in society, the latter being activities of a serious, adaptive or functional nature.[11] Play with Katie seems not to obey this conception. For Katie it is, alternatively, a basic mode in relating to people in many everyday situations, rather than being set off from them. Most situations Katie faces each day involve Diane and me, and occasionally other dogs and dog guardians. Given the generally benevolent character of these encounters, Katie tries to play in virtually all of them. As described in the introduction, it is first and foremost on her mind, generally speaking. Rather than being set off from everyday life, for Katie situations are seen as opportunities for play. I assume that this is partially context-dependent—i.e., she lives in situations that motivate her and reward her for such activities. I assume that if the context changed radically, for example, and God forbid became abusive, her response would not be to try to play. This imaginative variation aside, the ubiquitous nature of play in Katie's everyday life stands in contradistinction to how humans generally produce and recognize play in theirs.

Vocalizations as Part of the Orderliness of Play

> Animals are creatures that lead silence through the world of man and language and are always putting silence in front of man. . . . Animals move through the world like a caravan of silence. . . . A whole world, that of nature and animals, is filled with silence. Nature and animals seem like protuberances of silence. The silence of animals and the silence of nature would not be so great if it were merely a failure of language to materialize. Silence has been entrusted to nature and to animals as something created for its own sake.
>
> —Max Picard, *The World of Silence*

In some general way Picard's words ring true, and while I am often taken with the power and beauty of silence during my morning walks with my dogs, generally vocalizations are part of our interactions. While play with Katie was relatively quiet when compared, for example, to human play, it was not silent. The following general notes about vocalizations display some of ways they were constituent elements of our play.

Vocalizations in Play—March 23, 1997

I realize that I have been loath to write about this topic, mostly due to an anticipated embarrassment at having to own up to the crazy things I say while I play with Katie, as well as the babyish way I say them. More on that as I get into these notes.

The role of vocal exchanges in my play with Katie is evident, although totally asymmetrical in that I vocalize far more—before, during and after play. This is not to say that Katie does not make significant and influential contributions. For example, it is very common that Katie will use a whimpering sound in the morning to remind me that I have to take her out to play. She will stand near the kitchen cabinets, where we keep the balls, whimpering and/or making attempts to jump up at the balls. She will do this usually when I have lingered too long after awakening, or when I get up late and she has been waiting too long for me. Katie also whimpers occasionally, apparently out of excitement or joy at the prospect of play. This she might do when she is particularly excited and I say to her, "You want to play bally?" but it is not common.

Katie will vocalize during play, but often her communicative intent is not exactly clear to me. She will occasionally bark when I talk to her and stroke her before throwing the ball, getting her revved up, so to speak. When she was a pup she would bark vigorously when we talked with her during retrieving games. My son and I even had a kind of contest to see who could get Katie to bark more times (a three-bark throw was considered a really good throw). These barks appeared to reflect her level of excitement at the task, rather than any attempt to influence me in a particular way.

Another very ordinary vocal contribution by Katie during our play, happening in almost every instance, is her barking at the point she wants to change from ball to stick. Commonly she will do this by failing to chase after a thrown ball, and then running over to the stick she would like me to throw. If I do not come over to the stick and throw it, but say, for example, "Bring me the stick," she often begins to bark vigorously, in an obvious and evident request that I come over to her and pick up and throw the stick. She does not do it when she switches back from stick to ball, but ritually insists in this fashion when she switches the other way.

Katie also makes a variety of "small sounds" related to play. One typical one is a soft "whimper-bark," for lack of a better term, she makes at a particular part of our play. This occurs usually after she has been eating the stick we are playing with and I request her to "bring the stick." Apparently, it is as a response to this request that Katie "whimper-barks," although I am not sure what it signifies. Another small sound Katie makes is not so much a vocalization as an expression of her athletic concentration and effort. This is a sibilant out-breath when she begins to chase, similar to the kinds of sounds ballplayers in games make when they exert themselves.

Finally, Katie has occasionally communicated her pain during play through a yelp followed by prolonged and intense whimpering sounds. This happened several times due to accident—she ran over something sharp once and another time was kicked in the head during doggie soccer. On another occasion I was massaging her body after play and apparently hit a sore spot, and she yelped in pain.

My Vocalizations during Play

During the initial taping of our play sessions, I listened to some tapes and noticed that the sessions were unusually quiet compared to how they normally were. I realized at that time that I was purposefully withholding certain "embarrassing" vocalizations during taping—that I did not want to have a record of my vocalizations. The reason I think I was (am) embarrassed by the vocalizations is because they are incredibly babyish and foolish. The pattern of speech used, and particularly the over-reliance on paralinguistic features of vocalizations, make me sound foolish or babyish by any normal adult standard of speech. Reflecting about my own vocalizations, they are so absurd by adult standards that they may be even more embarrassing than the vocal productions made by adults to small infants and children. There is a certain parallel between my own sense of embarrassment at producing these crazy utterances and that reported by fieldworkers who do participant-observation research with small children— what the researcher says or does is perceived to be so un-adult and extraordinary that he or she is subject to corrections by other adults, who want to bring the researcher's behavior back to normal (see especially Mandel [1991]).

When reflecting on instances of play with Katie I have a sense of what my vocal work does. First, its notable absence, on days when I do not make any or few vocalizations during play, indicates a relative lack of enthusiasm. Normally, my utterances communicate enthusiasm for the play. I use paralinguistic elements such as high-pitched sounds, utterances that have a crescendo-like volume, exaggerated, overly pronounced statements of her name, etc., to "rev her up"—that is, to get her excited and motivated to play hard. These same paralinguistic features are used when I am verbally and/or physically rewarding her for good and enthusiastic play—for example, after chasing some balls thrown long and fast and bringing them back to me with minimal prompting. Often I will stroke her and say things like "What a good girl" in high-pitched tones.

Another kind of vocalization I use indicates seriousness and command—it is a stern tone of voice that Katie immediately recognizes and responds to. During play I may say to Katie, "Come to poppy," then wait and say, "Come to poppy and bring the stick." She often ignores me if she is busy chewing away on the stick. Yet if I use a stern tone of voice and say the same thing, she will almost always immediately do what I request. Katie can accurately distinguish the difference between the two kinds of demands: the serious and not so serious.

Another thing that I sometimes do is whisper while we play. I try to use hand gestures and whisper to get Katie to orient to my gestures more than my voice (this will teach her signs for the same things we have words for). Sometimes I whisper and forget to gesture—I have seen a couple of these on tape—giving the session a strange whispery character. I say, "Katie get the ball," but in a whisper, as I throw the ball for her.

Hearing my recorded vocalizations, I cannot be sure what Katie actually perceives. Research and experience tell us that dogs have extremely keen hearing compared to humans. Katie undoubtedly hears more in my vocalizations, and in our play, than I. Perhaps body movements, breathing, and clothes rustling are all parts of what she hears during play; but they are absolutely missing from my own aural experience of it. It may well be that such sounds, in addition to those I hear, constitute Katie's playing with me.[12]

The above reflections about our vocalizations are an incomplete assemblage of matters relevant to the topic. The notes bear an indistinct relationship to how vocalizations in play are actually produced and recognized in any instance. Because the video segments supplied on the disk do not contain the audio part of the original videotape, nothing more than my own reflections about vocal elements of play will be available to the reader.

A further thought about foolishness: when I play with Katie one of the most foolish things I do is call her by different pet names. These often have an alliterative element and are so silly-sounding that I loath to even write them now (despite my allegiance to science I will refrain from doing so). I think it is the content of the utterances as well as their paralinguistic features that are embarrassing. Yet I must also note that, as far as I can see, Katie absolutely does not find these silly-name utterances at all relevant to play. In a cartoon I once saw a dog guardian talking to his dog, but portrayed from the dog's perspective. In the balloon the cartoonist (I believe it was Gary Larson) used to portray what was in the dog's mind, human words appeared like this: "blah blah blah blah Ginger blah blah blah blah blah blah blah blah Ginger." It doesn't quite work that way with Katie and me. Paralinguistic elements and my "blahs" in play are not necessarily equivalent. Yet in general, "blah blah plus effect" may well be the content of many human utterances from a dog's perspective (for a further discussion of vocalizations, see chapter 4, my discussion of Mitchell, 2001; Mitchell & Edmonson, 1999). On the other hand, some extraordinary claims of word recognition by dogs have been made by various observers.

Initiating Play

In some ways the machinery of play resembles conversation, in that it is sequential and often involves an initiating action/utterance. The action/utterance constitutes the potential (potential in that it may or may not be responded to as such) boundary of play. Just as the conversation analysts write about the ways in which conversationalists open up conversational closings, or initiate openings to conversation, play also consists of the mutual production of signs and invitations to begin (and later to end) play. The following are field notes about the vulgar availability of Katie's request to play.

April 25, 1997—Chance Observation: "Tennis Anyone?"

Next door today there is a bridal party leaving for the ceremony. I am out in the herb garden planting and the neighborhood women, kids and my wife are going over to visit the bride. Katie is running over to everyone with a stick and trying to get him or her to play with her. At one point the mother of my next-door neighbor says, "Now I see why there are all these sticks all over." It is a friendly and mundane comment but strikes me.

Every darn person in this setting knows without hesitation that Katie wants to play with a stick. Even when they were extremely young the little kids next door, age two or so, knew that Katie wanted to play stick. With no training on my part the kids "vulgarly" accepted her offer and began throwing the stick for Katie, at an age when their language competence was minimal. I counted seven adults and children in the scene, each of whom knew in some detailed but non-credentialed way that Katie wanted to play ball. She ran from one to another with the play object, presenting it to whomever, to see if she would get lucky.

Through bodily placement, posturing, movement and vocalizations, Katie has the ability to express her intent to play. The ability is of course dependent upon others to read the bodily communications. The others in Katie's world are competent readers of these actions. In the case of my neighbors—we have four—there have been up to eight neighborhood dogs. Local children and adults are familiar with dogs and read their signals well. For Katie, there has never been a problem in getting people to realize what she wants. (Of course one could imagine naive and fearful others who would or could not read Katie's communication attempts; these persons are by definition unavailable to dog communications).

As an example of vulgar availability of a dog's request to play, yesterday the neighbor's golden retriever escaped from his yard. Teddy, a three-year-old male, was roaming around our home, looking for someone to play with as he had several times before when he escaped. Diane told me that when she went to get him he had gotten one of Katie's balls and had approached her to play bally. Teddy watches Diane and me throw the ball for Katie all the time from his yard; he must have figured this was a good chance for some ball retrieving action and actually came to Diane, idea already in mind. ("To heck with freedom; this lady plays ball.") Teddy is a "neotenous" animal, a big adolescent who is so sweet and kind that there is never a question of his intent. His whole comportment and attitude just says, "I am a guy who just wants to have fun." At least this is how he has always acted with Katie and me.

Katie's reaction to Teddy's being free was also interesting. She was very wary of him at first. He is a large male—perhaps 120 pounds. Katie generally is afraid of such large dogs. Yet Teddy is such a sweetheart that there was really nothing for her to fear—that is, until he decided to play with her bally. There were two balls on the driveway. When Teddy went to pick one up, Katie was right in his face, barking and growling. She did not want any part of his playing with her property on her property, and she let him know it. Teddy barely paid her growling and barking any mind, still ready to play at anyone's suggestion. He simply ignored Katie, luckily.

Teddy has been watching Katie and me play bally each morning. "Gee, I wish I could do that," was what I always thought Teddy had in mind, and his behavior upon achieving freedom from captivity indicates the priority of his interests. Katie's reaction to Teddy is interesting. She was intensely jealous of his appropriation of her play object. For this she was willing to fight what would have been clearly a losing battle for it. Playing with her ball was at that moment for her very serious business. Diane says that Katie is developing a "nasty" disposition, but I think this has been part of her disposition all along. It is also part of other dogs' repertoire, but it is only activated in the appropriate situation.[13]

The Field Surfaces and Boundaries of Play

In most games a field of play is required, usually a geographically stable field of play.[14] This was generally true of play with Katie, which occurred for the most part on the driveway in front of my home (see on the CD the JPEG images FIELD-01–03 for three different conditions of play). As we shall see under the discussion of "Contingencies of Play," geographical constancy should in no way be understood as providing for a "same" field of play in any instance.

Physical features of the driveway area serve as play surface (the actual driveway surface), physical bounds of play (the house and garden walls and garage door, which constitute both boundaries of play and edges against which a tennis ball can be thrown), and out of bounds or not preferred playing areas (the herb garden and dog run at the end of the neighbor's property that runs along one side of the driveway surface). The herb garden is not a preferred area for throwing the ball—from my perspective because I do not want Katie to destroy the herbs, and from Katie's perspective because she dislikes the coniferous ground cover that runs along the herb garden's edge. The dog run at the end of my neighbor's property, which usually constitutes the right-hand boundary of play, occupies a similar status for players. For me it is not an area I want to throw the ball in order to avoid soiling it with various dog "products," and also because I can see that Katie would rather not chase and retrieve balls in this area. She has two distinct reactions to balls going into this area. The most common is to chase the ball to the end of the asphalt surface and then with some abandon "pounce" on the ball as it hits the run. Having decided that she is going to retrieve the ball in the dog run, she does it intensely. In contrast to this reckless abandon, when a ball is on the dog run it is quite difficult to coax her into the area to get it. Many times I have to be the one to pick it up and put the ball into play.

The driveway near the house is slanted and becomes flat about thirty feet from the house, where it merges with a small road. At the far end of the playing surface, on the other side of the road, is another wall, perhaps seventy-five feet from the front door. This constitutes the back edge of our playing field. In all our forms of play and since its beginning and without instruction, Katie seems to have related to this back edge of play. She pursues balls vigorously and appears to not want to let them hit the back edge of play if at all possible. She frequently runs so hard at the wall that she has to "put on the brakes" with some real intensity in order to avoid smacking herself against it. At such times her behavior is suggestive of the outfielder in baseball chasing a fly ball to the stadium wall.

Contingencies of Play

Each instance of play is a lived orderliness of play; it is an organization of what Garfinkel calls "haecceities."[15] Each instance of play reproduces certain motifs or orders of play (generalities), but is also a configuration of various contingencies that have to be discovered in the doing of the play at just that time (in details). In the following notes I share some of the regularly encountered contingencies play.

Depending on weather conditions (she does not like to play in either very hot, humid weather or very heavy rain), Katie will retrieve the ball and/or try to prevent me from getting it past her again in serious fashion. Climatic conditions, as experienced by *players*, are part of their mutual constitution of *play*. The same is true for the health and lively inner states of the players, which vary according to life's unexplainable rhythms, as well as its victories and insults. Other contingencies include the physical status of objects and surfaces of play. The actual physical condition of the ball is constituent of play, older balls being less lively, more quickly to become saliva-soaked and unpleasant and difficult for me to throw. New balls are more fun for me and, from observing Katie's reactions to them, for her too. The surfaces of play also vary in regard to condition, temperature, wetness, dirt, ice, etc. An apple tree at the top of the driveway at certain times during the year produces green apples that look very much like a tennis ball when they fall on the driveway, and their presence affects Katie's play. These are constituent features of any occasion of play together, contingently oriented to on any occasion. Orienting to such features provides the reasonable grounds for me to say to Katie, "You (or I) really don't feel good today, so let's go back inside," or "It's too hot (or icy) to play today," or for Katie to run outside with a ball to play but turn right around and come back in because it is raining too hard. These contingent features will be explicated further.

The presence, or lack of presence, of multiple play objects on the driveway affects the organization of our play. This is often the case, with many balls and sticks commonly available. This contingency of play can be either relevant or not in any instance of play. Multiple objects can sometimes be ignored entirely by Katie, and at other times become a central feature of our playing. One common thing she does is stop pursuing a ball and instead stop near a stick (this was previously discussed under the topic "Switching of Play Motifs"). She will wait next to the stick and often bark until I come over and throw it for her. At that point she may or may not retrieve the stick. We may continue to play retrieve-the-stick for some time, and she may then switch back to the ball by running to get it and presenting it at my feet. This switching between "what-happens-to-be-available" play objects is not indefinite and perhaps not random on her part. It will usually only occur three or four times in any one session of play. The presence of both sticks and balls on the playing surface makes available to us two sets of play motifs/structures/orders, those associated with the tennis balls, and those associated with sticks. Switching from ball to stick is apparently also related to Katie's tiredness, the stick providing for an easier retrieve (it doesn't roll). Capturing a stick is often followed by a part of play during which she "dissects" the stick, i.e., eats the play object. I can think of no comparable human sport in which the players eat the play object.

Because we play outdoors, weather profoundly structures each occasion of play. On days when it is raining heavily, both players are negatively affected. I will not play outside in heavy rain and will only stand in the garage or on the porch under the verandah during play. Katie must adapt her play; for example, her presentation of the ball to me if I am on the porch must be on the first step (this prevents me from getting wet), or if I am in the garage must reach where I am standing inside and not require me to get into the rain. Katie is also negatively affected by rain, and if it is heavy she will only play in the morning, when she also has to do her "business." Very recently I witnessed an example of this, where in the morning in a heavy rain Katie elected to play (she presented me with a ball inside the house and then again in the garage). I threw the ball from the garage and she chased it several times. I coaxed her to do her business with the phrase I taught her for this purpose ("hurry up"), and on the third throw she went to the run and peed. As soon as she was finished, she came running back into the garage and into the house, wet and unhappy (she does not like to be wet), to be toweled off. She clearly indicated the termination of play after three throws by urinating. This kind of modification of our normal play, which is coupled in the morning with her need to go out and relieve herself, is a common way one form of bad weather affects but does not terminate the routines of play. The occasion of play is integrated into the lives of players, in this case into the subplot of having to get Katie to do her morning business in heavy rain.

With respect to our playing together, the weather has particularly understood meaning and effects. When conditions are physically dangerous, such as intense thunder, lightening or wind, I decide to preclude play. "Bad" playing weather for Katie includes heavy rain and/or intense humidity, heat and play surface icing. All other kinds of weather, including intense cold and heavy snow, moderate wind, and lightening and thunder (which she does not like but apparently will tolerate for playing purposes), are for Katie acceptable playing conditions. She is particularly comfortable in the cold and very much enjoys chasing the ball in snow. In snowy conditions, because the ball will not roll, and depending on depth her effort at chasing may be considerable, the entire look and feel of play is altered, as are its motifs, as the snow becomes deeply constitutive of our play together. To say that snow is a contingency of play is not to imply that it does not occupy a central role in it.

As a contingency of play, climatic conditions partially constitute the physical conditions under which play must be realized if it is to occur. Climate is thus contingent in the sense that players have absolutely no control over what climate might be in any instance of play. Climate happens. But the players' responses to these contingencies are orderly and regular. Heavy rain in the morning is immediately understood to lead to the kind of play described in the preceding paragraph, and will not mean a happy and energetic player on Katie's part. Katie, in turn, seems to have learned that I will not stand in the rain and adapts her play to that fact on rainy days. As mentioned above, snow, a condition of play that Katie thoroughly enjoys, is immediately understood by me as a good play condition and also is linguistically formulated by me as such through such remarks to Katie as, "It's snowing today and someone is going to have a really good time playing ball," or "Ready for snow-bally?" Katie has learned to like and understand the word "snow."

The last "regular contingency" to our play about which I am going to write is the presence of wild animals, notably in our area deer, squirrels, or ground hogs. Initially, for Katie the presence of any of these animals superseded play and required her to give chase. Over the long run, perhaps due to the regularity of the presence of deer and squirrels, Katie has learned to tolerate playing ball even when deer graze quite close to her. She no longer chases squirrels as predictably as she used to, although the rare appearance of a ground hog continues to be a reliable interrupter of play. The arrival of the neighbor's cat or dog also will, in almost all circumstances I have observed, end our play. Related to this is the pestering of insects, especially wasps and bees. These insects can abruptly end my psychological willingness to play, and have on occasion stung players.

The Subjective Meanings Experienced by Players on a Field of Play

As the following notes indicate, different venues of play may be seen to have different "motivational value" for players. Put alternatively, geographical location of play is observably not a matter of moral indifference to players.

Playing Sticky at Madison Square Garden, April 5, 1997

One of my earliest memories as a game player was as part of my public school basketball team. We visited the gymnasium of the local high school and scrimmaged. It was the first time I became aware of the effect of the venue on play. The gym was so big, it was "big-time," and we played intensely, without the usual sixth-grade complaints and breaks in play. The next experience like this that I remember was playing in the gymnasium of Queens College as a freshman. The gym was so huge and intimidating that I (and many others there for the first time) played with an intense nervousness uncharacteristic of "normal," everyday, schoolyard ball. My nervousness was partially due to my first trip to Madison Square Garden (the old MSG) the year before. The experience was completely overwhelming. I was there to watch a high school game, and I insisted that Coach (I was a junior varsity player) take me on the floor during halftime. That brief walk, not even as a player, was for me an intense sports experience. It was the experience of being on a truly great playing court. I also played basketball at Pauley Pavilion for the seven years I attended graduate school at UCLA. I am not a stranger to the experienced effects of playing at great venues.

It is not therefore surprising to me that the same phenomenon can be seen in my play with Katie. We have as part of the overall theme of play in our lives a regular occurrence that is something like a change of venue to "big-time." This change is part of our going to the local reservation, a huge green belt reserved for animals, hikers and horseback riders, and playing "stick."

Part of the reservation consists of horse trails in dense woods, with many ascents and descents in and out of a glen. There are many streams and run-offs. There are also very large, open, manicured fields. In such a setting the number, quality and size of play sticks is considerable, and Katie is constantly checking out potential sticks as play objects for us.

When my wife is with us on the walk we do not generally pause and play with sticks very much. Because the walk is her main exercise for the day, she objects to the standing around and prefers to keep moving. When she is not with us, there is a routine that Katie and I follow with regard to stick playing. As we descend into the less publicly visible part of the park, we are looking out for a "good" play stick for us to use. "Good" means, from Katie's point of view, a large, preferably very large, and edible branch. "Good" means for me a stick large enough to cause me to exercise during throwing but not so large as to give me a hernia or prevent me from throwing the stick far enough to interest Katie. From my perspective the stick should also be relatively clean (this feature does not interest Katie) and free from small stubs and branches so that I can throw it easily, without injuring my hands. In my view the play stick cannot be rotten, as that will cause it to break during play. Preferable (although less available) are sticks of hardwood trees, since they are sturdy and, due to their density, very good sticks to throw long distances. While we both search for potential play sticks, it is ultimately my responsibility to select a stick before we get to "the field." That is how we do it.

"The field" is a phrase Katie understands. It refers to our Madison Square Garden of "sticky," where we have been going since she was a little pup. It is located about a quarter-mile into the park, and when we are alone it is a mandatory stop for play. This has become a virtually routine part of our walks together, and both of us orient to "the field" as a mutually understood forthcoming event within the walk. "The field," in a wild surround normally without other persons or animals, is an ideal place for Katie and me to be able to play. We do so in quiet, beautiful, relaxed, physically comfortable (the grass surface for her) circumstances without regard for spectators or interruptions.

By the time we reach it, unless we have been unlucky, I have selected a large branch, sometimes as much as (without having weighed them) thirty pounds and six or more feet long. That's the large end of the spectrum, when I want to make things athletic for me. Smaller sticks will also serve. They are acceptable to both players, and I use them when I want Katie to run long retrieve paths and need to throw the stick as far as I can. The ideal stick for this is about ten to fifteen pounds and a couple of feet in length, and on days when I feel particularly strong perhaps a bit larger and heavier.

When at the field, I approach the whole throwing part of the throw and retrieve as a genuine athletic workout. If the stick is big I limber up for a minute or two before beginning play (this makes Katie crazy, and as she waits for me to begin she often whimpers and barks). I throw the stick as far as I can, depending on weight. I use "thought-out" techniques in lifting and throwing, and try to perform as efficiently as possible. With the proper stick, I can throw it as far as 120 feet, with trailing wind perhaps even farther. Depending on weather conditions we stop at the field and play for ten to fifteen minutes, or until Katie collapses. Then we continue with the walk. Katie's approach to playing stick on the field has always been similarly intense, although I cannot say for sure that she simply picked up my own seriousness about the athletic aspect of play at this venue. From the very beginning, she seemed to have an excitement of her own related to the field, perhaps from the smells of the animal residents of the reservation who congregated, grazed and engaged in other activities there, perhaps from the spectacular soft grass surface, which was so comfortable for her to run on, or perhaps from her being "pre-wired" for such open fields as a member of a herding breed. I have already written about Katie's desire to chase deer, which she has occasionally done on the field. Yet these "perhaps" are conjectures on my part, natural theorizing. I am not really in a position to speak about why, but she took to "the field" immediately in her own ways.

This is not to question my contribution as specifically defining the field as a place of serious athletic performance. From the above the reader can see that the field was an opportunity to play more athletically with Katie—something that the small playing area in front of my home makes almost impossible. Katie took to this athletic definition of the situation on the field immediately and without hesitation, as if it was something for which she had longed. Over time the intersubjectivity of this ritual encounter has taken on intense meaning for her; she sometimes whimpers when I do not pick up a stick to throw (there are contingencies like rain, tick infestation and mud that prevent play on any particular day). During play on the field, Katie works as hard as she can and I supply very loud and regular verbal praise. I also pat and stroke her if she permits (she is often so intense that she is totally rejecting of affection, and one again gets the sense that petting is particularly demeaning to her in this circumstance). If tired, she rests between throws by gnawing away at the ends of the sticks and at the broken branch stubs on them. For Katie the field is also the Madison Square Garden of gnawing, and she does it so intensely that she sometimes whimpers and snorts from joy, often accompanied by my laughing at her attempts to orally destroy five-foot branches.[16]

Even though the play on the field is clearly athletically demanding for me, it is far more so for Katie. She runs extremely long retrieve patterns and often carries back branches that appear to me to weigh as much as she does. She has figured out a technique to carry the branch by biting at its balance point— something it took her several years to become reflexive about and not just stumble upon. She also does a lot of barking at the moment of the throw, due I think to the highly motivated character of the play. She is often so intense in her pursuit that she will tumble and roll in the snow while trying to stop and bite the snow-covered stick. On several occasions she was so abandoned in her chase that I was afraid she had hurt herself in the tumble. Because the physical demands of play are so high for her, it is usually after the third or fourth collapse to the ground with the stick, and extended gnawing, that I call an end to

play and move us along to the rest of our walk. Depending on weather conditions, we can play anywhere from ten to thirty minutes. The longer sessions are
often in winter, in cold conditions when snow is on the ground. This is Katie's
favorite situation to play sticky at "the field," in the snow, in the cold. Under
these ideal conditions her joy, her self-abandonment, her unlimited energy in
play, are incredible to behold. On several very cold winter mornings, while watching Katie's endurance and athleticism on the playing field, I have thought to
myself, "It's almost unbelievable." Her experience is evident in the look of
things, a scene almost anyone could appreciate. She maintains this intensity even
as a middle-aged dog (at ca. 4½ years). For Katie, "the field" is the stick-playing
version of Madison Square Garden, which, luckily for her, she gets to visit
several times each week.

Temporality of Play

Occasions of playing ball with Katie have a certain natural temporal progression,
at least some of which appears to be related to the layout of the field of play. In
front of my home the driveway is on quite a slant, and Katie immediately realized
that eventually the ball would roll down the driveway even if she did not pursue
it. This allows her to engage in a lazy form of play in which she actually does not
retrieve the ball, instead allowing it to run back down the hill toward me. She does
this especially when she is tired. Katie also realized that she could chase and
capture a thrown or kicked ball and then rest at the top of the driveway. At that
place and time in play she could stay and hold the ball or return the ball to me by
opening her mouth and allowing it to run down the driveway in my direction. As
part of our routine play she sits there and holds the ball in her mouth, whether I
request her to "give me the ball" or not. She often appears to do this because she
is tired and panting heavily, but it is also perhaps as a matter of "control" of the
situation (see sequence 1: CONTROL-01–27 and CONTROL.AVI, discussed above).
A friend who has played a lot of ball with Katie says she is playing "mind games."
This is reminiscent of behavior of young children who might "hold the basketball" so that other kids cannot play with it. The periodicity of the play with Katie
often seems to follow a pattern of initial excitement and intense retrieving and
shadowing me, followed by these resting sequences during which she engages in
lazy play or sits with the ball in her mouth at the top of the driveway. For
players, lazy and intense play provides for temporalities of play that are experienced differently.[17]

The Inner States of Play

Garfinkel wrote about the "lively inner states" of members interacting (1967,
chapter 7). Katie and I display such lively or less lively inner states during our

play with one another. Our play reflects the various conditions of our "inner" states—for example, play when both are highly motivated and focused, or play when one or the other is highly motivated or focused, or when neither of us is. These "inner states" and their relative liveliness (not only liveliness but "whatever," and whatever's quality and intensity) are observable matters to players. That this is observably the case should in no way be taken to mean that "accurate" reading of these states is a necessary part of, or precondition for, play.

Katie sees and senses when I am really "into" playing with her, or when I am not. I can do the same regarding her. Her ability to sense my relative motivation and energy in the activity should not be mistaken for sensitivity, i.e., consideration or care about me or respect for my situation. In fact she often appears to be unconcerned about whether I want or do not want to play. When she is very intense about her play she appears to take my "will to play" as simply a contingent circumstance of her ball playing.

Nor is it the case that our inner states consist of only the motivated character of the play. Occasions of play themselves constitute in their doing players' lively inner states. For example, our inner states of play after my being away for a long time, on a beautiful cool morning, or with a brand-new ball reflect this specific kind of excitement for both of us. Other lively inner states may follow in this example as a result of the circumstances of play. If she has not exercised while I was away, she could be overweight and out of shape. She could be disappointed in the play, unable to perform. On the other hand, if she had been staying with my friend in the country, she would probably be skinny and in great shape, and play impressively. In Katie's and my play, all sorts of lively inner ways of participating in the play can be found. There is no particular reason to make a comprehensive list of these. We could lose the new ball in the forest; this would be bad, something neither of us would like. We can find ourselves in the midst of disheartening or uplifting matters.

Katie appears to react negatively or disapprovingly to certain plays that I make in the game. For example, if I miskick the ball several times in a row, she often picks it up and runs to me with it, standing at my feet, looking into my eyes as if to say "get it together" (she does have a limit to her patience and will terminate play on occasion due to my inability to get kicking together). Katie does not appear to resent it when I accidentally hit her with the ball or even with my foot (if she is hurt she will come to me with ears down, indicating that she needs to be petted and reassured). If I hit her too many times in one play session she appears to react negatively. On two occasions I can remember she terminated play for this reason and appeared very disturbed with me.

The following section will consist of specific observations of Katie's "lively inner states" during play.

General Notes: What Is Playing Ball with Katie

(8/27/96) Today was a hot and humid morning. I took Katie out with the ball
about 8:00 A.M. and proceeded to throw the ball for her, then a little football.
She tired easily and sat at the top of the driveway holding the ball, panting. I
tried to coax her several times to "play bally" but with no effect. By this time it
was 8:10 and I decided that I would begin to work on plugging a hole in my
asphalt driveway. I went into the garage to get the broom, and as soon as I did,
Katie ran up to me with the bally in her mouth, wanting to play. This is the
phenomenon I want to write about, how Katie always wants to play ball when I
want to work around the house.

I began to notice this pattern because frequently I would decide to work
around the house, to shovel snow, to work in the garden, to fix up around the
yard, or in this instance to fix the driveway only after having played with Katie
and exhausted her. What struck me was her sudden renewed energy at the
moment I headed for the broom, shovel or what have you. She suddenly wants
to play fetch and becomes quite adamant about it, constantly interrupting my
shoveling by dropping the ball at my feet, whining and whimpering if I let her
stand too long without throwing the ball to fetch. My wife tells me Katie does
the same when she is working. It does not matter what the conditions are or how
tired she might be. When I begin to do outdoor work around the house, she is
always ready to play, wants to go—indeed, needs to play. If the weather is right,
cold and dry, she will continue to bug me with her "requests for bally" for as
long as I work.

This behavior is illustrated in the video sequence WORKING.AVI. It is a
short, twenty-one-second sequence in which I am sweeping leaves off my newly
surfaced driveway. Katie presents the ball three times for play to me in this
period. At each presentation of the ball I accept it with my left hand as I continue to hold and sweep with the broom in my right. While I hesitate in my
sweeping, the organization of my response to Katie's requests for play is an
efficient way to allow both my work and her play to go on. What the sequence
definitely does not capture is the surreptitious and perseverant nature of Katie's
requests to play while I work. This is true whether the task is shoveling snow,
raking leaves, washing the driveway, or whatever. The occasion of my working
provides Katie with an irresistible impulse to play with me. She will literally do so
until I stop working, wear her out, or she bugs me to the point that I verbally
indicate my serious displeasure at her efforts, at which time she usually desists.
This is why in this sequence I am efficiently responding to her requests, anticipating that they will continue for some time and potentially interfere with sweeping.

The question that occurs to me at such times is, "What does playing ball
mean to Katie such that it so important for her to be doing it at these particular

times, while I am working around the house?" What about my working activates her interest in playing ball so consistently? One theory could be that playing ball for Katie occupies a kind of substitute role for the farm work, such as shepherding or ratting, activities that her breed was created to do. If one were on a farm that herded with corgis, Katie would have her work cut out for her every day and would probably be up to the task, as indicated in the brief introductory remarks about her breed. I lean towards the theory that Katie needs to work, as part of her nature, and that, to use the Freudian metaphor, she has cathected this work-energy to playing ball, not as a substitute for work (because she does not know that there is a real work), but as a way to focus the impulses she was created to have.

How this focusing on play occurred in Katie's life is a mystery to me, since it occurred before she was a part of our family. The reader will remember that when we first brought her home at age four months we discovered that she already loved to fetch a ball. Whether she learned this from her initial human "mother" or "father" in Missouri, where she was born, or from the personnel in the pet shop in New York City, where she lived for six weeks before we got her, I cannot say. In fact, I cannot say if she learned it at all from any human, or any other dog for that matter. All I can report is that Katie was always an insistent and highly focused ball player, and more generally object retriever (stick, toy, sock). As soon as we got her, we noticed that she thoroughly enjoyed fetching various objects. She would take the object and play tug with us, then drop it at our feet and bark until we tossed it for her. This routine was fully developed when we got her, and none of us in the household, even my wife, who complained initially of Katie's stubbornness about playing ball whenever she wanted, did anything to break her of the habit. She was an especially cute ball and rolled-up sock retriever when she was a pup!

To understand today's display of Katie's having to play ball with me while I am working, I think you have to see the continuity of playing practices that Diane and I, and to some degree Peter, have provided for Katie. I am not sure that other than by very drastic measures we could have done otherwise, but by continuing to play ball with her we have allowed her to keep using this form of activity to satisfy whatever pressing needs it does.

Despite the fact that she appears to be driven when she is playing—and as mentioned above sometimes she is completely oblivious to my discomfort or comfort or happiness or unhappiness at doing so—I think Katie plays ball in the very incessant and insistent manner she does when I am working because she thinks it is what we want her to do, to work for her keep. She wants to work for her keep, and has to date found no other way to do so. At least this is a reasoned line of argument (natural theory) from her guardian's perspective.

The Social Situation of Play: Showing Off

Another apparent motive for Katie to play is to show off, and she will take any reasonable opportunity to do so. The presence of both Diane and me in front of the house both playing ball with her sends her into a ball-playing frenzy. If I have been playing with her, and Diane comes out to join us, Katie will have a burst of play energy, whatever her previous circumstances. Katie will only present the ball to Diane, requesting that Diane throw it for her. I have noticed that Katie much prefers to show her stuff to human females and will regularly ignore potential male players in their favor.

Diane and I notice this same showing off behavior with persons outside of the family, for example with the couple and their corgi with whom we sometimes walk in the local park. During these walks she is particularly keen on having one of the walkers throw a stick for her. She likes to show what she can do, a mark of a good herding dog. But she is also likely to engage in this kind of showing off behavior with total strangers. If she can find a human audience, she loves to show her stuff to them. This has been observed in both working and companion corgis.

Reactivity to the Videotaping of Play

While all videography shapes the thing it documents, videotaping in this analysis was noticeably a reactive procedure at times, to certain degrees and in certain ways. The following are some general (autoethnographic) notes and field notes about the ways videotaping observably affected play.

There appears to be an asymmetrically felt effect of videotaping on the course of play. The best and most involving play we have is discovered, i.e., is never planned but only encountered. Plans to have great play usually do not work out accordingly. Great play is a mutually discoverable thing. We have not had great play recorded on the video, and one reason may well be because of the recording of the play.

Videotaped play is planned, perhaps posed, and not just encountered. The way videos were done at my home was to open the garage door, set up the camera in the garage near an available outlet, and shoot play from inside the garage. The process of carrying out and setting up the camera already affected my routine of play with Katie, which normally would be to just come outside on the porch after she had done her morning business, and begin play. She is usually very excited and impatient to get started, and the setting up of the camera is frustrating to her. I take a minute or two to plug it in, set up the shot and then press record. This leaves Katie dealing with a period of prolonged anticipation, dropping the ball repeatedly at my feet while I fumble with the apparatus. The quality of the play occasion may thus be seriously compromised for her from the outset.

After the shot is set and the camera abandoned by me, play begins. The quality of play also seems affected by the video. On my part there is a certain self-consciousness imposed by the data-gathering procedure. Since the camera is still and unmanned and since I want to get good audiovisual data, I am quite limited as to where I can move when playing ball with Katie and remain in frame. This makes me conscious of how I move and at what angle, i.e., I am at every moment aware of where the camera is. As opposed to the videotaping I did at State Hospital, where the activities being taped were often so engrossing that it was impossible to maintain awareness of the camera or cameraman, playing with Katie is more playing-in-order-to-get-audiovisual-data-from-an-un-manned-videocamera. Because of my dual role in the affairs, I am always aware of the angle of the camera, and when I speak I am aware that I am speaking both to Katie and the camera, for the record.

For Katie the situation is quite different. She has no awareness that the videotaping has anything to do with play once I leave it. She does not share any of my concerns above. Yet she seems to change her play when the camera is on. This appears to me as a kind of tentativeness or suspicion in her play that is not usually there. It has occurred to me that Katie may sense indirectly my own alteration of play for the camera, the fact that I am limited in the space in which play is going to occur, and that I alter my vocalizations self-consciously. Katie's duration of play also seems to be slightly affected, as she appears much less motivated to continue. Perhaps my own analytic interest in our play destroys the fun of play for her. This may be a strong way of putting it. Perhaps "trans-forms" rather than "destroys" is better. I have sensed her unwillingness to ap-proach me while I am operating the camera. At certain points on the tape I try to get her to approach the camera and take the ball. She does not appear easy during these attempts and does not want to approach me. Summarily, from the look of things, Katie does not like the camera.

Field Notes on Katie's Stopping Play

(9/25/96) It has been two days since Katie has played ball with me. This is the first time in the almost three years that I have known her that she has been unwilling to play ball. To my recollection her refusal was a sudden event in the middle of play two days ago. She was chasing a ball when she simply turned around, stopped chasing it, and then went into the house. Aside from her general negative reactions to the camera, there were no clear warning signs within the play. Since that time she has refused to chase the ball or otherwise engage me in ball play.

Thinking that this was a possible sign of illness or boredom, Diane and I have each taken her to the park the past two days. In the park we notice no deviation from her normal behavior. She appears to have energy and chases the sticks we throw for her into the stream in the reservation as usual.

She refused again this morning, even though she seemed anxious to play when I announced "bally." She chased after me. We went to where I usually keep the balls, but there were none. We found one eventually in the garage. I set up the camera. She presented the ball to me and when I threw it she would not chase it. This is to me odd and remarkable behavior.

Diane echoed my own feelings when she said maybe Katie was sensitive to the presence of the camera, and that it was destroying her fun in the play. I have not used the camera since the incident and will refrain from doing so until our play situation straightens out. That way I will also be able to understand in what ways the camera may be an issue.

Katie has evidenced some other odd behaviors in the past two weeks. Especially shocking was her jumping into Gail's car (the guardian of Chester the corgi we walk with in the park) after our walk. This height of disloyalty occurred while I was in school, but was almost repeated the other day when I was present. Katie showed great interest in getting into the back seat of Gail's car. Diane and I wonder if she is simply not happy with us—although I cannot understand why that would be. It may not have to do much with our particular behaviors toward her. We treat and care for her quite well. We are affectionate, and it is clearly she who is ambivalent in her assessment of us.

So it is possible that her ceasing to play ball may be related to more general problems she may have with us. It remains to be seen. As of today anything is possible, from Lyme disease to neurosis or depression.

Katie's Hiatus Continued

(10/4/96) It has been ten days since my last field note entry. Ten days of resisting any urge to begin writing about playing ball with Katie.

On the suspicion that the researched character of Katie's play life might have contributed to "bumming her out," I stopped videoing and taking notes about our play together. For a solid week her unwillingness to play and her other unusual behaviors continued. She was particularly distrustful of me, as opposed to Diane, and would engage in unresponsive behaviors when I would command her to "come." Because of the extended character of this change, it began to concern me as a possible symptom of illness, even if expressed inconsistently. It also occurred to me that Katie's response, being apparently specific to me, could be due to something unique to me, perhaps even that *I* was ill or "smelled bad," and that her behaviors indicated that she had picked up on something wrong with me. On the other hand, Diane noted that even when she tried to play bally with Katie during this period she would be very lackadaisical and lethargic in her play, as if generally depressed.

I noted that during this period Katie did a lot of sleeping in Peter's room, on his bed and on the comforter that was folded on the computer printer. She could indeed have been missing Peter, whom she relates to in a way quite different from Diane or me, more like a brother, an equal. It occurred to me that it could have been Peter that she was missing, and perhaps that was why she was behaving as she was. Peter had departed a few days before she had stopped playing. And I was obviously and visually linked to Peter's leaving. I packed him into the car and U-Haul with Katie watching and then drove him to school. Maybe she is angry with me? With dogs it can be hard to tell.

For more than a week Katie remained indifferent to Diane's and my attempts to get her to play. It had reached a point where I had resolved to call the veterinarian and ask him what he thought of the situation and what I could do. Then, suddenly, with no overt or apparent difference between that day and the one preceding it, she began to play bally again. It is true that I had been especially nice to her in the days of her "depression," but there is no apparent explanation for the fact that she suddenly began to play again as quickly as she had stopped.

When she started to play again I was careful not to introduce the video camera, in case it was the culprit in the drama. After playing with her for a couple of days and establishing a normal rhythm of play, I introduced the camera again today, with no apparent ill effect.

Summary and Discussion of Autoethnographic and Videographic Data

The accounts and visual representations of playing ball with Katie display our mutual work as a continually elaborated theme of our everyday life. This mutual work has a particular history to it, in the sense that any instance of play reflects what each of us brings to it individually and our "mutual biography" of playing ball together. For Katie and me playing occurs as lived, concrete, specific occasions within that shared history. Instances of playing ball are made to happen with regard to these long-term historical features, as well as contingent ones such as weather, field of play, relationship to immediately previous occasions of play, health of players and so on. In this sense, each occasion of play is what Garfinkel refers to as a "lived orderliness." It is "orderly" in praxiological and historical ways described and shown by the data. Our playing is not random, it is methodical. Yet it is "lived" in that playing must be made to happen, brought off, under just these conditions, just now, with just these players. The written and visual data are attempts to convey to the reader the "in vivo" course of David Playing Ball With Katie.

There could be many methods and ways to convey this to the reader. In social science writing, the attempt is to de-gloss or deconstruct "playing ball with

Katie" and formulate it into its constituent, witnessable, observable, everyday events and practices. These practices consist of specifically describable, mutual bodily movements and posturing in relation to the play object. They are done within intersubjectively shared productions of particular game motifs and moves. Upon these "evidently" understood game structures, described and displayed above, players make play moves with regard to their specifically understood possibilities within that motif or game order. The game structures for Katie and me consisted of "simple" throw and retrieve, "football-style throwing," playing field offense/defense in doggie soccer, playing kicker/goalie in doggie soccer, lazy play, various stick retrieve variations, and holding/controlling the ball, with most instances of play being a mixture of these. These game motifs were recognizable themes that were elaborated upon in each occasion of play. They were not simply static, invariant, formal structures. Part of "structure" consisted of what each player had learned about the other's moves, what he or she had done in response, and then what was in turn done in response to the response, etc. Despite this historical character to the details of the structures of play, as well as their asymmetrical availability to either player, they were repeatedly and reliably used by both players in an ad hoc'd, mutually responsive and immediately contextually sensible way.

While not entirely programmatic or static, repeated and reliable use of these game motifs was a not a matter of moral indifference to either player. This was observable in the actual details of play, from the look of things. Players could be seen to be joyful at great play, disappointed at uninspired play, angry at unreliable responses to obvious game moves, showing consternation when the other player could not get his or her act together, and so on. In essence, play proceeded based upon trust that the other player would do his or her best to conform to the "normal" ways of play within that play motif. When that trust was violated or confirmed, appropriate emotionality could be observed. In this way, from the perspective of the human player and from the apparent displays and actions of the dog player, play consisted of an observable moral and praxiological orderliness.[18]

In writing the phrase "David playing ball with Katie," it is the above embodied, mundane activities that I intend to invoke for the reader. It is for that work that this phrase is a gloss.

3

Mitchell and Colleagues' Videographic Research about Dog-Human Play

> *More atomistic interpretations . . . of play as a collection of actions . . . fail to describe the overarching objectives of the players in performing these actions. It is as if one were told that someone was cracking eggs into a bowl, whipping them together, pouring milk into them, stirring this mixture together, and so on, but lacked the knowledge that the person was making an omelet. (Mitchell & Thompson, 1991, p. 214)*

Building upon some of the themes presented in the introduction, this chapter utilizes the work of Robert Mitchell and his colleagues to explore the relevance of the previous chapter to the extant literature about dog-human play. Robert Mitchell has been investigating this and related topics for twenty years, and the body of work he and his colleagues have published is impressive, important and needs to be incorporated into this present writing. As described in the introduction, and in line with policies within EM that were already part of how I saw and wrote about things, collection of data was purposefully and for good reasons undertaken in ignorance of previous research in animal studies. Those reasons have now been satisfied and the explication of the current research in terms of previous research on this topic is a reasonable expectation of scholarly work.[1]

The chapter is organized into two parts. First the approach developed by Mitchell to dog-human play will be described, as will the basic results of that research. Then the data presented about playing with Katie will be discussed in terms of its relevance to Mitchell's work.

Mitchell's approach to play is a combination of theory and empirically derived concepts. As mentioned in the introduction, Mitchell employs an intentional, teleological frame to explain social play between dogs and humans, and specifically rejects more atomistic and behavioral approaches.

We present an approach to social play that views players as goal-directed agents whose goals function to maintain their play. In this approach, the actions of players are organized into projects, which are sequences of actions that are repeated in order to calibrate the organism's control over these actions or over the actions of another player. These social projects are coordinated into routines, or repeated interaction patterns. Routines are usually composed of compatible projects (i.e., projects mutually fulfilling to both players), and in this way play is stabilized through reciprocity between players. When projects are incompatible, players are expected to entice each other through self-handicapping, refusal to play, manipulative self-handicapping or refusal to play, and manipulation. In this approach, the activities of players are described at two levels: as actions and projects; and their interactions are characterized in two ways: as routines and enticements. (Mitchell & Thompson, 1991, p. 189)

I will explicate the meaning of this description of play below. It is founded on a view of dogs and humans as intentional players, by which Mitchell and Thompson mean "that the *animal* [i.e., nonhuman animal] is organizing its movements in a particular way to achieve, in a reasonable manner, a particular effect" (Mitchell & Thompson, 1991, p. 200). The authors propose that biological and behavioral views of play do not allow players to be seen this way and are "wrong as starting points" (Mitchell & Thompson, 1991, p. 200). They make observable instances of play unintelligible.[2]

Mitchell's Definition of Play Reflects This Intentional Approach

I claim that people perceive an activity as play when they perceive the organism engaging in intentional activity which either appears to be done for its own sake or for amusement, or appears intentionally to simulate end-directed activity for benign ends. (Mitchell & Thompson, 1991, p. 198)

This definition and theory of play as social and intentional emerged from both empirical research and an examination of literature. The empirically derived categories are the result of a 1986 analysis of videotaped play between 24 humans and dogs. In that study, the data from which has been used for many articles on dog-human play, dogs were paired with their guardians and with a stranger to play, with the restriction that if person A played with person B's dog, person B played with person A's dog. This resulted in 24 familiar and 24 unfamiliar play sessions. The guardians were present during unfamiliar play. The person videotaping was readily observable, and various play objects were available to players. "The person was told to feel free to engage in any sort of play he or she wished, and to end the interaction whenever he or she wanted" (Mitchell & Thompson, 1991, p. 196).

The tapes were viewed and two levels of coding, action codes and project codes, were developed. "Action codes were devised on the basis of theoretical and empirical considerations. The coding of action results in descriptions that indicate who performed the action, the direction of the action, who and what the action was directed in relation to, and whether contact was made or lost" (Mitchell & Thompson, 1991, p. 196). Dogs' actions were classified into 17 categories and people's into 19, with most of the action codes being fairly reliable. Some of these action codes will be utilized in the analysis of play with Katie.

Utilizing the data and various theoretical considerations, Mitchell and his colleagues developed the approach to play described above. The authors base their analysis on the idea of "projects" and "routines." In solitary play, "projects" are repetitive action sequences engaged in by the animal. "Simpson's term 'project' subsumes under one category those actions during an organism's solitary play that use different means to achieve the same goal (Simpson, 1976, p. 192)" (Mitchell & Thompson, 1991, p. 192). In Simpson's view the organism engages in repetitive projects in varying circumstances (the author uses the example of a monkey leaping, where leaping is "a project" that is done repeatedly but in a variety of circumstances). Simpson also maintains a teleological view of these projects. "In Simpson's account, the monkey is varying its actions in different contexts using different motor movements in order to calibrate its control over its actions." The idea is that through repetition with variation the organism learns to fine-tune its control over these actions. It "self-experiments" in order to "learn to control consequences of minor variations in [its] actions and to accommodate to continuing changes in bodily construction and coordination (Simpson, 1976)" (as cited in Mitchell & Thompson, 1991, p. 192).

Thus in Mitchell's view the elemental building blocks for play are these individual projects, the repetitive action sequences during which the players "calibrate control" over something: a ball, person, their bodies, etc. These individual projects change by virtue of accommodation in social play.

> In social play, one partner engages in its projects in coordination with the other partner's enacting of its own projects. Thus, unlike solitary play, social play requires adjustment between participants. If participant A is to engage in its projects, it must respond to participant B so as to bring about the opportunity of engaging in A's projects. But it must also behave in such a way as to offer opportunities for B to engage in B's projects. This interactive coordination between projects does not present any problem of adjustment when projects are compatible. Compatibility is present when A and B each engage in projects that require the simultaneous or near-simultaneous enactment of the other's project for their fulfillment. . . . Such social projects allow organisms to calibrate their control over actions of the partner as well as over their own actions.

The interanimal behavior sequences that result from the interaction of projects are called routines (Mitchell & Thompson, 1986). The most readily recognized routines are composed of compatible projects, though certainly routines composed of incompatible projects occur (Mitchell & Thompson, 1986, p. 193).

What is established in social play is mutual dependency and reciprocity between players. Each must adjust its own projects to those of the other player, although one should not assume that this mutual adjustment is done to the same proportion by each player; i.e., there is not an assumption that accommodation needs to be done symmetrically by both players.

Players employ various strategies when other players fail to enact compatible projects or when one refuses to play (engage in any project). "Enticements are methods (other than the full enactment of a project compatible with the other's current project) by which player A gets player B to engage in a project that is compatible with one of A's projects, or by which A gets B to engage in new activities such that A can accomplish the goal of A's project (and perhaps engage in a new project)" (Mitchell & Thompson, 1991, p. 194).

Enticements occur in two forms: self-handicaps and manipulative activities. "In self-handicaps, A practices its actions to achieve its goal in a less than optimal manner, because if it proceeds towards its goal in an optimal manner, B does not play. . . . Thus, A engages incompletely in its project while B engages in its own project" (Mitchell & Thompson, 1991, p. 194). The standard example is playing "catch me" while running away from your partner less quickly than one could. "An extreme form of self-handicapping is a refusal. In a refusal, a player fails to engage in a project compatible with the other's project, apparently (if not actually) withdrawing from play" (Mitchell & Thompson, 1991, p. 194).

"In manipulative activities, A performs actions that are not compatible with B's project in order to either (1) to get B to engage in a new project or (2) to get B to engage in activities discordant with B's current project, which might allow A to fulfill the goal of a project compatible with B's project" (Mitchell & Thompson, 1991, p. 194). The authors give the example for (1) above of a collie and a shepherd playing object keepaway in which one dog tries to switch the play object to a rag when it had failed to get the ball the other had. "In this instance, the shepherd uses an incompatible project to entice; any such use is manipulation" (Mitchell & Thompson, 1991, p. 194).[3]

As an example of (2) the authors discuss refusal, in which one player does not play in order to get the other player to self-handicap, i.e., stopping play as a way to get the other player to restructure the play interaction.

Another example of (2) is often present in object-keepaway: the collie, by bringing the ball close to the shepherd but moving away when the shepherd comes close, entices the shepherd to engage in its project of chase the ball. In this instance, the player uses self-handicaps manipulatively by giving the other the impression that the opportunity to fulfill its own project is imminent, though most likely it is not. . . . Self-handicaps and manipulations may themselves become projects and engender routines if they are repeatedly and playfully engaged in. And something like manipulations and self-handicaps may be inherent in some projects, as seems the case with the project of object-keepaway. (Mitchell & Thompson, 1991, p. 195)

Another important feature of Mitchell and Thompson's view of play has to do with embellishment of play routines and how deception can be used to elaborate upon previous routines. They note that routines are not fixed but are played with; that is, they are changed, thwarted or transformed by the players through variation over time.

In the example above, the dog may keep the ball away from the person, or the person may run after the ball along with the dog. Yet a play routine, as such, leads to some expectations, and hence to the possibility for manipulation and thwarting of expectations. Deception is possible in play because actions, due to their juxtaposition with certain outcomes, are the signs for animals of possible future events. (Mitchell & Thompson, 1986, p. 193).

The deception observed commonly in play between dogs and persons is integral to some forms of play. Interestingly, deception in such play is found in many cases of dog-human players who are familiar to each other and who play with each other regularly. In their 1993 article on this topic, Mitchell and Thompson note that familiarity breeds deception in certain forms of play, despite theories to the contrary. This was particularly true for deception during "show object," "throw object," and "retrieve object," where "deception simulated honest activities" (Mitchell & Thompson, 1993, p. 298). In such cases, where the dog and human player are familiar with one another and play regularly, players begin to react to the deceptive attempts of the other, i.e., develop an attitude of "skepticism" and begin to adjust their play to take deception of the other into account. This is a way for them to elaborate upon the previous routines, to innovate and make new moves that, if successful, capture the interest and require response from the other player.

The more contextually specialized the honest acts, the more familiarity . . . with another's responsiveness can lead to relatively more frequent deception—if the deceiver benefits from it. The fact that victims can assess reliability of a communicative act (i.e., be skeptical) can, in our view, lead to high frequencies of deception to counteract the effect of counter deception by the victim, but such skepticism may have no consistent influence on the frequency or rarity of deception. (Mitchell & Thompson, 1993, p. 299)

As acknowledged by the authors, the reason it has no consistent influence is that such deception makes play more fun; and fun is the reason players play.

In summary, Mitchell and Thompson present a view of dog-human play in which players intentionally engage in activities for their own sake or amusement (what was called in the introduction "autotelic play"), or as activities that simulate another end-directed activity but for benign ends. In doing this players engage in individual play projects that need to be accommodated to one another so that the projects are made compatible. For the most part compatible play projects form the basis for play routines, and much play between dogs and humans consists of routines based upon compatible projects. Compatible projects in routines are those whose objectives can be fulfilled through the enactment of the other player's project.

Various accommodations are required of dog and human players in order to achieve stable play.

> Enticements depend on self-handicaps and manipulative activities. A self-handicap occurs when a player's actions make the objective of a compatible project by the other player more likely to be attained, at the expense of fulfillment of the self-handicapper's objective. A manipulative self-handicap occurs when a player follows a self-handicap with actions that make the objective of a compatible project less likely to be attained. A refusal occurs when a player stops engaging in a project compatible with the partner's project or fails to engage in a compatible project but then enacts one. . . . And a manipulation occurs when a player, by enacting a project incompatible with the other's project, tries either to thwart the goal of the other's project or to get the other to engage in a new project. (Mitchell & Thompson, 1991, p. 199)

Mitchell and his colleagues report that this conceptualization is useful in "parsing" the interactions observed on tape and is parsimonious with current psychological knowledge of dogs and humans (Mitchell & Thompson, 1991, p. 212) (although they also rightly note that such knowledge is itself highly incomplete and not consistent). Their results are general, based upon aggregated data averaged over the course of 48 videotaped interactions (for example, that such and such a percent of routines were composed of compatible projects). The authors are interested in average play and not in explaining the experience or structure of specific cases of dog-human play. In their own view the utility of their work is to be judged by its contribution to a theory of dog-human play and not in terms of its relationship to the experience of particular players.

It is clear that these authors view play as understandable, motivated, socially organized and fun. Play is "autotelic," a feature that is often signified by its highly repetitive character. Play can also be "pretend" or "simulated," in which the play acts look like non-play acts (for example, sex or fighting) but are done in a way that is "incomplete, inhibited, exaggerated or uneconomical, repeated more often and relatively unordered" (Mitchell, 1990, p. 205). Mitchell also describes social play as having different levels of complexity hierarchically, such that the simplest forms must be mastered before proceeding to more complicated ones. The levels of play move from motor-perceptual play that is programmed and not dependent upon learning to forms of play that are learned and that increasingly require the player to display forms of intentional simulation. As the reader will see in the next section, much of the play engaged in by Katie and me would be at the third of Mitchell's five levels of play, and almost none of our play involved pretend play.

Before leaving this brief summary of Mitchell and his colleagues' research on dog-human play, I want to mention their research on talk during dog-human play. In two articles (Mitchell, 2001; Mitchell & Edmonson, 1999), the functions of talking to dogs during play are examined by a linguistic analysis of the audio portions of the videotape data described above. The commonly observed "baby talk" that humans employ with dogs during play (doggerel) was analyzed and compared to the talk employed by mothers with young human infants (motherese). Many common features were found, including high pitch, low mean length of utterance, high frequencies of grammatically acceptable utterances, repetitiveness, attention-getting devices and present tense verbs. There were also some differences noted, but basically both forms of talk involved communicating with an addressee who was inattentive and with highly limited comprehension. Both forms of talk often involved controlling attention or behavior and expressing friendliness and affection. Differences seemed to reflect the eventual speaking status assumed by the mother in the tutoring aspects of her speech with the infant, which is lacking in doggerel.[4]

Generally, the results of linguistic analysis of this data reveal that people talk a lot to their dogs during play, that they use simple, repetitive and grammatically correct utterances, and that these utterances appear to function in a way to control the actions of the animal. Some human players speak in a fashion that provides for a conversational feeling (a feeling of effective communication), although there was a noticed lack of speech by humans during play that attempted to represent the animal's view or to talk for or on behalf of the animal.

While no actual audio recordings of talk in play with Katie are presented, the autoethnographic data about talk to Katie will be explicated in terms of the above research.

Relationship of Playing with Katie to Mitchell and Colleagues' Research

Of all the work I encountered in animal-human studies, the perspective taken by Robert Mitchell and his colleagues, particularly Nicholas Thompson, is most consistent with the view that emerged from this research. Their observations and explanations of dog-human play are consistent with many of those in the current study. In this section I will demonstrate some of the ways their themes can be found in my own data, and also the ways some of their ideas may be slightly differently construed from a praxiological/EM perspective.

Mitchell (personal communication, 2003) correctly characterizes the similarity between animal and human ethology on the one hand and EM on the other. What ethology and EM share is a concern for the observable details of everyday behavior, and in this sense both are "naturalistic" sciences. Because of this, it is not surprising that there is a certain resonance between their methods and findings. However, this similarity hides what are some significant differences.

Perhaps because my data and the data used by Mitchell are based upon a detailed analysis of actual instances of play, the most significant similarity in our work is finding that play must be understood as detailed, socially organized, intentional activity. The written data about playing with Katie are naively but thoroughly intentional; there can be no question after reading the data that they present our "game moves" as motivated actions to be understood within the history and detailed practices of the game being played, or that the moves are often instantly understood and done without reflection. This is the same view of play that emerges in Mitchell and his colleagues' work.

> Dogs and people recognize the directionality of each other's projects and actions; if they did not, they would not be able to predict each other's actions. Much of this prediction is probably unconsciously processed by the organisms involved. For example, the dodges and ruses which both dogs and people use are done so quickly as to seem effortless. We think it is reasonable to say that dogs and people also recognize the intentionality present in action. Not surprisingly, people employ a rich intentional description and explanation of their own and dogs' actions. (Mitchell & Thompson, 1991, p. 202)

"Intentionality present in action" is a fine way to phrase things. Here we are very close to how EM would characterize players in a play situation. The lively inner states of others are evident, or not (as an empirical matter), in and of the interaction. They are not, at least entirely, private matters that cannot be "vulgarly" read in the course of interaction. They are, observationally and naturally speaking, not "inner" states. This will be looked at in some more detail in the next chapter.

Mitchell and his colleagues find that humans make sense of dogs' behaviors in play through contextual interpretation. What appears to occur is that the human player reads the movements of the dog player in a way that assumes the animal is acting similarly to a human in a similar context. That is,

> . . . when an animal's global body movements in a particular context are

similar to those of a human in the same context (where behaviors appear natural to the organism's described), people use this similarity of behavior-in-context to interpret the animal and the human as having the same psychological state. (Mitchell & Hamm, 1997, p. 177)

Humans understand human and nonhuman animals' motives and actions via this interpretive device, which is very similar to the way we interpret conversational utterances *indexically*.[5] We rely upon the movements of the animal, natural to the animal, as expressions of the animal's intentionality-in-action. The movements are read against a backdrop of understanding what the game is, and what the animal is trying to do, what game move it is making, then and there. This is precisely what is found in the discussion of play with Katie. However, as Mitchell points out, this form of understanding is not anthropomorphic projection of one's own mental state but, rather, witnessed intentionality-in-action. Even though the person has no direct access to the subjective psychological state of the animal, conventional usage of psychological terms used to describe animals is assumed accurate unless otherwise indicated, and this certainly appears perspicuously in the current data.

Another feature of play described by Mitchell, its "autotelic" character, is certainly evident in the data, especially in the repetitive character of Katie's ball and stick chasing. While the data contain speculations (I did not censor myself, but I do not give these speculations much analytic weight) about why Katie was so passionate and repetitive in her play, all that really can be said observationally speaking is that these activities appeared to have an intrinsic value to her and were not goal-directed towards some practical end. This extreme repetition suggests that her reenactments were not being done just to achieve the end (capture), but were performed for their own sake. While other forms of play were possible, with the exception of tug rope, which resembles "pretend" or simulative play fighting in some respects, all of our play had this extremely repetitive, not end-directed character.

Because Mitchell and Thompson inspected a large video data set and developed empirical definitions of the observed projects and routines, they identified all of the projects Katie and I engaged in, and more that we never played. They also identified other empirical phenomena that are consistent with the data and will be discussed, including embellishment, self-handicap, teasing, manipulation and deception.

Mitchell (personal communication, 2003), in reading the data on playing with Katie, remarked that much of what we did involved what he and Thompson called "fakeout" (David) and "avoid fakeout" (Katie).[6] We played in a way that is described by Mitchell & Thompson (1991, p. 214) in which the pet guardian clearly specialized in fakeout and the dog in avoid fakeout. The guardian clearly showed that he intended to play at fakeout, and the play consisted of various kinds of feigned throws and kicks designed to get the dog to fall for the fake. Aside from the straightforward throw and retrieve game (for example, throwing the stick at the park), this form of fakeout and avoid fakeout was what Katie and I did for the most part, although I did not time-sample our play to get a quantitative measure of exactly how dominant this particular form of play was.

The data about playing with Katie display the ways in which this mode of play was made to happen in particular instances, and also how the play was embellished over time to keep it fun and interesting. "If a person's enactment of throw the ball predictably makes the dog chase the ball, the person can test the limits of this predictability by varying the similarity of his or her actions to the actions of throw the ball" (Mitchell & Thompson, 1991, p. 213). The dog then develops the response of "avoid fakeout" to the guardian's fakeout, and similarly can test its abilities to distinguish between the real and fake throw and kick. In a guardian relationship such as I have with Katie this form of play becomes embellished over time.

Other dog projects (there were a total of 12 in Mitchell and Thompson's study) that are seen in the data are "chase object," "dropaway" (dog moves away and drops object), "retrieve object" (dog makes object available to person), and "surrender" (dog allows itself to be petted). Not specifically mentioned in the data but also part of Katie's play-related repertoire are "tug of war" and "object keepaway (where dog attempts to interest person in object but not let him or her get it)" (Mitchell & Thompson, 1990, p. 27). Similarly, in my own case I engaged in many of the 14 different human projects identified by the authors. In addition to fakeout, the data show that I engaged in "capture dog" (person exhibits control over dog physically), "hide object" (person interests dog by showing and hiding object), "instigate dog" (person attempts to engage dog repeatedly or by tagging it), "instigate with object" (person attempts to interest the dog by repeatedly contacting it with the object), and "throw object" (person makes object available to dog by throwing or kicking it) (Mitchell & Thompson, 1990, p. 28).

In enacting our play, much deception was employed.[7] This is most clearly visible in the tapes when I "hide object" and do "fakeout." That much of our play employed deceptive strategies is consistent with the finding by Mitchell and Thompson (1993, p. 298) that "familiarity does not make deception rare and indeed apparently breeds deception." Players familiar with one another, such as Katie and I, employ deception even though it becomes expected as part of play, and they are nonetheless susceptible to it. Players benefit from the deception in the sense that they use it to engage in play they find satisfying. They develop counter-deceptive (and counter-counter-deceptive) strategies. This was the way it was with Katie and me. I employed well-known deceptions in order to make the game more fun for us to play, and she developed a skeptical attitude and counter-deceptive strategies. Based on her counter-deception, I altered my deceptive strategies, and so on.[8]

As described by Mitchell and Thompson, "self-handicapping" was an essential aspect of play with Katie and was engaged in by both players. Katie regularly used the extreme form of "manipulative self-handicap" when she would sit with the ball in her mouth and refuse to play, despite my enticements. This was the basic way she employed self-handicapping. I, on the other hand, had a host of self-handicapping devices, used to make the play more interesting, that were inherent to the play. These occurred in forms of throwing play where my physical superiority would have allowed me to throw the ball so far that she could not have chased it and captured it. Inherent to the throwing play was giving Katie "the impression that the opportunity to fulfill . . . [her] own project is imminent, even though most likely it is not" (Mitchell & Thompson, 1991, p. 195). The whole trick to play being fun lies in the "most likely" part of it. It may be appropriate to think of "fun" as consisting of the possibility of success, and thus, in order for "avoid fakeout" to be fun for Katie, she has to have a chance to succeed. In order to play throw ball, the ball must be thrown in such a way that she has an opportunity to pursue and capture it. Thus self-handicap was an inherent aspect of these forms of play with Katie. Self-handicap did not seem to occur in certain other forms of play, and these motifs were a real contest between us. This could be seen, for example, in the form of "doggie soccer" where Katie guarded me and I had to attempt to get the ball by her, or in "free kick goalie" play where I tried to kick the ball past her from a distance. During these games it appears that both Katie and I tried our hardest to "beat" the other player. So it may be, as Mitchell suggests, that in only some games self-handicaps are employed by players when they need to make playing more fun.

There is a slight difference in how I experienced self-handicap in play and how it is defined by Mitchell and Thompson. In looking at my play with Katie, my self-handicaps were not completely at the expense of fulfillment of the self-handicapper's objective. When I self-handicapped in play with Katie I directly benefited from the strategy through having a fun game to play with her. I had no sense of giving anything up at all and felt that in doing so both Katie and I immediately benefited.

It is also possible to typify play with Katie via the hierarchical levels described by Mitchell. Specifically, play with Katie resembled what he describes as third-level play, that is, learned play that builds upon the organism's existing behavioral repertoire. As noted by Mitchell, much of this play takes the form of "teasing," by which is meant "actions . . . used to instigate or manipulate others in a surprising or irritating way" (Mitchell, 1990, 208). Many of our play motifs had an element of teasing to them, including the fakeouts used in throwing/kicking and Katie's extreme use of self-handicapping to control the ball. It is interesting to note that there was extremely little schematic play, such as play fighting or chasing, and virtually no play that involved intentional simulation (fourth level) or intentional communication of the simulation (fifth level).

Finally, some brief remarks about talk to Katie during play: there was no systematic investigation of this property of play and no audio data are presented (i.e., audio tracks are absent from the compact disk video versions of tape). However, the textual data reveal features that are highly consistent with those noted by Mitchell generally.[9] I employed a form of "doggerel," whose features were described in the previous chapter. The talk was highly repetitive and often attempted to influence Katie's behavior (I do not think "control" is quite the correct word to describe what I did with language, and I believe Mitchell also recognizes this when he says that commands in play were friendly). The way it worked has something to do with the ways dogs participate in conversation through bodily action and gesture.[10] I talked to Katie in the course of the play to exhort her to action, to tell her what action I wanted her to do, to ask her how she was feeling or if she was hurt, etc. Her "answer," her turn of talk, was made in the form of behavior. Talk was thus meaningfully embedded in the unfolding, *in situ* course of mutually produced bodily events.

My impression is that talk was generally and often part of our play, although since I have not examined it systematically I cannot say to what degree this is the case. I cannot empirically claim that my talk as embedded into the playing had a particular structure or periodicity (for example, that in playing talk occurred more at this or that juncture, or with respect to this or that play activity), although it is my impression that it did. I also suspect that talk was a somewhat variable aspect of our play, that on some days I was not at all talkative but on others more so, but this is also recall data and suspect on that ground.

Given the above discussion the reader can appreciate that it is both possible and profitable to read the data on play with Katie as an extension of the work of Mitchell and his colleagues. In a way much of my field notes fills out in detail or provides flesh to Mitchell and Thompson's writing about variations in projects—i.e., repeated action sequences around a same theme but showing variation. To some degree the data present a natural history and praxiological description of how this worked in our particular case.

The reader also needs to appreciate the differences between the object of their study and my own. Their work was aimed at an understanding of average play, or play in general. The methodology used—videotaping and coding many instances of play, and then counting, aggregating and statistically analyzing the results for all cases—creates "average approaches" to the phenomena and measures of central tendency. Such a method locates average distributional features (the overall percentage of utterances that were commands, or the overall percentage of routines that were composed of compatible projects). Average approaches are of interest to many scientists, as they represent general tendencies in a population or phenomenon. Yet it is important to note that general tendencies can only be found in academic writing. They cannot be found by observing actual instances of play, which consist of "just" these particular players, there and then, with just these resources, under such conditions, and so on. Thus one main difference between Mitchell and his colleagues' work and my project is that I am not concerned with producing "average approaches" to playing with or talking to dogs.

This is not to question the value of a general understanding of how play works between dogs and humans; one gains a tremendous sense of what is involved in dogs' and humans' playing together when you read Mitchell and his colleagues' writings, the breadth or complexity of which has not even been indicated in my brief summary. However, there are costs to the kind of methods used by Mitchell. One loses a sense of how actual instances of play work, of plays unfolding as a lived, natural process, of all that is involved, its emotions, its lived embodiment, of how particular dog-human players pull it off, the joy of victory, of getting it done, and what "it" for them particularly is or, in the current instance, how it evolves over time between a particular dog and a human. It is the price of a general understanding, I think, which is not to say that it is not worth paying for some reasons. Additionally, while Mitchell provides written accounts of play taken from video, they function toward a different end, as illustrative of the analytic elements being discussed. Just as one cannot gain a sense of general dog-human play from my work, one cannot get a sense of what it consists of in all its detail for any particular dog-human players from Mitchell's studies.[11]

The purpose of the descriptions in this study, as explained in the introduction, is to explicate the lived order of play with Katie—to display it and to show what it consisted of for players in local terms. So Mitchell and his colleagues' and my own are two approaches, emphasizing two different ways of studying play and with different ends—Mitchell aiming at understanding general and distributional features of dog-human play and I at a detailed description and natural history of practices involved in a particular instance of dog-human play. If dog-human play exists only as actual, specific instances of it, as EM proposes, describing the natural organization of these instances and figuring out how they work is a critical scientific task.

There are some unclear terminological issues in comparing our work. Mitchell asserts that the idea of "project" is very similar to my idea of motif, although I actually think it is his notion of "routine" that is most similar to motif. In any case, our terminologies differ in significant ways. As defined by Simpson the term "project" is clearly psychological, i.e. based upon individual behavior. Mitchell and Thompson's use of this term to organize observations creates an understanding of play that is social-psychological; play is the result of compat-ible or incompatible *individual* projects. Despite their description of their model of play as social, this sounds very psychological—play as the result of individual psychological initiative and the individual decisions to coordinate these or not.

In reflecting on the data about play with Katie, it does not appear that play is the result of individual projects that happen to come together, nor is it based on the players' decisions in play. I will use two analogies, one jocular, to help explain the difference. It is not the case that drivers on the thruway have come to the thruway with individual driving projects in mind and then decide to coor-dinate these or not. When the crowd screams at the finish line at a racetrack, it is not the case that each person has come to the track with an individual scream-ing project that each decides to coordinate at the end of the race. In reflecting on the data it is my view that the unit of analysis for studying dog-human play naturalistically is the game, the motif being utilized by the players; and that motif contains or entails asymmetrical forms of participation for players (i.e., the projects are more derivative of the social form than constitutive of it). The issue is really one of emphasis and nuance. In EM, we tend to look at the social event as providing for what its individual members could be doing. *The event, the lived order, is the unit of analysis, and the individuals populating it are "enacted features of the setting."*[12]

There are additional matters regarding play with Katie and its relationship to the work of Mitchell and Thompson. They have to do with how to under-stand the nature of play.

Mitchell and Thompson write that their viewpoint sees players and play as teleological, which means that the observed behavior is organized by the inten-tions of the players. This view can be contrasted with a "teleonomic" view, which recognizes the organization of play but is less concerned with explanation or cause of the organization. If what is meant by intentions of players is intention-ality-in-action, as is described above, then the ethological view advanced by Mitchell is similar to that of EM (or vice-versa, given the long history and numerous practitioners of animal ethology). However, as I look at play there is no theoretical requirement or empirical evidence that all play is organized by intentions of players, even when it might appear to be to an outside observer or player. A lot rests upon exactly what one means by intention and what the intention's external and internal representations consist of (see note 2 above). Given the discussions in Mitchell and his colleagues' work and my own data, it is probably wise to refrain from taking a stand about what play does and does not consist of, at least a hard stand. I am undecided about the ways play is organized by players' intentions, and even exactly how such a proposition might be true.

A final discussion having to do with the nature of play concerns whether play is done to practice and gain competencies in non-play situations. Many scientists who study play believe this, which I refer to as "the practice hypothesis." It is based upon developmental, evolutionary, and behavioral evidence. For example, the belief that play is practice is inherent in Simpson's usage of the term "project." Recall his monkey leaping, using the occasions to gain calibration over the project of leaping to self-experiment in order to "learn to control consequences of minor variations in [its] actions and to continue to accommodate to continuing changes in bodily construction" (Mitchell & Thompson, 1991, p. 192).

Let us look at Simpson's monkey. If his proposition is that the monkey is playing in order to practice, i.e., that the monkey is aware that he or she is practicing in order to practice for real life by playing, then the monkey would be very smart! In that version of the play-as-practice hypothesis, what is being advanced clearly indicates the logical fallacy of affirming the consequent (inaccurate anthropomorphism). Getting better at jumping may well be the result of repeated jumping, but this does not in any way entail that the animal performs the jumping to get better at it. Of course, if having intention does not require either awareness of intention or control over it, then it may or may not be that the jumping is intended to be practice. In one case the animal would not know; and in any case, upon what basis could the human observer decide?

The formulation of leaping or jumping as an individual's project "psychologizes" it and neglects the social situation in which the behavior occurs. Seeing it this way fails to appreciate the way that actual instances of jumping are part of a flow of mutually produced and witnessed events, a cooperatively achieved "lived order." If I may expand the frame of reference just a bit to humans as well as monkeys, consider the following list: jumping for joy, jumping from having been startled, jumping while playing tag, jumping as a result of witnessing something horrible, jumping to avoid a predator, jumping over a creek while being chased in play, jumping from one branch to the next while mating, jumping while trying to get a piece of fruit out of reach, (now the human stuff) jumping off a bridge, long jumping, jump shooting, etc. This is not a list of events to which the organism came with a preexisting project of jumping. While jumping can be used to refer to a specific anatomical set of behaviors, this description of it cannot make any sense of what an individual jumping does in any actual situation. Focusing solely upon jumping as an individual behavior ignores how it is a form of social participation. This is what Garfinkel refers to as creating a "psychological dope"; one emphasizes the psychological features while ignoring the social ones.[13]

This being said, there is a way of thinking about the practice hypothesis that makes sense developmentally. It is just the fact of the matter that children and dogs play before engaging in non-play activities. There is no question that the outcome of play, of repeating bodily motions over and over again, is that the animal or child becomes better at those bodily motions as well as the judgments involved in their employment. When babies or dogs play they are gaining skills that can later be used to walk, run, eat, fight, or what have you. But this developmental observation and reasoned argument (almost a combination of observation and tautology) does not imply anything about intent or awareness. The practice is only seen from hindsight. Young children are specifically not aware of what they are doing from an adult point of view. They do not look upon the organization of their own activities as practice for being adults. That view of them is specifically adult and must be distinguished from how children see themselves and organize their world in their own right.[14] One needs to appreciate the practice seen in dog-human play in this same way.

My basic point is that reasoned argumentation concerning play as practice that implies anything further than this obvious observation needs to be evaluated carefully, and on the basis of naturalistic data, not theory. At least in studies of children there is great reason to believe this, and as I have asserted all along, play between dogs and humans needs to be "naturally" appreciated in its own terms.[15]

There are additional important issues that the current research raises for animal-human research, the most important of which may be how to interpret the free use of anthropomorphism and anecdotalism in the data. To utilize Ryle's (1949) distinction of knowing *that* and knowing *how*, the data clearly indicate that in writing about play I appeared to know that Katie felt this or that way about something, and without reflection I used human psychological states to describe these feelings. *How* I knew these things, or whether I *really* knew them are matters that will be further investigated in the next chapter.

4

On the Use of Natural Language to Describe Dog-Human Interaction

This chapter reflects upon whether the use of human characteristics to describe Katie while playing is an inappropriate exercise in anthropomorphic epistemology. Reflecting upon the written data, this issue is something that cannot be avoided, so we shall look at it in some detail.

It would not be possible to decide upon the validity of this method by looking carefully at the written or visual data. The validity of the method might not be easily decided by two observers looking directly at my play with Katie. If one of the observers had a behavioral bent, and the other a phenomenological one, they might well not agree about what it was that they were, in fact, seeing. Even if they could agree about the behavioral details, they would not then necessarily agree about what these meant, or to whom, and on what basis. Both the sociology of knowledge and the philosophy of science have argued that the analyst's ultimate beliefs (what Ernst Grünwald [1934/1970, p. 222]) called the ens reallissimum) or ultimate assumptions (or what Carl Hempel (1966) called "auxiliary assumptions") never get directly tested in science, since they are built into the very methods used to test things. I agree with that observation of science and thus cannot appeal to my own data as a way to ground my method.

I have instead decided to examine anthropomorphism from the perspectives of several critical thinkers from different disciplinary backgrounds: Eileen Crist, D. L. Wieder, Vicki Hearne, Bruno Latour, and Robert Mitchell. My purpose is not to resolve methodological and epistemological issues attendant to each author's discussion of anthropomorphism. I want to point to them and explore their pertinence to the current research.

"Piteous, Hopeless Dejection": The Re-emergence of Darwin's Anthropomorphism

I admit anthropomorphism was a concern even during the data-collection phase of the research. I tried to put it in the back of my mind as much as possible, to proceed as naively as I could, but previous experience in research with children without formal language had sensitized me to its relevance and importance (see Goode, 1994a, chap. 2). Still, I attempted to remain as indifferent to the topic as I could and certainly read nothing until the data collection was over. When I finally asked friends about whom I might read on the topic, a number of them recommended the work of Eileen Crist.

In the observations presented above, both the ethnographic and auto-ethnographic data "assume" the use of natural human language to describe human-dog interaction. This is a widespread, massively observable epistemological practice among dog guardians, aside from the current study, and needs to be explicated critically.

Describing animals anthropomorphically has been debated in one form or another since the invention of modern sciences, and continues today. A critical examination of the practice was taken up by Eileen Crist (1996). She details accusations that Darwin was anthropomorphic in his writings about animal expression (see especially *The Expression of Emotions in Man and Animals*, 1872). Her discussion of Darwin's work, and the tradition to which it led, is of particular import to the current analysis.[1]

Darwin's writings were generally seen as an attack on the religiously inspired notions of "man" as an "emergent" being, qualitatively different from "lower animals" and superior to them. The discontinuity between animals and men (embodied in what Crist calls "the mechanomorphic" viewpoint of animal behavioral sciences, the legacy of Descartes's mechanistic view of animals)[2] was attacked by Darwin in his theory of evolution and also in his writings about the behaviors and actions of animals. These writings often relied on anecdotal evidence and contained language suggesting a "natural interpretability" of animal expression by human beings, and vice versa. Darwin was/is criticized for "lapsing" into anthropomorphic language. Crist disagrees and instead advances the idea that this was not a lapse at all or some relic of nineteenth-century writing. Instead, she proposes, "his [Darwin's] approach reflects his perception of subjectivity—namely, the dimensions of meaningfulness and authorship—in the animal world" (1996, p. 35). Darwin saw animal and human subjectivity and expression as aspects or outcomes of the same evolutionary process.

Thus, rather than seeing Darwin's language as mistakenly anthropomorphic, Crist characterizes it as consistently evolutionary:

> Darwin's language of representing animals makes a resounding statement for evolutionary continuity of animals and humans. Darwin's implicit advocacy for continuity takes shape through a generous, unabashed use of commonplace terms of (human) mind and action as resources through which to witness and understand animal life. Relying on the vernacular vocabulary of action to describe and interpret both animal and human

behaviors is an additional way of arguing for evolutionary continuity. (Crist, 1996, p. 36)

Crist further explains that Darwin's language was descriptive and not just created from a theoretical position:

> Darwin's work does not reflect the fact that he is making unfounded inferences about what goes on inside animals. Darwin's application of anthropomorphic terminology is well documented and does not amount to placing *homunculi* inside the animal: his deployment of mental terms is not derived from rash imputations of specifically human qualities to other animals. Rather, Darwin is concerned with the behavioral and physiological manifestations that support the ascription of subjective phenomena.
> ... [T]hat he believed in a close correspondence between human and animal mentality may be viewed as something of an understatement. There is abundant evidence that Darwin held such a view. His lack of skepticism regarding the attribution of what have often been regarded as specifically human qualities to animals originated from his commitment to the entailments of common descent. The evolutionary perspective compelled him to acknowledge continuity not only at the level of physiological and morphological traits, but with respect to behavioral and mental attributes as well. (Crist, 1996, p. 41)

This latter commitment was the final stretch of the evolutionary path, which even his contemporary supporters could not travel.

Crist describes how animals as subjects emerged in Darwin's writings, subjectivity having two elements identified by Schutz (1974): the meaningfulness of experience and authorship of action. Crist writes that Darwin had a naturalistic view of animals as subjects who authored and experienced action as meaningful. However,

> Darwin does not present subjective states of being in animal life on the basis of inferences from "observable" behavior to "unobservable" mind ... his view of subjective experience is based on observation of particular behavioral and physiological manifestations.
> In other words, Darwin does not speculate about subjective states from behavioral expressions, but rather *witnesses* subjective states *in* behavioral expressions. The constitutive link between a conceptual characterization and the behavioral expression it predicates is often achieved by the presentation of the characterization as a description, as opposed to a hypothesis or a deduction. (Crist, 1996, p. 57)

Thus in Darwin's writings thoughtfulness of an animal comes about through the witnessing of particular overt expressions and actions. That this is the case is a result of the detailed look of things and his belief that those details can be interpreted as they appear to be.

> ... [T]he idea of thinking divorced from overt action or perceptible expres-
> sion is only one class of the phenomena of "thinking," and relatedly, only
> one of the senses in which the concept is used. There is another sense of
> thinking which is internally and locally connected with (some course of)
> action. By "internally," here, an emphasis is intended on the compellingly
> intelligible character of ascribed thinking, under particular circumstances;
> and by "locally" an emphasis is intended on the necessity of concrete be-
> haviors and events which occasion such an ascription. (Crist, 1996, p. 70)

In Darwin's view, animal reasoning is essentially and observably circumstantial. Seen in this fashion, animals display certain "lively inner states" (of
course the same argument can be made about human reasoning and experience).

Crist presents anecdotes about Labrador retrievers to show that the interpretation of dog behavior is both circumstantial and biographical. In one incident a retriever kills a bird purposefully by biting it. The dog was a trained field
dog. It faced two live birds on a retrieve and solved the problem by killing one.
This was seen by the guardian as a deliberate act designed to solve the problem
the dog found itself in, namely, having two live birds to simultaneously retrieve.
The background of the dog, that it had never killed or even ruffled a feather of
any game previously, was also used by the guardian in reasoning the specifically
willful character of the kill. The guardian saw the dog as reasoning and experi-
encing with respect to the situation (situation as understood by the guardian, the
most intimately knowledgeable person about the dog) in which it (that particular
dog with its specific biography) found itself. That is, in the guardian's perspective
the dog's actions were specifically interpretable from within the biographical
event sequence in which the dog, with its unique kill in this instance, evidently
participated. For the guardian, this dog's inner states (what he or she was thinking when he or she killed the first bird) came to be understood within these
events, clearly, observably and without ambiguity.

Darwin provides a marvelous example of such reasoning with his own
dog:

> I formerly possessed a large dog, who, like every other dog, was much
> pleased to go out walking. He showed his pleasure by trotting gravely
> before me with high steps, head much raised, moderately erected ears, and
> tail carried aloft but not stiffly. Not far from my house a path branches off
> to the right, leading to the hot house, which I used often to visit a few
> moments, to look at my experimental plants. This was always a great
> disappointment to the dog, as he did not whether I should continue my

walk; and the instantaneous and complete change of expression which came over him as soon as my body swerved in the least towards the path (and sometimes I tried this as an experiment) was laughable. His look of dejection was known to every member of the family, and was called his *hot-house face*. This consisted in the head dropping much, the whole body sinking a little and remaining motionless; the ears and tail falling suddenly down, but the tail by no means wagged. With the falling of the ears and of his great chaps, the eyes became much changed in appearance, and I fancied that they looked less bright. His aspect was that of a piteous, hopeless dejection; and it was, as I have said, laughable, as the cause was so slight. Every detail in his attitude was in complete opposition to his former joyous yet dignified bearing. (Darwin, 1872/1998, pp. 57–60, emphasis in the original)[3]

Crist comments on the above passage:

The description of the dog's expressions assembles the attentive reader's perceptual focus. Along with Darwin, the reader does not infer joy and dejection from the dog's bearings, but rather, by imbricating visual memories into the described scene, sees joy and dejection in the dog's bearings. Darwin's understanding, without a moment's pause, skirts by the idea of mind as a private domain, and in this unassuming fashion delivers a serious blow to the chimerical dualism of observable body and unobservable mind. (Crist, 1996, p. 78)

Crist's description of Darwin's witnessed mindedness, witnessed "lively inner states" of the dog-Other, is resonant with the autoethnographic data about playing with Katie. My anthropocentric use of terms referring to her subjective experience of play is inconsistent with the idea of her mind as a private domain, or as something ascribed to her. They describe forms of participation. Admittedly, the words employed to describe her lively inner states are those of a particular human language and culture. The language contains certain glosses of what "inner states" could be, even what "dog inner states" could be, and how such matters are to be perceived and described. These are the tools/resources that the mother tongue provides to social members, which we (members) in turn "use" to describe and characterize these phenomena. The interpretational "tools" of the mother tongue structure the reportage of the witnessing, but the witnessing itself is not primarily a language event. The tools of language do not create the event; they are part of it. They do not involve matters of inference so much as socially accepted and sanctioned ways for recognizing and describing details of readily interpretable events—in the above case, for Darwin and his family, a dog's "hothouse face."[4]

Language and Behavioral Operationalism

I anticipate that many who read and watch the data will want to provide a behavioral interpretation of it. This approach is also worth examining, since I believe it to be an unavoidable view of the writing. I use the work of D. L. Wieder to critically examine behavioralism while at the same time to explore a more phenomenological approach to the interpretation of animal behaviors. I will end the discussion with a general model of intersubjectivity that, I believe, makes clearer the epistemological underpinnings of human descriptions of animal behavior. [5]

The phenomenology undertaken by Edmund Husserl is relevant to a critical appreciation of language's place in description. This phenomenology is both explained and applied to the analysis of animal-human interaction by Wieder (1980) in his seminal work on EM's conception of animal-human interaction. Wieder extends Garfinkel's often cited comment about "behaviorizing" a perceived event or action:

> [T]he investigator can choose [certain methods] and achieve a rigorous literal description of physical and biological properties of sociological events. This has been demonstrated on many occasions. Thus far the choice has been made at the cost of either neglecting the properties that make events sociological ones, or by using documentary work to deal with the "soft" parts. (Garfinkel, 1967, pp. 102–103)

Wieder's work shows how chimpanzee researchers professionally *behaviorize* chimps while at the same time treat them as sentient subjectivities acting in a life-world. He provides a phenomenological description of the life-world, following Husserl in the Fifth Cartesian Meditation. [6]

He shows how, through what methods and practices, chimp researchers behaviorize their approach to the work with chimps and the chimps themselves. What Wieder terms "Behavioral Operationalism" is a conscious way of life for these researchers and is discussed openly among them. Behavioristic Operationalism methodogenically transforms the life-world into a world that is consistent with the scientific *desiderata* of academic psychology. It is not that this world is not a real world, but it is that the cost of such a transformation is, as Garfinkel points out, a loss of comprehension about the sociological properties of the events, and/or a bifurcation of reality into "hard" and "soft" parts. "The behaviorized order is truncated from the lived order and stands over against it. If it is taken as referring at all, it no longer refers to the originary events but instead to a hypothetically constructed mechanism" (Wieder, 1980, p. 100). The results of behaviorizing are "fully detached from the originary events," similar to the way in which sociologists code and create tables from face-to-face interactions such as interviews and treat the coded data as standing on behalf of the actual events (see especially Cicourel, 1964, p. 174). Another result of the procedure of behaviorizing others' action is that they are transformed from sentient living subjects into "automotons" through suspension of perceived signification in their actions. They are made into biological dopes whose actions are viewed as organically programmed.

Ironically, Wieder demonstrates in his data that the chimp handlers, in spite of their formal commitment to the scientific rationale of behaviorism, could not deal with chimps on a day-to-day basis without violating that rationale. Their interactions with them recurrently evidenced chimps being seen by handlers as individuals, sentient and meaningfully acting.

Wieder's basic observation can be read as 1) a justification for the use of a natural vernacular rather than a scientific language to describe Katie's and my play together; and 2) a rejection of the adequacy of description of Katie's and my play together in primarily biological or behavioral terms.

A General Phenomenological Model of Intersubjectivity

Wieder's summary of and reflection on Husserl's phenomenology of the life-world is also important, as it provides the phenomenological "grounds" for many of the descriptive elements found and assumed in the autoethnographic data. An extension of Husserl's phenomenology and research results from my previous book *A World without Words* (WWW) is presented in figure 2, a general model of intersubjectivity (adapted from Goode, 1996). Figure 2 displays the recursive role of language in "naming" what is ontologically given anterior to language, asserting its essentiality in any reflection on the life-world. At the same time it shows that, antecedent to communication, much more is given in the life-world than can be communicated, and more can be and is communicated than can ever be codified into language.

Figure 2 can be administered as an analytic device to map out the phenomenal layers of Katie's and my play: matters assumed but not communicated; matters communicated but not spoken; and matters formulated into language. Under such a conception, "what is known or taken for granted in common" is not a reflection of language but of "assumed" intersubjective phenomena anterior to formulation into language. Much of the play between Katie and me proceeded based upon a sharing of (pre-, non-, a-) linguistic features of play. By saying that play (or anything else) involves these prelinguistic features, I am not maintaining that "intersubjectivity" and "communication" do not reflect cultural machinery or organization. As described above, perception of and action upon naturally given features of the world do reflect the social membership of participants. For example, while my dog and I can share certain perceptual features of snow with any human, the description of those features could be radically different; i.e., an Inuit and a Bambudi Pygmy would not experience, react to, or communicate about snow in a comparable fashion. The model presented in figure 2 is a formal analytic device intended to synthesize empirical and philo-

> **Intersubjectivity**—The broadest sense of a world-experienced-in-common includes "communalized" apprehension of an objective world also called the life-world, the working world of everyday life, the paramount reality, the plenum, the ens realissimum, or concrete facticity. Shared by all subjectivities (all possibly imaginable monads or experiencing beings), intersubjectivity includes transcendental nature, time, space, an apodictally given ego, others, here, there and other features of "objective" reality. The intersubjective world includes communication (for all subjectivities) and language (for subjectivities who employ language) but is not reducible to them, and serves as the raw phenomenal structures with and out of which both are constructed. No language is required to participate in this level of sharing the everyday world. All subjectivities share this level of sensual intersubjectivity.

>   ↓

> **Communication**—Communication includes formal language and non-linguistically formulated expressions that serve to convey information to other co-present subjectivities. Formal and informal language, bodily gestures, representational expressivity (art, photography, dance, etc), esoteric and "idiosyncratic" practices (for example, "ESP"), bodily exchanges (rough-housing, kissing), cultural rituals (greetings, toasting, waving), including culturally specific elements as well as what Augustine and Husserl called the universal or natural language of all men. Not all subjectivities share these forms of communication. Cultural membership is required to participate in many of these forms.

>   ↓

> **Language**—Formal and informal language, including codified and non-codified language (for example, native sign among the deaf). Internal and idiosyncratic languages are included. Shared/used only by those subjectivities who participate in the particular language system.

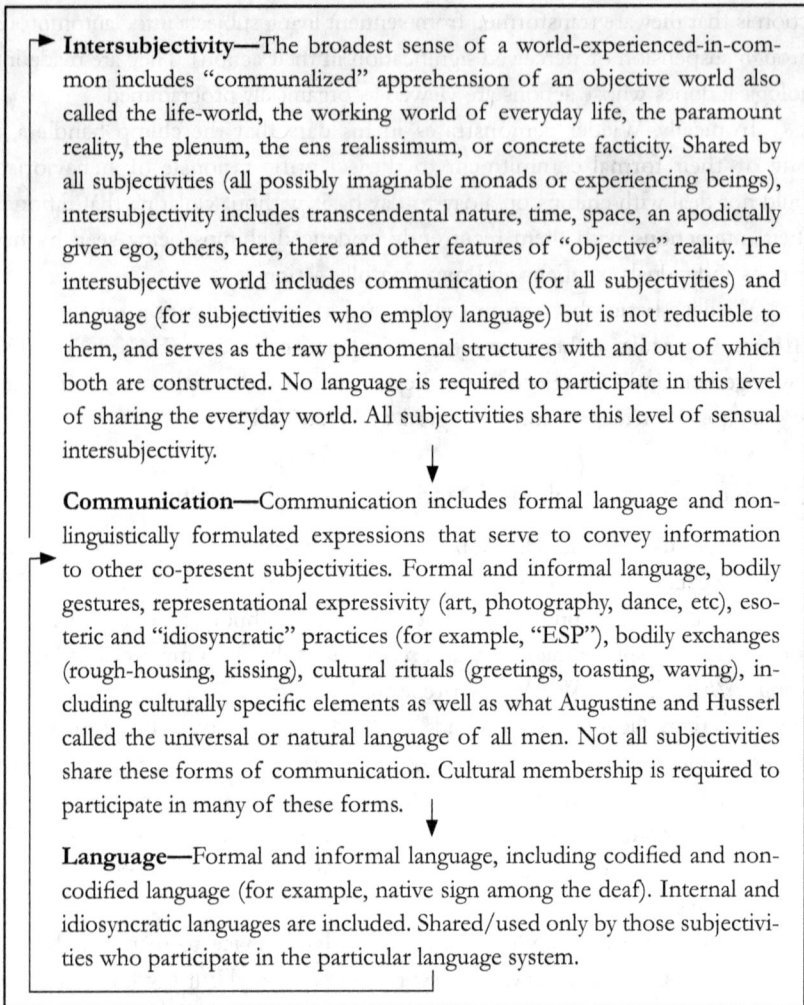

Figure 2. A General Model of Intersubjectivity (modified from Goode, 1996)

sophical observations about intersubjectivity. Like the writings of Schutz or Husserl, it is not intended to be read as a description of how things might work in any instance. It does, however, show how anthropomorphic description might be based upon shared aspects of dog-human intersubjectivity that are in some sense anterior to linguistic naming.[7]

Vicki Hearne on Intersubjectivity between Humans and Dogs

> The investigation of animal consciousness, like the investigation of human consciousness, is centrally an investigation of language, and ought to remind us what an investigation of language is. (Hearne, 1987, p. 74)

Vicki Hearne, the late philosopher, poet and animal trainer, wrote some of the most insightful books about dogs to date. Here I will present some of her views about language in the study of dogs.

Hearne's insights were based upon her extensive experience as a guardian and trainer. This experience allowed her to place language in an appropriately important and yet ambiguous role in her relations with dogs. Although she did not use the term "intersubjectivity" directly, Hearne's writings about how humans and dogs "talk" with one another contain many insights about the role and place of language in such affairs. The following example is about a dog she was training:

> There are a lot of things we don't have yet. Among others, we don't have a subject—a grammatical object, that is—for our primitive language to engage. Even Salty's creative management of the food dish and garbage can does not allow her to name the garbage can. Naming is an advanced activity of language and not the prior, essential act some of our allegories about ourselves and matters such as signing chimps make it out to be. Names for anyone or anything but the speakers of a language are not necessary for knowledge or acknowledgement until we actually do name objects, and then they will be necessary. (Hearne, 1986, pp. 57–58)

Note the consistency between this observation and the general model of intersubjectivity offered above. In that model, the naming of objects in formal language terms would be the most advanced of the intersubjective sharing actors achieve together (that is, it is possible to have massively available sharing about things without communicating them to each other let alone formulating them into formal language, i.e., naming them). Hearne's observation that what needs to be known is the "name" of the speaker (I interpret name here as meaning the identity of the speaker, not literally the language formulation of his or her name) is also consistent with an interpretation of expressions as understood "indexically."

Hearne writes that syntax is prior to semantics. This is a point she makes in her reference to Cavil's teaching of the word "kitty" to his daughter and in the following remarks:

> This is the sort of moment in my thinking when it seems clear to me that syntax is prior to semantics—that you can't have meaningful communication without grammar—without a structure that is embedded in time. Even in the case of what appears to be a gesture or signal consisting of a single counter, as when Belle barks to be let out to run, the bark or the tail-wagging or door-scratching is meaningless without what goes on before and after coming in certain ways, in a rule-governed sequence. (Hearne, 1986, p. 97)

Here she appears to get very close to EM's conception of the role of language in structuring everyday social life. Rule-governed sequence brings to mind the orderliness of everyday affairs (the way in which these are actually "rule-governed" in a traditional sociological sense being a complex issue). The idea is that communication and meaningful expression are "found" within the context of an evolving situation and require of participants knowledge of that situation, its actors, and history in order to what they see and hear. This is similar to what Bar-Hillel and ethnomethodologists describe by the term "indexicality."

Hearne notes that writing about dogs focuses the analyst upon the concrete features of the language he or she is employing. The specific ways in which language fails, or is limited, with regard to the descriptive task unavoidably becomes a central part of the inquiry.

> . . . [O]ne of the things that might lead someone to wonder about what looks like the wildest sort of anthropomorphizing is the sketchiness of the tokens of this language game. One thing I should say is, I'm not filling in all of the details. . . . More to the point, a reason for trying to get the feel for a dog-human language game is that it sharpens one's awareness of the sketchiness of the tokens of English. Wittgenstein says, "It is as if a snapshot of a scene had been taken, but only a few scattered details of it were to be seen: here a hand, there a bit of a face or a hat—the rest dark. And now it is as if we knew quite certainly what the whole picture represented. As if I could read the darkness." When we learn a language we learn to read the darkness. (Hearne, 1986, p. 72)

The data about playing with Katie are, for me, mnemonic—they represent snapshots of a total reality, a reality of which they serve to remind me. But for the reader the relationship between the words and the events is quite different, even with the augmented data of video and sequenced images. The words and images are representations of aspects of the lived orderliness of our play, which cannot be reflected upon or analyzed except through such representations. Wittgenstein's insight is about the glosses of language and how, when used descriptively, they represent "a few scattered details." This is completely consistent with the general model of intersubjectivity offered above. The epistemological error of which he speaks would be to read the diagram in reverse; that is, to naively read the language tokens at the bottom of the chart, to represent what is mutually understood in its entirety.

Perhaps most important for this current analysis is Hearne's proposal that studying dogs can provide "corrective insights" about the hidden commitments of our mother tongue (twenty-first-century American English). Hearne is writing about the human experience of scent versus a dog's.

We can show *that* Fido is alert to the kitty, but not *how*, for our picture making modes of thought interfere too easily with falsifyingly literal representations of the cat and the garden and their modes of being hidden from or revealed to us. I say "falsifyingly literal," not because the literal is automatically false, but because our attempts to think about scent locate one the areas where the mind's lust for the literal, what Wittgenstein called "grammar" and Frege "speaking," *misleads us in ways we can find out about.* My very impulse to say, for example, that thinking about the problem of tracking "clarifies" or "brings into focus" certain aspects of language suggests how profoundly oriented I am to sight. . . . But here is the thing: we do talk with dogs about scent, and some people do it quite well. . . . (1986, pp. 80-81, italics added)

Much of the current analysis reflects the commitments of mid-twentieth-century white, middle-class American English when it is used to try to describe and analyze playing with dogs. What am I doing when I play with Katie? How am I to write about what we are doing? In what ways does the gloss "playing" descriptively reveal or mislead us about what we do? In what ways can the describing reflect real phenomenological differences between species? The analysis is thoroughly one of and through language, but at the same time needs to be concerned with the way language can possibly mislead us when we use it naively in our writing about animals.

Latour's Automatic Door Groom

Bruno Latour's wonderful 1988 essay, "Mixing Humans and Nonhumans Together," is not, as one might surmise from the title, a reflection upon relationships between humans and animals; in fact his "nonhuman" is not an animal at all but a machine, specifically an automatic door-closer. Latour's purpose is to question the distinction made by social scientists between human and nonhuman actors in everyday society, and to pursue the theoretical implication of this intellectual move.

> You discriminate between the human and inhuman. I do not hold this bias but see only actors—some human, some inhuman, some skilled, some unskilled—that exchange their properties. (Latour, 1988, p. 303)

Latour's general formulation of the accomplishment of everyday life is basically consistent with an ethnomethodological view. His approach can be used to locate certain implications of this study. Consider his construction of a social order based upon what he calls "scenes" and "scripts." Latour's are not solipsistic subjects exchanging properties in some random or psychologically motivated way, but in fact "properties" themselves are partially a reflection of how other "actors" structure our possibilities, i.e., are "social objects." Despite his language,

Latour's view, like Garfinkel's and Sacks's, is that subjects and their properties (staffing cohorts) are themselves defined by the scene, by the activities and practices it requires and how these are enacted. In this sense, at least, Latour begins as ethnomethodologists do. Also, he constructs a similar criticism of "sociologism" in which some simple reading of human behavior (and nonhuman behavior) is achieved through a programmatic, scripted account. This idea he dismisses as an absurdity.

In an unintended rationale for the current writing describing human-dog play, Latour writes,

> The bizarre idea that society might be made up of human relations is a mirror image of the other no less bizarre idea that techniques might be made up of nonhuman relations. We deal with characters, delegates, representatives, or, more nicely, lieutenants (from the French "lieu" "tenant," i.e., holding the place of, for, someone else); some figurative, some nonfigurative; some human, others nonhuman; some competent, others incompetent. You [i.e., sociologists] want to cut through this rich diversity of delegates and artificially create two heaps of refuse: "society" on the one side, and "technology" on the other? That's your privilege. (Latour, 1988, 308)

Latour's intent is to blur the apparently natural distinction between the animate and inanimate, between the human actor and the automatic door groom (that is, an automatic door, sliding or revolving). In looking at the automatic door groom, he distinguishes three different senses in which it is or can be characterized in anthropomorphic terms.

> ... [T]he automatic door groom is already anthropomorphic through and through. "Anthropos" and "morphos" together mean either what has human shape or what gives shape to humans. Well, the groom is indeed anthropomorphic, and in three senses; first, it has been made by men, it is a construction; second, it substitutes for the actions of people, and is a delegate that permanently occupies a position of a human; and third, it shapes human action. (Latour, 1988, p. 303)

These defining anthropomorphic characteristics of the door groom can also be used to characterize Katie. She is clearly produced by humans in the sense of her breed's creation and her own particular physical breeding. She can be seen as permanently "substituting" for the actions of people (i.e., other human players).[8] Finally, in the same way the characteristics of a mechanical door groom shape the actions of the humans for whom it was intended to serve, Katie's playing shapes the possibilities of what it could mean for me to be a player with her.

This description of door grooms in anthropomorphic terms, and Latour's blurring of simplistic distinctions between human and nonhuman authorship, underwrite the possibility of anthropomorphic, or at least a common, language in the description of interaction with animals, and, in Latour's proposition, mechanical actors. However, and here I may differ from Latour, the idea that Katie is an actor in very similar ways to human beings or door grooms does not mean that she is or acts in ways just like a door groom, or even similar to them. In my view these similarities are formal—i.e., exist as abstractable features from lived orders. They exist in a formal sense but are not the "same" for human and nonhuman actors; and the witnessable details of their concrete enactment display deeply asymmetrical features. Yet I do not think Latour's point was that humans and door grooms (and dogs) are the "same"—just that they all must be seen as consequential participants in a human social order, and that any model of social order must provide for their participation. In this sense, and following Latour's discussion, the current writing could be read as contributing to a practical and theoretical understanding of everyday society that includes "nonhuman actors."

Mitchell and Colleagues' Treatment of Anthropomorphism

> [T]he notion that one can distinguish anthropomorphic from neutral descriptions is *a priori* fallacious because it presumes an "amorphic" perspective—paradoxically, a perspective from no particular point of view—by which to determine which description is more accurate. Rather, recognition of some description as anthropomorphic occurs only after one has made presuppositions of what is the correct description, and these presuppositions can themselves be anthropomorphic . . . the presumption that animals are machines . . . is itself just as much an unverified assumption as those designated anthropomorphic. (Cenami Spada as cited in Mitchell & Hamm, 1997, pp. 4–5)

As mentioned in the introduction to this chapter, anthropomorphism refers to the extrapolation of human characteristics to nonhumans, while anecdotalism can be defined as the psychological interpretation of an individual's actions presented in a brief story. "When combined, anthropomorphism and anecdotalism create a method of interpretation" (Mitchell, 1997a, p. 151).

Mitchell (1997a, 1997b) examines the controversy about the use of this method to describe animal behavior, and proposes an integration of the various perspectives and arguments surrounding both anthropomorphism and anecdotalism.

Mitchell (1997b, pp. 407–408) distinguishes between three overlapping types of anthropomorphism:

Global anthropomorphism (which includes the other two forms) is an expectation (perceptual or theoretical) that things in the world are like human beings or are caused by human beings or humanlike entities. Inaccurate anthropomorphism is an erroneous depiction of animals as having (uniquely) human characteristics (usually psychological). And subjective anthropomorphism is attribution of mental states or other psychological characteristics to animals (whether accurate or not).

The attribution of mental states is more complex than simply anthropomorphic projection of human states into animals' minds. It involves, among other things, the current behaviorist bias against positing any mental states, human or otherwise, with regard to other subjectivities (animal or human).

Global anthropomorphism can be viewed as a basic process of human cognition and perception, or as a methodological attitude toward animals. Viewed as a basic human process, global anthropomorphism reflects our "experience of the world in terms of what is most important to us— humanness." [Indeed, all objects of experience, sentient or not, have been portrayed] "as having characteristics redolent of humanity." (Mitchell, 1997b, p. 408; cf. Latour's door groom)

When seen as a methodological attitude toward animals, anthropomorphism can be traced in large part to the influence of early animal observers such as Darwin and Romanes. While these early descriptions of animals are naïve and unconcerned about questions of language and accuracy, they were based upon the assumption that evolution provided a basis for describing animals as having humanlike qualities, especially those animals that were biologically close to humans.

With respect to anthropomorphic method, the authors included in Mitchell, Thompson and Mile's (1997) edited volume on anthropomorphism seem to fall into two ways of approaching the topic: 1) the use of mental state attribution to understand animal and human psychology; and 2) the evaluation of the accuracy of attributing mental states to animals and other human beings (Mitchell, 1997b, p. 409).

Those concerned with inaccurate anthropomorphism include both crude or uncritical anthropomorphism and more sophisticated uses. They distinguish between categorical anthropomorphism, in which species are incapable of the psychological characterization in question, and situational anthropomorphism, in which an inaccurate characterization of behavior occurs within a particular situation.

Detection of inaccurate anthropomorphism usually is done by someone outside the situation, not the anthropomorphizer, and is usually attributed to the beliefs of the anthropomorphizer with respect to "our perceived place in nature." Inaccurate anthropomorphism is thus detected when someone reinterprets the description from outside the use of human psychology to come to grips with animal psychology.

It would be a "reduction to absurdity" to say that human beings cannot or do not make errors with respect to their interpretation of animal psychology. On a mundane level, such mistakes occur all the time and many are recognized as such. But in academic writing, in order to be inaccurate, there is a presumption that "an accurate" interpretation exists, what Spada calls an amorphic description, a description untainted by any point of view (in EM we call this a transcendental perspective). Because, as Mitchell points out, "any observation statement is based on the observer's subjective experience" (1997b, p. 411), the distinction between accuracy and inaccuracy can, and often does, become quite blurry. Given that all descriptions reflect the language we use, what we are doing, the way we think about what we are doing, our past experiences with regard to the thing(s) described and so forth, "to distinguish between the description from the object described requires someone who knows what the object truly is, which again presumes an amorphic perspective" (Mitchell, 1997b, p. 411). If such a perspective is impossible, when we talk about inaccurate anthropomorphism our narrative consists of a description of a psychological state that can be made to be seen as inaccurate from another observational perspective, whose weight in the particular case persuades the reader. Involved are a comparison of different observational procedures and perspectives rather than with an amorphic perspective.

Some factors that influence the perspective of an observer include: culture and period, scientific paradigm, socialization and training, reflexivity (self-analysis), and biases due to anthropocentric thinking and other stereotypes. Most writers in Mitchell, Thompson, and Miles's book feel that anthropomorphic ways of thinking are either linked to evolution and have become outside our awareness, or are otherwise linked to being a human being and innate.

All judgments about anthropomorphism rest upon our knowledge of 1) humans, 2) animals, and 3) the relationship between the two (Mitchell, 1997b, p. 12). Building on this argument, assertions with regard to the accuracy or inaccuracy of anthropomorphic description are being made without established bodies of knowledge about animals or people. Indeed, the very same issues of "accuracy" that are often posed in anthropomorphic thinking can be found in our thinking about human beings. The same issues concerning when one is entitled or not entitled to ascribe similar mental states to the Other can be found in our writings about human beings and animals. Thus to say that a description is categorically anthropomorphically inaccurate implies that we already have a good grasp on what are "uniquely" human characteristics. Although some scientists would disagree, particularly those who tend to believe that their particular viewpoint is amorphic, there appears to be considerable debate about human characteristics, i.e., what they are, and whether or the degree to which they are shared with other species.

Human uniqueness was what Darwin and Romanes sought to explain and erode by detailing comparable psychological examples in nonhuman animals, and to achieve this task they and their intellectual descendents sought evidence of identical or simpler forms of human psychology in animals. Their reasoning was homological (i.e., animal and human cognition and experience are the same because they derive from the same source). Today much of the reasoning against anthropomorphism is analogical, i.e., extrapolation from (what is taken by the researcher to be) a well established domain. Interestingly, positions with respect to both forms of reasoning range from outright dismissal to acceptance, at least on the common sense level. Others see analogy and homology as ways to generate hypotheses that can then be tested.

With regard to analogy from one's own experience to a nonhuman other's experience, the authors in Mitchell, Thompson, and Miles's book are divided. Some are sympathetic to the idea that subjective inference by analogy provides us with knowledge about animal (and human) experience. Others argue against the accuracy of such a procedure. Shapiro's work argues that empathy is not analogical subjective inference, maintaining instead that empathy allows one to directly connect another's bodily experiences with our own body (Mitchell, 1997b, p. 415). This is a similar position to that taken in my data.

Subjective anthropomorphism, or mental state attribution, is the device most thoroughly relied upon in the written data. Mitchell considers the viewpoint that using psychological terms to describe animals (or anything) is not based on analogy but is an "appropriate use of language" (1997b, p. 416). Thus friendship or grief in their common meaning can be applied to animals as well as to people. The issue becomes, with regard to animals or humans, on what evidence does the application rest? To be scientifically acceptable "the evidence needs to be more specific," (Mitchell,1997b, p. 416) by which Mitchell means more behavioral or operationally defined. The operational definitions do not make reference to the inner states of the animals involved. "[T]hey are applicable . . . even without knowledge of these organisms' subjective states" (Mitchell, 1997b, p. 417).

In Mitchell's view, psychological terms "commonly refer to or entitle the circumstances in which animals act, . . . the bodily actions of animals, or both" (1997b, p. 417). The terms themselves can be seen as summarizing, abbreviating or entitling a variety of manifestations that can be included under them. EM calls this "glossing"—that is, the term "angry" can refer to a variety of specific manifestations that will share some essential same element even though they may look and sound substantially different (for example, "fuming with anger" versus "exploding with anger"). The psychological terms we use are linked to the situations (verbally rendered as anecdotes) within which animals and humans manifest their behavior. They are psychological characterizations of animals and humans acting in circumstances (in EM, in "lived orders"). We find, learn and use these patterns of behavior within circumstances.

> Given that our anthropomorphic psychologizing is an expectation based on observing people's statements about other people (including ourselves), subjective anthropomorphizing is not a projection of one's own mental states. Rather, it is the result of other people teaching us, and our discerning, the requirements for conventional usage. . . . Therefore, using such mentalistic terms as "angry" does not require one to "introspect" another's experience . . . or even one's own. (Mitchell, 1997b, p. 418)

This is a very Wittgensteinian way to explicate psychological terms in descriptions.

Mitchell describes how the child might learn such rules of proper usage about psychological states. "He/she learns to integrate two sets of evidence, one having to do with how others use the terms to describe themselves and others in situations, and the other having to do with the child's own experience of his/her body and face. The child learns to use appropriately these terms for self and other by connecting these two diverse senses of the same term" (Mitchell, 1997b, p. 419).

> The result is that the two forms of evidence are simply assumed to be mutually cohering; that is, the self and the other are expected to have most experiences in common when any salient manifestation—visual, kinesthetic, somatosensory, et cetera—indicative of a particular mental state term is presented by either. In this way, the other's experience is imbued with experiences comparable to those of the self, even though the self has no direct access to those experiences; and the self understands how his or her behavior appears to others, and experiences that appearance as also imbued with subjective aspects for others. (Mitchell, 1997b, p. 419)

Mitchell does not believe that mental state attribution is a result of the observer projecting his/her own mental states into the mind of the human or animal he/she is observing. He bases this partly upon the fact that we have a very unclear and indistinct grasp of our own mental states. Our understanding of our own psychology is typically riddled with falsehoods (and I would add, contradictions and paradoxes), not the kind of knowledge we could use with confidence to extrapolate to other actors.

> If mental state attribution is indeed dependent upon access to one's own mental states, then our knowledge of other organisms' psychological attributions may be exceedingly difficult to discern in that we do not have access to their mental state; . . . but if mental state attribution is dependent upon

perceptual access to others' behaviors and circumstances . . . then our knowledge of other organisms' psychological attributions is likely to be more
readily apparent. (Mitchell, 1997b, pp. 419–420)

Some authors, including Shapiro and Mitchell, argue that the study of
"private mental states" can be done through careful observation coupled with
knowledge of the individual, species, behavioral and neuroscience research, as
well as upon human empathy. Mitchell seems to suggest that "a new methodology re-appropriate 'ordinary common sense' but with additional skepticism"
(1997b, p. 421). This recommendation could very much be taken as a rationale
for the method used in producing the written data about playing with Katie, in
which common-sense knowledge of play is refined and re-specified to a degree
of detail unfound in ordinary society.

Anecdotes

Mitchell also points out that the way animals are studied usually involves describing the animals' behaviors through anecdotes. "[A]necdotes are narrative
depictions of animal behavior interpreted psychologically" (Mitchell, 1997b, p.
421). If the anecdotes are constructed by careful scientific observers, there is
usually agreement about the patterns of behavior or action that are observed.
What is contested about these anecdotes generally is not that what was observed
did not occur, but rather how to interpret the patterns observed. Comparable to
how we interpret videotape, what is argued about are not the detailed patterns
of actions seen on tape (the "syntactics" of events) but their interpretation (the
"semantics" of events). Possible interpretations of events are not built into
events or recordings/renderings of them but are the product of the observer(s)
observing either the event itself or its record/rendering.

Mitchell points out that a carefully constructed anecdote about an animal
will tend to be an appealing basis for understanding that animal's psychological
processes. Further, in a discussion of "ambushing" in humans and non-humans,
he argues that evolutionary parsimony bears upon the function of a behavior
but may not be as easily interpreted in terms of experience or cause. Thus, and
this is my own view, when one finds similarity of praxis between different species, or between seeing, hearing persons and those born deaf-blind, one can
conclude with some sureness that the praxis contains major elements which are
similar, similar enough to be called the same, but that is all. One cannot, because
of the similarities in these major elements, conclude that the praxis in its entirety
is the same, or that the experience of that praxis by the practitioners is the same.
This is what I referred to as the asymmetry of Katie's and my access to the
events and moves of play.[9]

Scientific acceptance of anecdotal evidence varies. Certainly the naive use

of anecdotes is not regarded as good scientific practice, but the range of thinking about anecdotes is from complete mistrust to overly trusting. Many accept
that persons who are close to animals, trainers and pet guardians for example,
without reflection use anecdotes to tell about and/or control (predict) behavior
in their animals.

> Some authors provide anecdotes to give readers some of the flavor of
> watching their animal subjects . . . or to illustrate established behavior
> patterns of a species or an individual animal they know very well . . . , but
> such flavorful or illustrative anecdotes can sometimes take on a life of their
> own, creating an image of the animal (or species) that is more complex and
> humanlike than is warranted by the animals behavior patterns. . . . Again, in
> the study of animal behavior the issue is not whether the behaviors de-
> picted in anecdotes happened, but rather how they are to be interpreted.
> . . . *[S]ituating animal behavior within the story structure (i.e., to use the story as the
> frame of reference for evaluating the behaviors) and to look to consistency among all
> the elements of the story, rather than to the behaviors of the animal, to decide if the
> story is accurate.* (Mitchell, 1997b, p. 423)

The problem is that there is more than one story that can account for
observed behavior. Mitchell feels that deriving complex psychological explanations from anecdotal evidence is therefore problematic. This is not to say that
careful descriptions and anecdotes should not be used but, in Mitchell's view,
that there psychological content would need to be tested experimentally.

Describing animal behaviors within stories enhances the perception of
animals as intentional, perceiving agents. There is research showing that when
various mammals are described within a story indicative of a complex psychology, all animals are seen to have the same psychological characteristics that the
story implies. That is, Mitchell is suggesting that it is the story that endows the
actor with the psychology it (the story) requires.

If we accept anecdotes as legitimate forms of knowledge about animals, as
for example reflecting psychological terms that are applicable across species, then
we need to deal with the idea that there may be more than one story into which the
observed behavior can be fit. This is why the same behaviors need to be looked
at from a variety of views (from within a variety of stories) in order to find
maximum consistency. In fact, this is not how science appears to work. Instead,
we get numbers of competing stories rather than triangulation between them.

Mitchell comments on intimacy as a factor in producing stories about animal mentality. On the one hand are those who mistrust intimacy between observer and animal as a hindrance to objectivity. On the other hand are those
(Shapiro among them) who see the long-term observer as better able to understand the animal than someone without a long-term interaction or observation
history. Mitchell also adds that long-term observation allows evidence about the

animal's developmental history to be collected, which can be examined for new developments in the animal's understanding. This bears directly upon studying play with Katie.[10]

Mitchell's conclusion section summarizes the overall argument he makes well:

> The discussion of these ideas leaves one with some degree of consensus. Global anthropomorphism is a pervasive aspect of human perception and cognition, the use of which as a methodological tool to understand animals must be examined critically and empirically. Inaccurate anthropomorphism is by definition an error, but how one is to determine when one has erred is problematic: the method suggested is to use diverse perspectives (translated into hypotheses) to evaluate data, where these perspectives vary in their degree of anthropomorphism (from none to a great deal). Subjective anthropomorphism—mental state attribution—is just one perspective on how humans and perhaps animals understand other beings, and evidence for it and the conditions under which it occurs need to be critically examined. Subjective experience of both humans and animals should be studied empirically (if possible) and methods adequate to the task may be developing. Anecdotes by reliable observers can be accepted as believable evidence that specific behaviors occurred (that is, this animal did this action and that animal did that action). When these behaviors can be accurately observed under the viewing conditions employed, anthropomorphic terminology can be reasonably used to label or entitle these behaviors, but the interpretation of these behaviors as scientific evidence for mental state attribution demands the same method used to evaluate the accuracy of anthropomorphism: data should be examined using multiple hypotheses varying in sorts of mental states they propose (if any). As with any science, the accurate interpretation of evidence depends upon the hypotheses and perspectives available; and, the available evidence may support multiple hypotheses and perspectives. Note, however, that people concerned with ethics toward animals or control of animal behavior, or those just wanting to interact pleasantly with animals, might reasonably use anecdotes and ordinary common sense to fulfill purposes associated with these concerns and desires. (Mitchell, 1997b, p. 426)

In my view, and that of EM, the most interesting is the last sentence. It's all very practical, and in the everyday world apparently there really is not much choice about this matter.

Concluding Remarks

In this chapter we have come at issues related to anthropomorphism from many different views. However, when we look at these views collectively I believe there are several points of powerful agreement about the method of anthropo-morphism.

The first is that the method of anthropomorphism, of describing animals (and in Latour's case, objects) with human-like traits acting within situations, is natural to human beings. By natural I mean to say that it is observable in everyday life, that it occurs as a natural, not theoretical, object. It is a form of language use that is common to humans interacting with animals, even to people like Wieder's "chimpers" (persons who worked with chimps in laboratory set-tings) who tried otherwise to deny humanlike characteristics of their charges. The kinds of descriptions presented of Darwin's dog, or Lucy the chimp, or Katie, are naturally occurring ways of seeing the animals in question and consti-tute instances of the method described by Bob Mitchell, anthropomorphic readings of the animals' actions and psychology as meaningful with respect to the events at hand. While other forms of describing animal-human relations are also naturally occurring in the sense that they are observable (for example, behaviorist accounts, or evolutionary accounts), these are theoretically reasoned methods and are not methods one would see in use with the vast majority of people interacting with animals.

Like all methods, an anthropomorphic method can lead to various errors, although the determination of wrongness itself can be problematic. For ex-ample, it is hard to determine if we are wrong or right about what distinguishes animal thoughts and actions from human ones (i.e., to be sure that one has committed the error of categorical anthropomorphism) because we lack a clear or consensual understanding of either. Similarly, it is not always a simple matter to agree that situational anthropomorphism (misreading an animal's actions within a situation) has occurred, if both observers do not share the same definition of the situation. Plus, since we lack an amorphic or transcendental perspective upon which to judge alternative descriptions of the same event, we are unable to make great claims about wrongness or rightness, and are only able to compare one humanly authored account to another.

I agree with Mitchell that, in practice, situational anthropomorphism can occur without the anthropomorphizer knowing it. In his review of my data, Mitchell asked questions to the effect, "How do you know that Katie thought that catching the ball in stride was a 'good catch'?" or "How do you know whether she was showing off or just seen to be that way by others?" Adding to Mitchell's concerns, any dog guardian involved with his/her dog will have had the practical experience of having misread that animal's behaviors, that is, as having committed an error of situational anthropomorphism. So I think his questions are good ones, and even further specification how I knew what it was that I thought that I knew would be appropriate. Could I have been "wrong" in some of my descriptions? Absolutely. Was I "wrong" in empirical detail with regard to any particular interpretation? That question is more diffi-cult to answer.

I also agree with Mitchell's proposal that anthropomorphic method, when practiced critically and in conjunction with other bodies of information about humans and animals, is a valuable form of scientific inquiry. It can tell us much about, for example, how we play with dogs. I do not share his optimism that multiple methods will lead to what scientists will consensually agree to be accu-rate interpretation of evidence, or to resolution of the various problematic matters related to anthropomorphic method.[11]

The chapter also presented a general model of intersubjectivity in which levels of reality can be "shared" by dogs and humans without predicating a "shared" language. Vicki Hearne's observation that much understanding be-tween dogs and humans is based upon pre-semantic matters, that "syntax is prior to semantics" (1986, p. 97) is consistent with the findings of this research. On the occasions when humans and animals play or work together, many of the communications and understandings that occur do not require naming in any formal sense. They may elicit recognition and response, but not formal identifi-cation in language. Indeed, many practices observable in interaction between dogs and humans are completely tacit and do not require reflexive awareness of any type. They are done praktognosically, without reflection and without con-scious awareness, like the artful practices of conversation.

Involved in the documentation of playing was an appreciation of Katie's and my own "lively inner states," although documentation of such states do not generally preoccupy the data. The object of the analysis was not to account for Katie's experience, motives, or feelings; although these matters do crop up in the data, and while in my own view understanding Katie's inner states is a possible element on any occasion of play, *the documented play practices were not contingent upon my accurate reading of Katie's psychology.*

5

At Play and Work: Some Reflections on Companion Dogs and Working Dogs

There are different types of human relationships with dogs, and thus far our concern has been understanding play between a companion dog and her guardian. In this chapter we will look at continuities and differences in relations with companion dogs such as Katie, and with working dogs, such as guide, scent or field dogs.

The Social Invention of Companion ("Pet") Dogs

This book is an analysis of playing with my companion dog. What it means to be a "companion dog," or for that matter any other "kind" of dog, is clearly a construction of society. The ways of looking, speaking and writing about companion dogs are cultural productions of a particular society and language. The social production of dogs has a history, and it is to this history, as well as its associated outcomes in our thinking about companion dogs, to which we now briefly turn.

There is much evidence that the primary relationship between humans and dogs was a functional one until the eighteenth and nineteenth centuries. In the same way that the nineteenth century is described as the "golden age of the child" (see Aries, 1962; Postman, 1982), so it may also be seen as the "birth age of the household pet." Until this time, dogs without function were limited to the wealthy, the popular lap dog of the eighteenth century being a good example. Even among the wealthy, larger breeds were rarely kept simply for enjoyment, the greyhound being a notable exception.

Kathleen Kete, in her 1994 book *The Beast in the Boudoir*, describes what she calls the "embourgeoisment" of dogs in nineteenth-century France. A brief examination of that process will allow us to characterize our current social conception of companion dogs, and to place it in a sociocultural context. This is important when we reflect upon how I "constructed" Katie, in terms of my

expectations about the relationship with her and how I use particular terms to
describe this companion dog/guardian relationship.

"Pet dogs" were seen as an identifiable social problem in the beginnings of
the modern state. By "pet dogs," bureaucrats and legislators in France and En-
gland, for example, intended those dogs that were kept but did not serve a
clearly and exclusively economic purpose. In the nineteenth century, the pet
dogs of both the rich and poor began to experience a negative social reputation,
in the former case because of excesses and deviancies, and in the latter because
of their sheer number and daily social impact. One Parisian commentator in the
mid-nineteenth century wrote, "All of these animals too great in number, con-
tribute neither to the health nor to the repose of the city" (cited in Kete, 1994,
p. 40). Further arguments about the control of companion dogs stemmed from
their growing number and their social cost (for example, their drain on the food
supply of France). Thus in the mid-nineteenth century we see the modern state
enact laws designed to curtail "useless" dogs.

The French state instituted a tax on dogs in 1855. This was a clear attempt
to socially legislate the desirability of "useful" dogs over those that were "useless." This initial distinction was to hold a powerful influence on all later dog
classifications and thinking, despite its own problematics. The basic idea of the
legislation was to tax heavily those dogs that did not have a basically productive
(in the strictly economic sense) function. Thus the law was posited upon the
distinction between "working dogs" and "luxury dogs," or "useful dogs" and
"useless dogs" (Kete, 1994, pp. 41–42).

> ... [D]ogs integral to the economy of the working classes were to be taxed
> minimally, but dogs of no economic value were to be made expensive, so
> that only the rich could maintain them. The mid-century pet was by defini-
> tion a luxury, reserved as the privilege of a small class, as a matter of
> consumption. ... The luxury tax was directed against the poor people's
> dogs in a system that recognized "rich" and "poor," "useful" and "use-
> less," but ignored the distinction categories of modern bourgeois life.
> (Kete, 1994, p. 42)

With the institution of the tax of 1855 there began a long theoretical and
practical battle between bureaucrats and French canophiles/dog guardians about
the meaning of "utility." "To bureaucrats, only working dogs were useful. For
bourgeois pet owners, affect and defense against the onslaughts of modern life
were essential functions of the companion dog. Decrees ... thought to settle
matters to the benefit of the law ... was [sic] a feeble attempt to contain
modernity within bureaucratic bounds" (Kete, 1994, p. 46).

The counterargument took an interesting and particularly modern turn. "As
the multifunctional family beast took shape in the bourgeois imagination, it vehe-

mently contradicted the bureaucratic notion of the useless dog. Decrees ruling that a canine could be either pet or guard dog but not both went against the grain of bourgeois experience and angered canophile writers" (Kete, 1994, p. 46).

Instead, they advanced a bourgeois conception of utility, basically the cultural conception with which we live today. The very feature used to place dogs in the category of "useless"—that they served as objects of and sources for affection—was now argued as an important antidote to the isolation of family life characteristic of modern cities. Dogs in modern life did not fit neatly into the old categories. All dogs, it was argued by the canophiles, were guard dogs, whether living in an apartment or chained in a yard. Dogs served the purpose of protecting the household against the gangs and ruffians in cities. Dogs in the modern city had to perform all these functions, it was claimed, essentially to buffer against the problems modernity had created.

A bourgeois history of dogs was created as part of the owners' answer to the state's attack against them. This history emphasized the intimacy of the dog-human relationship, which had been until the Middle Ages based primarily on survival on an elemental level. Only in modern society, where the functions of hunting and shepherding were no longer required of the city dweller, had dogs lost their survival function and taken on an affective one. (A debate existed in the mid-nineteenth century, with some arguing that dogs in the modern world had no real function and should be destroyed.) By the latter part of the century, the position taken by the majority of writers, however, was that dogs had evolved with humans and their society, that in modern society they had become cultural objects of affection, and that they served other modern functions. "By the end of the century legal and moral attempts to contain dog guardianship within the categories of the ancient regime had clearly failed. . . . *Le Petit Moniteur Universel* noted in 1876 that in Paris there was one dog for every twelve humans" (Kete, 1994, p. 53). The attempts to "tax poor dogs away" abated, and their roles as companion dogs were accepted:

> By 1907 . . . luxury and pet guardianship were now contingent themes. The definition of a pet had changed. Its indispensability was acknowledged and the old categories of function could not be maintained. The dog, useless when considered in light of productivity, had become an essential household figure—a "love machine," a *machine à aimer*. . . . Ensconced within the family, the dog had become an affective end in itself. (Kete, 1994, p. 53)

The attitude toward pet dogs at this time mirrors very closely the attitude today. Companion dogs (to use today's accepted nomenclature) are socially constructed with these features in mind: that they are objects of and for affection and that they may serve other modern functions, such as enhancing socialization between isolated family units and guarding against intruders. This is the way most "pure" companion dog guardians think of their animals. By pure guardian I mean those who do not engage in formal and ongoing training of their companion dogs in some practical context.

Contemporaneous with and joined to this Victorian legal and intellectual battle was the development of a set of bourgeois, class-based institutions associated with the nonworking dog. The creation of social and legal conditions that provided for the growth of large numbers of dogs (in nineteenth-century France this growth was extraordinary) also created the possibilities for an associated economy. Companion dogs became the bases for forms of production and profit for capitalist society. The control of strays led to a large set of organizations and places devoted to this problem (we are here reminded of Marx's essay on the productivity of crime). Other institutions participated in the development and the selling and showing of breeds. Also during this period we find the creation of businesses that specialize in veterinary medicine for companion dogs, dog foods, dog-care products, dog clothes and accoutrements, dog kennels and dog sitting, dog training, dog control and euthanasia, dog grooming, dog taxidermy and dog burial.[1] Such institutions sponsored and structured the cultural identity of bourgeois companion dogs—that is, they provided for their possibility and forms of social participation, and they continue to do so today. In the United States, dogs are a truly big, multibillion-dollar business. Because of the growth of these institutions and businesses, the twentieth century can be described as the golden age of "pet" dogs.[2]

The bourgeois pet was clearly a creation by and for the bourgeois classes. The image of the companion dog as "quasi-human and quasi-toy-like" was and continues to be primarily an image for classes with disposable wealth, for it was only these classes who had the resources to coif their poodles or buy the expensive products from Spratt's or other dog-supply houses, or bring their pet dogs to a veterinarian, or to board their companion dogs. While no reliable data exist on the social class distribution of purely nonworking dogs, one gets the impression from a variety of sources that the poor continued to treat and use their dogs in primarily instrumental ways, certainly at the outset of the twentieth century. One readily can find in that era (late nineteenth and early twentieth centuries) in photos, paintings, children's book illustrations and elsewhere evidence of the economic use of dogs (for example, as cart pullers for products and human transportation, herding dogs, and guard dogs) by the working classes, uses that continued well into the twentieth century. To some degree this class difference in the treatment of dogs still exists today, as a drive through many urban or suburban poor neighborhoods will demonstrate.

For the vast majority of companion dog guardians in the United States, the images and practices employed to construct them are akin to the Victorian ones described by the historians of companion dogs. The birth of the bourgeois pet dog at that time has led to the social frame and situation within which we find ourselves and our companion dogs. Certainly I would include Katie and me within such a frame and within such institutions. Katie is my companion. She is a dog I enjoy, take care of and engage with mostly when I feel like it for my pleasure. She is not a dog I depend upon in any functional way. She is not a dog that I train in any formal or ongoing fashion or for a pragmatic, serious reason. I take her to the vet, feed her a special dog food diet, exercise her and groom her, and kiss and stroke her. She provides me with unconditional acceptance and affection. She is my *machine à aimer*.

Working Dogs

My first close encounter with a working dog was in 1992 on the experimental farm station in Mols, Denmark. The dog was a Border collie who worked the animals on the experimental station and, as I later found out, was also being trained for the European competition for herding dogs. I met him one early morning while walking. He was with his guardian, who was fixing a fence. After an initial greeting I said to him, "He's a spectacular-looking animal." "Thank you, and he's more than that," was the reply. And then, "He's not just fantastic *looking*." The farm worker proceeded to tell me that he had bought him in Scotland from a special breeder. "He's a good worker. Watch," he said. Then he called the dog's name, and when he came up to him he said something in Danish. In one leap, the dog jumped over a three-foot fence. He said the same word, and the dog jumped back. As he worked, he would say that same word, and each time in one leap the dog would sail over the fence. He must have jumped the fence twenty times before I asked, "How long will he do that?" The answer came absolutely without hesitation, "As long as I tell him to."

The working dog is not such a "machine." He/she obeys his/her master out of *moral duty*, not knee-jerk reflex. The features and qualities of a working dog differ from those of companion dogs. Working dogs are not companion dogs; what we do with them is different, and the social-historical situation within which they are constructed differs. By "working dogs" I refer to relationships with dogs that are established upon serious, practical or pragmatic ends and that often involve intensive and ongoing training. Examples of these kinds of relationships with dogs in contemporary society include guide dogs, hearing dogs, personal assistance dogs, rescue dogs, police dogs, military dogs, field dogs, herding and shepherding dogs, and various forms of competition dogs who require ongoing and intensive training (schutzhound work, for example).

While the biological building blocks of human relations with working dogs are the same as those for companion dogs, the *social context* of the relationship and its construction on a daily basis differs significantly, in ways that ultimately transform the relationship into something qualitatively different. You can see this in the examples of the guide dog and the trainer's dog.

The Dog-Guide

Rod Michalko (1999) describes his relationship with his guide dog, Smokie. His book, *The Two in One*, already indicates the profound difference between his relationship with Smokie and my own with my companion dogs. Michalko is a person with blindness and Smokie is his pupil, friend, guide and teacher, all in one. As the title of his book implies, Michalko's identity is bound up with that of his dog, and consequently his account is filled with observations about the nature of this identity, from his own perspective and from society's. The author and his dog have an intimate and functional relationship (i.e., one directed at the achievement of some practical end, and entailing serious ongoing training). Relationships with companion dogs often lack these two elements. While pet guardians can be very emotionally tied to their animals and feel very strongly about the affective importance of their canine relationships, this kind of bond is quite different from the "two in one" described by Michalko. That would never be a phrase that would even occur to me to describe my relationship with Katie or with Jack. For Michalko, that change from "me" to "we" occurred almost immediately and was part of his initial training experience with Smokie: "I had arrived at the school as 'me,' but I was leaving as 'we,' as part of a dog guide team" (Michalko, 1999, p. 82).[3]

Michalko describes this "we" relationship in the following excerpt:

> This is the quintessential reputation of a dog guide team. We are a team, a dyad; we are a "two-in-one." This two-in-one concept, in some ways, is not unique to Smokie and me. Good friends or intimates are often seen as two-in-one. They are two people who "belong" with each other by virtue of their relationship and how it is perceived by others. At the same time, of course, they are separate individuals . . . for Smokie and me things are somewhat different. Unlike a relationship between two human beings, ours is animated by the distinction between human and animal, society and nature. We are "man and dog." Like society and nature we are different from each other but interdependent. In terms of our social identity— blind person and dog guide—we cannot be separated. *My*self is now *our*self. Smokie's self too is *our* self. We are "at home together," which means that we are continuously making a home for our self. [Note Michalko's use of the singular form of reference.] This "home-making" manifests itself in a web of social relations that identifies blindness as a feature, but an undesirable one, of home. (Michalko, 1999, p. 91)

Such a conception of his relationship with Smokie grows out of their daily life together. Day in and day out they engage in constant work together, work that has as its purpose the successful guiding of Rod by Smokie. To do this they have both been trained, and they both are required to continue to train each other. They are engaged in a constant conversation about the guiding and about their shared lives, and it is out of this conversation that Michalko's appreciation of Smokie (and Smokie's of him) grows. Michalko sees the dog's participation in this process as a form of "moral" work, in the Aristotelian sense.

> "... [M]oral virtue comes about as a result of habit ... from this it is also plain that none of the moral virtues arise in us by nature; for nothing exists by nature can form a habit contrary to its nature ... nor can anything else that by nature behaves in one way be trained to behave in another. Neither by nature, then, nor contrary to nature do the virtues arise in us" (Aristotle, *Nichomachean Ethics*).
>
> Conceding to the wisdom of contemporary culture, we may say that "working with blind persons" is a virtuous occupation. If we further concede that a dog guiding a blind person is engaged in work—that the dog is a "working dog"—it follows that the dog guide, too, is engaged in a virtuous occupation. Trainers use repetition and reward as their primary techniques for training dogs for guide work. Dogs learn to guide when trainers repeatedly take them through the tasks required, until that work becomes habitual. If work with blind persons is virtuous and if a dog guide is understood as working with blind persons and learns so as a result of habituation, it follows that a guide dog, in Aristotelian terms, possesses "moral virtue."
>
> The end to which dog guide training aims may now be understood as the inculcation of virtue in a dog. Dogs do not, by nature, guide blind persons; this virtue is the result of habituation achieved through training ... there is nothing in the nature of a dog that is contrary to such a habit[uation]. (Michalko, 1999, p. 74)

Companion dogs and their guardians also engage in their own forms of moral behaviors, such as the play described in this book. But Michalko's description stands in contradistinction to that of a simple "pet" relationship. In the relationships I have with Katie and Jack there is a moral element, but it is not the same kind of morality described by Michalko (or below by trainer Vicki Hearne). The morality of both Hearne and Michalko results from sharing some form of virtuous work together. The practical nature of that work ensures that it is a never-ending process of mutual discovery and practice, held accountable to some practical, consequential outcomes (good scent work or good guide dog team work). This is precisely what is lacking in simple pet relationships, in which morality develops but not with respect to virtuous, practical work. Instead, it often involves a morality that emerges through "play" (specifically not practical) or "household routines" (specifically pragmatic but not virtuous), "walks in the park," or what have you. Of course when formal training is also a part of the "pet" relationship, or other kinds of virtuous work, the relationship may have a morality more like that described by Michalko and Hearne or observed in the Border collie in Mols.

There is a tremendous amount at stake in guide dog work, literally the life of both of the dyad's individuals. Thus it should not be surprising to find that the degree of trust that exists between dog guide and master differs from that of companion dog and guardian. Michalko writes about this trust:

> When Smokie is guiding me, I trust his judgment, his decisions and his abilities. I also trust his loyalty to me. I am trusting my interpretation of Smokie as a "working" animal, as an animal with a job to do. Unlike most human workers, Smokie is always loyal to work, will work for free, will work to please me, will work because he is bonded to me. I interpret it as "natural" to Smokie to do these things. . . . This interpretation, trusting as it is, permits me to use Smokie to enrich my own life. Very often as I work him, I feel the presence of cruelty when Smokie breathes car exhaust fumes, burns his feet on salted winter streets, and breathes smoke and other fumes while we sit in bars and cafes. Very often I think of how "unnatural" this must be to Smokie. (Michalko, 1999, p. 146)

A dog guardian (in everyday parlance, "pet owner") would not have written this paragraph, which is not to say that he or she would not have some things to write about the naturalness and unnaturalness of his or her dog's life, or about the degree of trust that he or she has with dogs. Insofar as dogs are "just companion dogs," i.e., not worked in some practical way or trained in some organized fashion for athletic or beauty competitions, the relationship does not possess the same kind of degree of trust, devotion, mutual work, and loyalty as the working dog team relationship. As stated above, with companion dogs there is not as much at stake; indeed, very often, other than the mundane practicalities of managing everyday life (feeding, cleaning, walking, bodily functions) there may be nothing (other than emotional support) at stake in the relationship. In the ethnographic data, I speculate much about the role of play as "sublimated" work for Katie. This may be the case; play may be her way to make something "at stake," to create "virtuous work." To some degree the function of play for her may be similar (enough) to that of work, in setting up certain mutually understood affairs and attending to them ethically, morally, physically, emotionally, and so on. That is, play becomes that part of the "pet–pet guardian" relationship in which at least some of the trust, loyalty, training, and so on required for deeper relationships with dogs can be made to come into play.

Another feature of Michalko's relationship with Smokie that differs significantly from that of a companion dog is the nature of the *learning* that Michalko experiences in that relationship. What can be gleaned by the human from this intimate, ongoing form of virtuous work together is truly remarkable. Michalko writes about how he has learned to appreciate his blindness through his relationship with Smokie:

> What is not mysterious but very clear is that Smokie does not treat my blindness as a bother, nuisance or inconvenience. He gives no indication that he cares about any social conception of blindness; he is not concerned with self-pity or the pity of others. Blindness does not seem to be a particularly positive thing to him, either, but simply an occasion for him to work, to be a decisive actor in a social world. This is what I have learned from Smokie. My blindness is an occasion for me to act decisively and to think about what is important. When Smokie is working, he is making decisions, decisions that I emphatically abide by. I too make decisions when Smokie guides me, and he emphatically abides by them. We operate decisively, alone together. (Michalko, 1999, p. 105)[4]

At other points in Michalko's text he describes how Smokie has been able to lead him into a deeper appreciation of his blindness, to discover it, to be at peace with it and even to see it as enabling him in specific ways:

> The independence I get from Smokie includes this natural movement of my body, a movement I now have independent of sight. The grace with which I move with Smokie has given me an independence that has very little to do with independence as it is conventionally understood in relation to blindness. Smokie has given me movement "in blindness." The goal of any person is to live and move and work in a world even though that world is visually absent. Yet independence is more than that, for blindness is not merely the absence of the visual; it is also a presence. Blindness is an occasion to make the visual present through means other than sight. The senses of touch, smell, and hearing can bring one in touch with the visual. This is what I mean by the "grace of independence." Smokie has given me a glimpse of my homeland from the point of view of my home-in-blindness. I am "in home" with my blindness and, with Smokie's help, I carry this home gracefully through the homeland of sightedness. Blindness is now essential and no longer a happenstance. (Michalko, 1999, p. 123)

This kind of profound learning is not characteristic in relationships with companion dogs.

Yet another form of learning that Michalko describes has to do with his own mobility and grace, a form of bodily learning:

> Smokie and I move in and out of pedestrian traffic in the same graceful, well-choreographed way. Everything Smokie does comes to me through

the harness. I feel each of his steps and I step with him. I feel every variation of speed, every change of direction, the most subtle variation in the path Smokie is taking, and I feel myself moving with the subtle smoothness and grace that Smokie gives me through the harness. With him, I can start, stop, and "turn on a dime." He often has to stop suddenly or turn quickly to avoid a carelessly moving pedestrian, a cyclist, or even an automobile, and he has prevented injury on many occasions. . . . Smokie has given me movement in blindness. (Michalko, 1999, pp. 122–123)[5]

Michalko's appreciation of Smokie's grace in their work together is built from the same building blocks as my appreciation of Katie's pursuit and capture during retrieving play. Indeed, while many of the above notations about Michalko's relationship with Smokie would appear to distinguish that relationship from that of the companion dog guardian, as described above, these differences reflect how essentially similarly defined "methods" are put to use in the context of a social relationship. This transformation from companion to working dog is, as we shall see, one that results in a change in the quality of relationships. Yet it is a matter of degree as well; "pet" guardians also learn from their dogs, they engage in moral behaviors with them, they appreciate their pets' grace, and so on. What they do not do is place these happenings within an overall relationship that is highly serious, consequential and pragmatic, and that requires ongoing mutual learning/training.[6]

The Trainer's Dog—Vicki Hearne

As stated above, Vicki Hearne, a philosopher, poet and animal trainer, was one of the most insightful observer of dog-human relationships. Her book *Adam's Task* (1986), is one of the finest texts ever written in this regard. Aside from her ability as a writer of prose and poetry, and her familiarity with the academic literature about dogs, what makes Hearne's writing unique is that it is anchored in her expertise and experience as a trainer. It is sometimes said that those who study art do so because their artistic work is inadequate. For Hearne, this kind of critique does not apply.

Vicki Hearne was first and foremost a trainer of animals. Her practical experience training dogs thus bears heavily on her writing about them. This basic social relationship, dog trainer and dog, is manifest in the everyday, mundane experience of her dogs and obviously informs her perceptions of and writings about them. Thus it is not surprising that her writings proceed from what I call her "trainer's axiom."

For Hearne, the authority of human over dog creates the responsibility of dog training for dog guardians. This axiom forms the basis for understanding human-dog relationships. The relative coherence of this authority, its concretization in and through training, is what allows dogs and humans to have moral and "healthy" relationships with each other and to genuinely "talk" with each other. For the trainer and dog being trained, retrieving is a game to be taught, not just one to be played. This view of play contrasts with the form of play I had with Katie, which had no formal, clearly designed training element, or even one-sided authority of human over dog. Yet this did not prevent us from enjoying playing with each other and from developing innovations that kept it interesting. To Hearne this would be "just play," in the sense that

> Fido [can be] perfectly happy to play fetch while refusing to bring the stick all the way back. The gap the dog insists on between us and the stick represents the gap between our ability to command, give advice and so forth and our ability to acknowledge the being of others. This is the taint in our authority. . . . It won't do to suggest that the dog can just live peacefully around the house while we refrain from giving him any commands that might deprive him of his "freedom," for that simply doesn't happen. We are in charge already, like it or not, and when a dog is about, everyone involved is going to be passing out advice and giving commands whether or not they have earned the right to do so. One might as well suggest that we leave off keeping toddlers out of the street or teaching anyone anything at all. We do assume authority over each other constantly. (Hearne, 1986, pp. 48–49)

This is the central recommendation of the trainer's construction of the companion dog. That is, *not* training is an abnegation of the authority that humans have over dogs; and *not* assuming this authority fully, through training and mutual "virtuous work," in some direct way fails dogs and their masters. Hearne's viewpoint is Platonic; that is, it postulates an ideal or healthy form of human-dog relations, against which others are measured. The authority of the human, the obligation to train (both formally and informally) and the necessity of talking together, form the basis against which other people are seen. It is this "vision" of human-dog morality that illuminates her writing, like the fire that created the shadows on the wall of Plato's cave. It is her "foundational" belief. In this way, Hearne's writing as a philosopher/trainer and mine as sociologist/dog guardian proceed under different assumptions and conditions.[7]

This difference is clearly displayed in Hearne's comments about dogs playing the game of retrieve:

> But dogs and people, unlike wolves and people, have the impulse to "play fetch" with each other, and the impulse to play fetch is the best predictor of good working dogs. . . .
>
> The impulse to play fetch is also a pretty good indicator of which of a group of eight-year old human beings is likely to be a good trainer. Dogs

are domesticated to, and into, us, and we are domesticated to, and into, them. The potential dog trainer, obeying both instinct and myth, picks up a stick and throws it for his or her new puppy. The first time, Fido is fairly likely to bring it back. The second time, however, Fido typically says, "Well this is fun and all, but can I trust her with my stick?" So Fido compromises by bringing the stick to the point just out of reach and dropping it there so that the human, if she wants to play fetch, must accept this modified version and pick up the stick herself. Thus begins a game that can be played until the dog or the guardian dies. It is fun but it will seem to anyone familiar with it that no power on earth will induce the dog to bring the stick the extra three feet or ten feet forward, a move that would amount to a full acknowledgement of the human as an authority. (Hearne, 1986, pp. 28–29)

It is interesting that, for a trainer, the significance of a dog's "willingness" to play is that such behavior is a good predictor of the dog's ability to work. For a pet guardian, who does not intend to "work" his or her dog, the dog's willingness to retrieve is a sign of a good dog to play with, or at least a dog who is going to be requesting to play a good deal of the time, perhaps even too much of the time. He or she may well turn out to be "a real pain in the butt." The point here is the difference in the "texture of relevancies" for dog guardian versus trainer.

There is even more to Hearne's observation. Let us consider it as it applies to my play relationships with Jack, my Labrador retriever. Specifically, let us look at her observation, "no power on earth will induce the dog to bring the stick the extra three or ten feet forward, a move that would amount to full acknowledgement of the human as an authority." This is thoroughly a dog trainer's construction of the dog. In contrast, we can look at how placement of the ball upon retrieval was an actual matter addressed in play with Jack. At first Jack had a habit of holding the ball and chewing it, and then he would drop it wherever he was with the expectation that I would come, pick it up and throw it for him. That expectation lasted for a very short while, as I absolutely refused to comply, simply because it was a hassle for me. Then he began a series of moves that deposited the ball nearer to me, both in front of me and behind me. These moves I cooperated with for several years, finding them adequate to the practical circumstances of our retrieve play. It was of no particular consequence to me whether he dropped the ball a foot in front of me or a foot behind me. It really was of no concern to me as his guardian that he would only bring the ball back to me "while refusing bring the ball all the way back."[8]

Then came a time when an acute back injury prevented me from bending down to pick up and throw Jack's ball. In fact, I was only able to throw the ball at all in quite a limited fashion, while sitting down on the stoop in front of my house. His usual, casual way of presenting the ball to me was no longer acceptable, and I chastised him and pleaded, "Pop is in pain and you need to bring the ball to where I can reach it." The adjustment actually took very little time for Jack to make, once he picked up on my communication. In short order Jack was bringing me the ball so that I could pick it up without having to lean over or leave my sitting position. That is, we "spoke" about the issue of bringing the ball all the way back. Jack addressed it once it was evident to him that it was unavoidably important to our play together. However, I felt no generalized urge to "teach" him this refinement of the game of retrieve, as trainers such as Hearne do. Therein lies an important difference between the guardian's dog and the trainer's dog; they inhabit divergent sets of humanly authored orderlinesses, with associated divergent purposes, practices and descriptions.

For Hearne, training a dog results in a transformation of both dog and guardian:

> If training is completed properly, the dog makes an intuitive leap—joins the group, as it were—and may later display degrees of ingenuity and courage in finding lost objects and lost children that can astonish the uninitiated. The handler, too, changes through his acceptance of posture and responsibility. He joins the group, too, enters the moral life as well, and learns to talk to Fido. . . . The coherence created by training accounts for why it sometimes happens that the drunk or the juvenile delinquent, or the supposedly "autistic" adolescent will "reform" as a consequence of good dog training. They learn how to talk meaningfully with the dog, and then they learn to talk to the dog trainer . . . (Hearne, 1994, pp. 29–30)

I would not argue with that, and given her expertise I have no reason to doubt her assertion. Having never "properly" trained a dog in the way Hearne intends, I cannot draw on experiential or observational knowledge in this area. I can accept that such an intuitive leap takes place, and that the trainer and dog come to occupy a relationship that is qualitatively different from the pretraining one. Hearne's descriptions of her training a dog to do scent work give some good indications of the nature of these changes, palpable and observable. This is to say, there appear to be some very real payoffs for both dogs and trainers who engage in serious work together. However, I want to characterize that difference from the perspective of a pet guardian.

The difference is one of a quantitative change transforming into a qualitative one. This is one of Hegel's principles of dialectical reasoning, which he called the "transformation of quantity into quality." In this sense, working dogs and companion dogs both are subject to forms of habituation that result in a moral and objective order, that is, an order that can be enacted "rightly" or "wrongly." Both the companion dog and the working dog are subject to forms of humanly defined habituation. Yet the degree to which this is true, the pragmatic character of training/working versus "companion dog–socialization" (for lack of a better term), the self-consciousness and consistency of the trainer versus the dog guardian, and the content of the cultural forms of habituation transform a "companion dog" into a "working dog" and a "guardian" into a "dog trainer." With the exception of wild or feral dogs who do not directly interact with human beings, we cannot but help to train dogs, i.e., habituate them, to the practices of human society. However, the distinction between training and habituation is an important one, a matter of transformation of quantity into quality, from tacit training involved in everyday play and feeding into the reflexive, rational enterprises of guide dog work, herding and guarding animals, schutzhound work, or scent work.

Conclusion: All Dogs Are Socially Constructed Animals

In this chapter we considered two general "kinds" of relationships between dogs and humans. Each kind of relationship provides for both human and animal a different texture of relevancies and associated practices. These relevancies and practices in some sense create the relevant characteristics of the humans and dogs to staff them. We used the terms "pet/companion dogs" and "working dogs," categories that are clearly sociocultural constructions, to describe these two different ways of dogs' and humans' relating.

Every attempt to describe any dog is an occasion in which the cultural machinery of perception, thought and language is brought into play, and is in these senses a thoroughly social event. Hearne writes,

> . . . [I]n the trainer's world different kinds of animals exist than the ones that I heard and read about in the university. For the trainer, there are hot working Airdales, dutiful and reliable German Shepherds, horses with intense, fiery and competitive temperament, other horses who are irremediably dishonest. In the universities, there were more or less Cartesian creatures of uncertain pedigree, revised by uncertain interpreters of Freud and Jung, which may be why in the world of letters in general animals are invoked to mark "primitive" and usually more unsavory impulses, while in the trainers' world they are more like characters in James Thurber, who insisted that dogs represent "intelligence and repose" in his work. The trainers' language was, if I could only unfold its story with the full acceptance of what Stanley Cavell has called "the daily burden of discourse," the right language, the philosophically responsible language. (Hearne, 1986, p. 14)

Here is another construction she writes about that we have already encountered, "the behaviorists' dog" (cf. Wieder's description of the behaviorists' chimp, cited in chapter 4):

> To the extent that the behaviorist manages to deny any belief in the dog's potential for believing, intending, meaning, etc., there will be no flow of

intention, meaning, believing, hoping going on. The dog may try and respond to the behaviorist, but the behaviorist won't respond to the dog's response; there will be between them little or no space for the varied flexions of looped thoughts. The behaviorist's dog will not only seem stupid, she will be stupid. (Hearne, 1986, p. 58)

The academic dog, the behaviorist's dog, the trainer's dog and the companion dog are all thoroughly creatures defined by social discourse. Academic dogs are somewhat dissimilar to the other categories in that they are found primarily in the formal analytic writings of academics (reflections about matters appearing in books and journals) and in scientific laboratories. On the other hand, behaviorism in the laboratory is more than just academic reflection. That is, reasoning as Wieder with regard to chimps, when dealing with dogs in scientific laboratories, the behaviorist, scientific construction of dogs does not simply rest on the pages of books or journals. It can be brought into play as an actual guide or action framework to which real dogs are subject. As Wieder described, in some settings behaviorism as a way of seeing becomes incorporated into everyday life with animals. Even so, aside from the case of the science laboratory, there is a very basic difference between the construction of dogs in academic writing and their appearance as real animals in everyday situations.

It is clear when reading the accounts of Michalko and Hearne that the consequences of inhabiting these differing relationships are profound for both dogs and persons. In working with an animal such as Smokie or Salty, the trainer is implicated in a self-referential way that does not seem to occur in a purely companion-guardian relationship. In these working kinds of relationships the dog comes to define the human in profound and transforming ways, and in ways that often have practical and serious consequences. And while the relationship between a guardian and companion dog is equally defining for its participants, and though the practices within that relationship do have practical and sometimes consequential outcomes for them, this occurs in different ways and in different degrees such that there appears to be a qualitative shift. One senses this most clearly in Hearne's insistence that the trainer's language is the socially responsible and correct language and in Michalko's description of how Smokie taught him about blindness. While heartfelt descriptions of companion dogs that emphasize their contribution to the guardian's understanding of life can be found in prose and poetry, these are usually philosophical reflections, often written in memory of a companion who has died. They stand somewhat in contradistinction to the kinds of ongoing, consciously self-referential and practically consequential reflection described by both Michalko and Hearne.

By describing dogs as constructed in social context, I mean to recall the discussion of ethnomethodology's program presented in the beginning of the book. Dogs and humans find each other within a lived orderliness that defines each reciprocally. In our society these orderlinesses are given the names companion dog/guardian, guide dog/guide dog user, scent hound/trainer, "junkyard dog"/guard dog guardian, etc. The historical and lived details of these "types" are embodied and lived in any actual case. This is what is meant by "all dogs are socially constructed." All dog guardians/users/trainers are socially constructed as well. For both dogs and humans, perceived features and actions of the Other are given form and meaning through participation in these types of social relations, providing for both the "grounds" against which their own "figures" emerge. Social construction refers to the orderlinesses, these general types, achieved in detail in any case. They consist of the embodied and historical details of just this instance—the generality made real in its details. That's flowery philosophical language, but we are really talking about mundane, everyday stuff here: miraculous stuff, but ordinary.

In a way we are reinterpreting Durkheim's aphorism. We need to know, to be able to describe and demonstrate, what kinds of orderlinesses these are, and how they are achieved as praxiological matters, in order to understand who are the dogs and humans who staff them. We will not find our answers in the academic literature about dogs, we will not find them by administering generic representational theorizing and we will not find them if we rely naively on natural theorizing. The only way they can be found and understood is by empirically studying the lived orders in their observable details as they naturally occur in specific instances. By practicing ethnomethodological indifference and by using data that hold the analyst responsible, at least in some ways, to the details of concrete things, the ethnomethodologist also constructs his/her dog. It is the object of EM studies to do so in a way that holds the analyst responsible to the observable details of locally achieved, indigenous order.

6

Continuities and Discontinuities with Other Observers of Dog-Human Relationships

This chapter examines recent works of observers of naturally occurring dog-human interaction. It shows how the current analysis is continuous with certain aspects of previous studies but also significantly departs from them.

In 1983, the sociologist Stuart Sigman, one of the first ethnographers to turn his attention to human-dog interaction, noted that there was a dearth of observational data. Despite significant publications in the past twenty years, this continues to be the case and reflects a general, characteristic lack of observational data in social science investigations, as well as a specific lack of interest in human-companion animal relationships. Sigman's own observation/interview study of companion guardians was one of the earlier reports by a sociologist about these matters. In doing his research, he utilized both interview and observational data in order to investigate aspects of interaction between elderly persons and their dogs, particularly with respect to communication between guardian and companion. He employed a perspective coming out of the tradition of symbolic interactionism, emphasizing the meaning structures that existed between guardians and their dogs. By focusing upon communication between guardians and dogs, Sigman identified many of the formal features of communication that are similar to communicative practices in human-human interaction in which one of the participants does not express or receive symbolic, formal language (see below for a discussion of the similarities and differences between such interactions and those that occur with dogs). Sigman's work is pioneering in several respects.

Do Dogs Have Minds?

Clinton Sanders is one of the foremost sociologists studying human-dog interaction and has published work in journals and two significant books (Arluke & Sanders, 1996; Sanders, 1999). His book *Understanding Dogs* closely resembles the work of Erving Goffman in many respects. It is an important work. His scholarship in this area has been substantial and of high quality. He employs a more or less symbolic interactionist approach to his interpretation of human-dog interaction, and this endows his work with certain strengths and weaknesses.

The concept of mind plays an important role in various disciplines, including introspective psychology, developmental psychology, comparative psychology and the school of symbolic interactionism in sociology. The latter's use of mind stems from the work of George Herbert Mead, and later by Herbert Blumer and others. But with the advent of radical sociologies, such as EM, and with the loss of the methods of introspective psychology, the concept of mindedness has become increasingly problematic.[1] Neither dogs nor people "have" minds. Nor from my data can they be said to observably produce "mind" as an interactional accomplishment. I can show you a good move. I can show you a game. I can even find "lively inner states" of Others in play. But I cannot show a mind playing.

The approach taken by Arluke and Sanders (1996, chapter 2), as well as Sanders's (1999) later work, is based on the idea that the understanding of animals' "minds" emerges from interaction with them. This formulation is a problem from the outset, since the concept of "mind" occupies a scientific status akin to "ego," "consciousness," "intention or motivation" (see especially Bekoff & Allen, 1998 for a discussion of animal intention in play), "instinct" (cf. my discussion of Huizinga in chapter 2, note 11), and "norms"—i.e., unobservable constructs creatively invented to solve the problem of reality, but which are actually admissions of inadequacy in the face of that problem.

"Mind" is a commonsense term employed within scientific lexicons to explain regularities of individual and collective action as seen in everyday life. The concept of mind commits the analyst to seeing actors in terms of having a "part" of them inside that controls their intentions, motivations, reflective awareness, planfulness, comprehension of meaning, and so on. While there is no question that these features are found in human-human and human-dog interactions, their explication via the concept of a mindful actor to account for their presence is conceptually problematic.

Of course, nothing of this is new. Anticipating critique from other sociologists, Arluke and Sanders provide a section of writing designed to answer these possible objections. In "Answering the Skeptic" (Arluke & Sanders, 1996, pp. 48–52), they argue that mind is not simply a questionable piece of scientific ideology, and that animals and humans engage in "minded behavior." Further, to answer the critics who would argue that mind is a psychological entity invoked to explain social behavior, they assert that mind is not an entity possessed by animals or people. Mind is a social accomplishment. Whether it be human-human or animal-human interaction, mind results from practical interaction in which actors estimate how others understand what is going on and how they would like things to proceed. "Mind is a social accomplishment" is a catchy phrase intended to make things clearer. It appears to cover a lot. It is as if to assert on the basis of its being written that mind is not an abstract, given entity, but a social accomplishment of actors, and that this was to clarify and settle the ontological reality of mind. It does not.

Far from clearing up issues, this text further obfuscates the concept of mind, as does the authors' challenge to skeptics, "Given the possibilities and constraints of studying animal mind, what standards of scholarship might be acceptable to our community?" (Arluke & Sanders, 1996, p. 51).[2] The authors proceed, assuming that the issue of mind has been settled by the above move. Yet it really has not. To assert in writing (or oral or sign language) via reasoned argumentation that "mind," "rule," "norm," "social structure," or any other entity is a product or constituent part of social interaction does not establish the empirical validity or correctness of invoking that concept or frame, in this case the frame of minded actors. The assumption of the Arluke and Sanders text, taken from then on as obvious and unquestionable, is that human beings have/achieve minds, and therefore exhibit/produce them in interaction. They can then argue similarly for nonhuman animals.

To some degree, detailed descriptions and representations of everyday life, such as those I provide for my play with Katie, are somewhat constraining to such theorizing. At least they can be used in this way. While ethnographic texts and videotapes do not themselves limit the frameworks that can be brought to bear upon them, examination of their detail provides a certain recalcitrance, and sometimes insensibility, to either scientific armchair or common-sense theorizing. In the case of symbolic interactionism, the descriptions and data provided in this study tend to question, or at least limit the utility of, a concept like mind. The same is true with respect to symbol, which is a central concept to symbolic interactionists that I believe to be overly or inappropriately used by them. While there are such things as symbols, and these do enter into human-dog play, symbolic interactionists tend to exaggerate their fundamental importance in social interaction. They make shared symbols a necessary precondition for interaction, and in this overestimation distort their role in it (see below on the symbolic character of human-dog interaction).

It is clear from the data that I was not able to rid myself of my own sociological convictions in their construction. I had hoped, by employing multiple forms of detailed data that reveal as much as possible about a mundane account and representation of play, to minimize scientific importing of etic, academic theory-driven ideas into emic accounts of humans and nonhuman social members. Without (and sometimes even with) the use of detailed, historically sensitive descriptions and videotape, film and photographic images as the basis for arguing the existence of phenomena, sociological analysis may be essentially unaccountable to concrete activities of a material world—i.e., entirely an armchair and literary form of work (see Garfinkel, 2002, p. 265). When it is done in a literary way it becomes an exercise in documentary method. One describes a priori the underlying pattern of things as the theory provides, searches for corroborating examples, finds them, and uses these exemplars to further explicate the underlying pattern, which is then used to search for examples, and so on. Even with detailed notes of a situated historical production by particular actors, even with videotape of it, importing theories to explain the data is facile. Moreover, at the point in the research when one reflects upon the sociological significance of the data, it is difficult to know exactly at what point one is incorporating extrinsic reasoning and theorizing. Ultimately the question is a matter of judgment as to how much and how one holds oneself to a historically situated, punctilious, praxiological account, or allows oneself to theorize from the outset, at the ground level. As stated above, in this writing I tried to observe the policy of ethnomethodological indifference. However, this did not mean I pretended to know nothing, either as a ball player with Katie or as a social scientist. Instead, I kept my sights on what I was after.

Understanding Dogs

Sanders advances that the quality/closeness of the relationship that a person has with an animal and the systematic way in which he or she collects information are what should establish the "truth value" of a study. While I agree that such factors can be considerations in thinking about the validity of observational work, I find the argument that scientific validity rests even upon familiarity to be somewhat naive. As Garfinkel points out, all sorts of theoretical frames can be brought to bear in a methodical fashion on human-human and animal-human interaction.[3] In their reading they are all demonstrable, at least in the sense that Ernst Grünwald (1934/1970) intended when he noted that the basic assumptions of a perspective do not get questioned but instead form a way of seeing that constitutes the grounds for their own truth, including ways to incorporate counterfactual information. This is the essential process underlying what Mannheim (1936) later described as the documentary method, described above, and is a mainstay of all formal analysis. The point behind this brief trip into the epistemology of social research is that asserting validity based upon *closeness* to one's dogs and systematic collection of information (while helping to make observational work interesting in its details) inappropriately reduces complex matters of epistemology and method to two simple ones, closeness and "systematicness." These may be necessary but are certainly not sufficient conditions to justify claims of valid knowledge.

Many studies of dog interaction report guardians' reflections about their relationship with their dogs, treating them as factual and accurate accounts. This is especially true in several chapters of Sanders's 1999 book, in which guardians' verbal accounts and claims are treated virtually as empirical data—i.e., as reliable observational data. He writes, "The dog guardians, trainers, veterinarians, and others presented in this book are, in essence, 'folk ethologists'" (Sanders, 1999, 148). Without denigrating the very real insights people have about the dogs with whom they interact, I would emphasize the folk part of the characterization. It is epistemologically naive and methodologically improper to treat such folk accounts (natural theorizing) as scientifically adequate. Notes from my initial reading of Sanders's book display this logic:

> It is no more sensible to think that people understand what they are doing with their dogs than it is to think that they understand what they are doing when they have a conversation. It is not that wonderfully insightful ideas have not been produced about both dogs and conversation, but it is true that until the conversational analysts began inspecting actual recorded conversation in a direct and highly detailed fashion, insights about what language meant and how persons communicate through language were almost exclusively driven by armchair (general definitional) theorizing. Discussion of these topics was not held responsible to actual occasions of conversation and language actually in use. Philosophers of language are filled with wonderful and powerful observations about language use. Yet these insights did not lead to the systematic study of conversation such as found in conversational analysis. There is a great difference between reflecting upon language use in general and studying it in the kind of empirical detail found in the work of Sacks, Schegloff, Jefferson and their followers.

Similarly, the literature on dogs and dog-human interaction is permeated with insightful notions and genuine knowledge about this or that phenomenon. Such ideas and accounts fill the work of Sanders (and many other sociologists), and are cited as evidential of certain "truths" about dogs and people—for example, that dogs are treated as "persons" and therefore *are* persons. Yet scientifically speaking, the natural theories offered by the everyday dog guardians or trainers are held accountable to the empirical details of everyday events in a very loose way, if at all. Yet they are commonly accepted in the literature, somewhat uncritically from an epistemological perspective, as in some way adequate, real or true to some actual state of affairs.[4]

It is entirely reasonable that dog guardians' talk about their dogs or their relationships with their dogs would be filled with items from our culture's stock of practical knowledge (Schutz, 1974) about human-dog interaction, and that such talk might be inadequate to an empirical description or scientific representation of these same phenomena.[5] If it were true that people understood what they were doing and expressed this adequate understanding in their everyday language and accounts, then sociologists would have nothing more or less to do than be good journalists, to veridically record what people say about their lives, and that would be the end of it. Yet as any ethnographer can tell you, this simply is not the way things work. This is why "folk" accounts have traditionally been mistrusted in sociology as inadequate. Even in anthropological ethnography, where emic (folk) knowledge is what is sought and holds a central theoretical position, it is rarely treated as objective, scientific or self-reflexive.

There is good reason for this. It has been demonstrated that living with and understanding an event or phenomenon from within, intimately and naturally, is very different from studying or observing that same event or phenomenon with the scientific attitude, i.e., critically. Garfinkel's exercise in which he assigned students to go home, pretend in their minds that they were boarders, and make notes about what they saw demonstrates the difference powerfully (1967, chapter 2). The instruction produced a profound shift in how students saw their own families, both in terms of the actual practices observed and the morality of those practices. Subjects knew these situations intimately but they had never been given the specific task of observing or reflecting upon them critically. Having done so, many of the students were deeply disturbed by what they saw, so much so that they felt required to morally justify their accounts.[6] Similarly, my study of the Smith family (Goode, 1994, chapter 3), a family with a congenitally deaf-blind child without any formal language, showed that while family members were incredibly expert at communicating with the daughter on a day-to-day basis, they did not have (nor should they have had) an analytic grasp of how they did this and exactly what they were actually doing. Such an account was something that I could write "as an observer," given that my research focused on that particular phenomenon, but would never have occurred to the family to produce. Importantly here, their accounts of their communication with their child, though highly informative, were not identical with the observed detail of communicative practices. Again, doing something and analyzing something are related but different activities, with the latter always assuming the former.

Thus, while remarks by guardians, trainers and others may be revealing of selected aspects of human-dog relationships, they should not be treated as overall adequate formulations or descriptions of these events.

The autoethnographic notes and visual data are not offered in this way. Let me remind the reader, with regard to the current inquiry, of the purpose of incorporating a reflexive analysis of the relationship between the phenomenon, its data and its analysis. Garfinkel's device, described in chapter 1, is to demonstrate that even a detailed analysis of a single case, utilizing multiple sources of data and the "strongest" ways of holding analysis responsible to the details of things, does not "solve the problem" of the relationship of accounts and representations to everyday events. The text and audiovisual data about my playing with Katie are more reflective of the identifying details of lived events than purely ethnographic studies. Yet the constructed nature of the display cannot be dismissed by any amount or type of description, recording or self-reflection. It is, in Garfinkel's words, "an irremediable condition of analysis," which again is not to say that every analysis is equally hopeless or off-base. On the contrary, the very discussion in which we are engaged in some sense demonstrates an attitude of analysis that, I believe, furthers understanding of everyday interaction with dogs in a way that is far too absent in other dog-human ethnographies. This degree of reflexivity, I believe, represents a methodological improvement in observational work on this topic.

While an improvement, it must be again underscored that the reflexive incorporation of epistemological and methodological issues in the study of dog-human play does not "do away with," in any sense, the constructed character of this or any other analysis. To reiterate, one can be "systematic," "detailed" and "comprehensive" from *n*-number of perspectives (*n* being limited only by human imagination) with quite contradictory results, even if detailed empirical representations and data are employed. Given this, researchers need to be guarded about offering general theories about human-human or animal-human relations. The inquiries about human-dog play described in this book represent about one hundred years of scientific reflection on this topic and are, in my view, investigations in their youthful stage of development and therefore "initial." It is thus appropriate to be hesitant about formulating a theory that explains dog-human play. Even to offer such a theory as provisional is dangerous, at least before we have seriously studied dog-human play as an everyday event.

As described in chapter 1, ethnomethodologists have argued that descriptions of everyday life must be in terms of practices available *in situ* and in real time to actors as co-constructors of a "social orderliness." That is, descriptions need to be in terms or forms intrinsic to the social order being considered. Further, since social orders do not happen in general, but only concretely, for actors with particular social histories and under particular, unrepeatable conditions, it is not possible to formulate a truly general solution to how social orders are constructed by members. When such general descriptions are employed by sociologists (for example that interaction between humans and dogs is managed through the mindful knowledge of rules, symbols, motives and experiences of self and Other), they may be intellectually pleasing in their apparent power to explain many instances and occurrences, but often shed little light on exactly "what" is being done and how. Garfinkel has characterized this phenomenon as "the missing what" of social analysis: sociologists writing all around and about a phenomenon, producing data and analysis that are part of an ensemble of relevant matters. They can do so without defining/describing exactly "what" the phenomenon consists of in its observable doing, i.e., as a praxiological matter. The phenomenon is thus simultaneously counted upon but ignored. Most dog ethnographers have proceeded in this way.

The Symbolic Character of Dog-Human Interaction

The approach employed by Sanders is that of symbolic interactionism. Without going through a summary of the symbolic interactionist paradigm, I will concentrate upon some common themes in this school of thought. One extremely common feature found among symbolic interactionists is illustrated in the following assertion: "coordinated exchange is possible because the actors involved employ the conventional symbol system of language to talk to themselves and to those with whom they interact" (Arluke & Sanders, 1996, p. 62).

As is typical of many sociologies, including symbolic interactionism and even some earlier versions of EM, coordinated social action is seen as primarily, if not exclusively, possible because participants share language, meanings and symbols. This is precisely the kind of reasoning that is questioned in *A World without Words*, which demonstrates that rich and orderly social relationships can and do exist without shared linguistic symbols. Shared meaning through shared symbols is the essence of the symbolic interactionist proposal. Yet in both the deaf-blind studies and in the field notes on play with Katie, much of the observed order in action could be accounted for without any reference to shared symbols.

We have to be very clear about what we mean by the word "symbol" and sharing a symbol system. The word "symbol," in the way I am using it, means "something that stands for something else."[7] The orderliness achieved by Katie and me on specific occasions of play was not primarily based upon shared understandings of things that stood for something else. In fact, very few of the things we shared, or share, in play are really symbols in this defining respect. Our play was/is not based primarily upon symbols. In fact, thinking of our play that way distinctly distorts what it is to be doing the play, which is comprised of virtually instantaneous readings of bodily positions and postures as they are related to the position and action of the play object, in the course of some particular occasion of play, in this or that play motif, under specific biographical and natural conditions, etc. Because they are biographically situated, play moves and actions are better understood by me than by any other person, and by Katie better than by any other dog. In this sense they require something other than "mere observation" to understand the action as a move in play. Yet even these moves are observable and understandable to a degree by outsiders, just not in the depth and detail that I can.[8]

In the same way that I had no choice but to see my playing with Katie in a praxiological fashion consistent with my training as a sociologist, Sanders (1999) finds shared symbols in his descriptions of his relationship with his dogs. One impression I have of his texts is that he is "primed" to see examples of shared symbols, and finds them in a documentary fashion. Some of the examples are unconvincing in their observable details. A very simple example of this is his description of the game "Stick" played by his Newfoundland dogs. He explains the observation that his dogs grasp the stick with their mouths in such a way that the longer end is kept away from the other player, who is trying to grab it, as "an interesting example of symbolic redefinition of an object" (Sanders, 1999, p. 46). While the game he describes is organized and does appear to have motifs that are elaborated upon (I would not use the term "rules" in a straightforward way for human or animal interaction), it does not appear symbolic. In my reading, it is the skillful, practical management of a game, "I have the stick and now (or thereby) you want it," and much, if not all, of this simple game can be explained without reference to mind (taking the role of the other), shared rules or symbol. The analytic referents used by Sanders are imported from his own education about how to account for social order, i.e., through his training as a professional sociologist. "Symbolic features" become a way of seeing or looking, and are thereby found in every occasion of concerted interaction. Yet they are notably absent in his account of the game. The stick becomes a play stick when the one dog takes it up as one. There is nothing symbolic about that action in the sense that it requires the other dog to see the play stick as something other than what it appears to be or refer to (i.e., "a play stick"). In fact, work involving play sticks is describable, and some dogs spend considerable time inspecting and selecting play sticks with just the correct play properties (see my discussion of stick selection in chapter 2).

The same kind of critique can be constructed for the idea that coordinated social interaction is possible because participants share "meanings." Again we need to be careful here about terminology, "shared meaning" implying a shared sense of intention or identical interpretation. In EM this criticism can be found clearly in the works of conversational analysts, whose praxiological view of utterances and their function in conversation does not admit to their being other than utterances in a conversation. Such an approach can also be found in ethnographic forms of EM, for example in the work of Lynch, in which actual instances of laboratory results are seen as products of many different definitions of "what happened" in the lab. Shared understandings are not a requirement for coordinated conversation or interaction among humans, which is not to say that shared understandings do not occur in human interaction, just that social orderliness is not predicated upon them.[9] This is a central point of disagreement between EM and symbolic interactionism.

This also applies to dog-human play. The records of my play with Katie show that while certain motifs and structures of play existed, these did not primarily involve what one might call shared symbols of the situation. I hesitate to call them shared symbols or meanings since they were not primarily interpretive and did not necessarily involve carefully reading the mind of the other player. For example, *"Katie getting impatient with me for not fulfilling my part of a game" motif, for several botched kicks in a row, is not an interpretive act so much as it is both of us finding ourselves instantaneously in the midst of a recognizable state of game affairs.* Her becoming seriously dissatisfied with repeated botched kicks was not a matter of shared meanings so much as repeated frustration at bad kicks. It was a mutual production/recognition of this sad state of game affairs again. If a symbol is to be understood as referring in some way to something other than itself, symbols were not primary devices used by us in order to play together.[10]

Dogs as Persons

Arluke and Sanders argue that the description of the characteristics of the social category of "person," as found in the work of ethnographers on relationships between severely disabled and nondisabled persons (including my work and that of Bogdan and Taylor [1989]), "open[s] the door for admission of nonhuman actors into the realm of personhood" (1996, 65). While there are certain features in common in interactions between persons without formal language and non-human animals without formal language, I believe this proposal, while well-intentioned, is basically misleading.

While some severely disabled individuals do not develop codified language, and thus in their relationships with other persons share certain formal features of interactions that exist between humans and non-formal language-using animals, one cannot on the basis of these shared formal features "equate" these very distinct social orderlinesses. In their detail, they consist of very different sorts of "doings" for participants, these differences being quite clearly observable and vulgarly available. Anyone who watched a videotape of me playing with Christina, the deaf-blind child I describe in *A World without Words*, and compared it to one of me playing with Katie would immediately be convinced of this assertion. That person would find extremely different-looking and -sounding kinds of things, sharing some formal communicative features, but otherwise incomparable. I will comment in more detail on this below.

Sanders describes companion animals as "virtual persons" and as "animal persons" (Arluke & Sanders, 1996; Sanders, 1999). Such statements represent natural, folk-theorizing entering into sociological knowledge. Reminiscent of sociologists speaking about children under the rubric of socialization, they represent slightly abstract statements of the sociologist as member, or the sociologist as common-sense theorizer (Mackay, 1973). Such comments are made frequently by dog guardians who might say, "My Roxy is just like my child" or "Biff is just one of the members of the family" or "Spot is a person like anyone else." While as a sociologist one can understand the everyday member's use of the term "person" to, as a practical matter, point out or underscore to the listener that this companion animal is far more than a biological piece of machinery, such descriptive nomenclature as a description of actual events cannot be accepted uncritically by an empirical sociology. There is a tendency towards a literary, loose, metaphoric use of terms in postmodern sociology. We find articles titled "The Body as Text" or statements such as "I am trying to read Staten Island like a text." One can get carried away with this kind of thing if one is trying to hold oneself responsible to a critical observation of some concrete state of affairs.

In its various etymological derivations, "person" means a human being. A "body," a thing that is alive, moves, breathes, excretes, copulates and so on, is not a "text." While postmodern literary conventions may be intellectually revealing of certain aspects of everyday life, accepting metaphors as descriptions can also be very misleading about phenomena as real-world events. In the everyday world, what Alfred Schutz (1974) called "the paramount reality," there are persons and there are dogs. There are bodies and there are texts. From the perspective of an empirical and praxiological sociology, I can see no reason why one would want to call one thing by the name of another.[11]

Describing dogs as "persons" or as "virtual persons," while pointing out certain features of human-dog relationships as everyday events, ultimately muddles our understanding of them.[12]

This common form of language use is based on certain formal similarities in relationships between human beings and between human beings and dogs. Such formal properties, while they are "real," are methodological abstractions from a lived orderliness that consists of far more than this particular language "snapshot" can reveal or represent. Once any set of formal properties of the lived order is allowed to stand on behalf of the lived order's entirety, it becomes relatively easy to find equivalent formal properties in other kinds of everyday orderlinesses. Yet, as stated above, in no way does finding them signify that these everyday orders, or the participants inhabiting their production, are in any overall sense "the same."[13]

Dogs Are Disabled, Symbolic-Interactionally Speaking

Arluke and Sanders (1996) carry through their symbolic interaction theorizing about human-dog relationships. On the one hand, having privileged mind and symbol, the following statement makes sense: "The animal person is, however, unable to employ language to respond to the guardian's talk or effectively express the content of his or her mind" (Arluke & Sanders, 1996, p. 66). The distinction between understanding, communication and language made in the general model of intersubjectivity presented above is critical here. Of course, Arluke and Sanders are descriptively correct to say that animals do not *express* themselves in formal language.[14] Even if, as some writers have claimed, some dogs can comprehend a hundred or more words, they do not speak them. To me this is a somewhat trite observation, and misleading, especially when it is incorrectly extended to mean that generally dogs cannot effectively express themselves. Such an assertion obviously does not bear up to observational scrutiny. Sanders's own field notes and interviews are filled with examples of dogs expressing themselves with clarity and intensity. Jack, my one-year-old yellow Lab, is one of the most expressive animals I know, sometimes to my chagrin and frustration. Yet, importantly, it is true that he cannot answer the question, "Does your stomach or your chest hurt?" In his 1999 book, Sanders somewhat reverses this position about the role of language in interaction with dogs, and particularly with regard to how we view dog cognition and expressivity. He writes about social scientists' having a "linguacentric stance" in their social construction of dogs.

Much of what dogs communicate to us is vulgarly available, as was described in my notes about Katie's presenting balls or sticks for play. As characterized by Crist, Darwin (1872) believed this vulgar availability to be non-culturally specific (for example, a dog's growling, snarling, and raising hackles will not be perceived as an offer to play in Java while a threat in Canada). It makes sense to think that such recognition of expression and demeanor is the result of common evolution, which is not to say that forms of dog expression are not open to cultural interpretation. These cultural interpretations will have to do with how to perceive and react to the communication, rather than an alternate interpretation of what it means on the dog's part. These forms of vocal and bodily communication by dogs require no particular training or intimate familiarity with dogs. They do require co-presence and sometimes a willingness to communicate and read the animal (thus persons who are terrified of dogs cannot communicate with Katie because they are either hysterical or running away, thereby unavailable to her expressions). At least some of what dogs can tell us is just as clear to us speaking-hearing persons as what humans without formal language can tell us. Then there are forms of communication between Katie and me that require more than what is available to the outside observer, i.e., vulgarly available. Expressions are indexical, and for some adequate interpretation requires knowledge of the history of the situation and how this or that expression has come to fit into that history. For example, Katie's scratching at the cellar door where the new balls were moved about a year ago means, "I want a new ball," or her particular expression of displeasure at a particular game motif gone awry needs to be understood as indicating a chronic problem in our play together (see Mitchell and Thompson's discussion of familiarity in chapter 3, pages 71, 76–77).

Utilizing a symbolic interaction perspective, in which words and language are critical for even the possibility of organized interaction, it is not surprising that dogs emerge as linguistically disabled. For example, in exploring the ways that dog guardians speak for their dogs, Sanders writes, "It is also through the process of speaking for the dog that the guardian actively constructs—both for him or herself and for others—the identity of the animal" (cf. Goode & Waksler, 1990; Sanders, 1999, p. 67). Here we find the same kind of reasoning discussed above, partaking of the same analytic device. A formal feature of relationships with dogs and with persons without language is that the language-using human is in the position to speak on behalf of the dog or disabled person. However, observing these two types of lived orderlinesses as everyday realities reveals massive differences between the two. In the case described by Goode and Waksler, Bianca is a child born deaf, blind and quadriplegic and developed no formal language and almost no ability to either initiate or respond to interactional events initiated by anyone unfamiliar to her. Bianca's multiple sensory disabilities immediately made many forms of mutual understanding (intersubjectivity) and action available to nondisabled humans and animals completely inaccessible to her. Under such circumstances, the mother's use of language to speak on behalf of her daughter, sometimes producing utterances in a simulated voice of her daughter, was the primary vehicle, virtually the *only* vehicle, for establishing Bianca's identity to others. Because of the disability of her daughter, the mother did actually define her child's identity in ways similar to those affirmed by Sanders as common to dog guardians. Yet, as the description below will illustrate, these commonalities belie substantive and qualitative differences between dogs and handicapped children.

A quick example will flesh out what I am saying. When my Labrador, Jack, was about eleven months old, a college archaeology class began to meet in the park where we walk. When he first saw the group, Jack took off like the playful puppy he was and jumped all over everybody in a kind of unmistakable "frenzy of friendliness." Jack was nearly 80 pounds at that time and formidable to deal with. In other words, he could be a nuisance. Despite his own inability to use words and whatever I might have said about him, he immediately began to establish his own identity with the group. Over the course of the weeks that followed I said a lot of things about Jack to that group. The things said did affect, I think, the way Jack was perceived sometimes to some degree. Yet the real "work" of establishing Jack's identity to this group was clearly and massively done by him. I could have said a lot of things about Jack to them that would have proven false by virtue of his behavior. I could have lied for him, but such lies would have been discovered. Instead, I told them on the very first day that we showed up, "Jack is a good boy, he is very sweet, and don't be afraid of him." Six weeks later, after spending a half hour alone with Jack in a field by an excavation, a graduate student on the project said, "You've got a sweet pup." There is "the talk," and then there is "the walk." I could have sung his praises or made excuses, but Jack established his own identity and communicated who he was in the course of events, and without the use of symbols. Only a theory-driven scientist could conclude otherwise.

It is in this sense that the perspective of symbolic interactionism, when applied to human-dog interaction, distorts and creates an unrealistic view of dogs as "linguistically disabled" animals. By focusing upon the linguistic and symbolic aspects of the interaction, this paradigm consistently produces an account of it in which the animal's contribution in these terms is made perspicuously absent. One might say that the focus upon verbal production in interaction masks the bodily ways in which the animal powerfully participates in establishing his/her identity and the event's course.

After arguing throughout that language is the basis for interaction and mind, Arluke and Sanders do a reversal and say that social scientists are linguacentric and that language is an overrated vehicle for interaction and cognition (Arluke & Sanders, 1996, pp. 78–81). Though these propositions are more descriptively accurate than some of the earlier proposals in the chapter, arguing this way after in the previous seventeen pages proposing something quite different is curious indeed. There is a deep ambiguity as to how language is portrayed. On the one hand, it is strongly argued that scientists are too linguacentric in trying to account for animal-human interaction, that the role of language is overrated and perhaps misrepresented. On the other hand, it is strongly advanced that shared language and symbols are the basis for concerted interaction and that the vernacular language of pet guardians and dog trainers giving voice to their companion dogs, because of their acquired expertise in reading and understanding the animals, should be trusted as a characterization of dog-human interaction. Either proposition focuses squarely, though differently, on language and not on a critical understanding of the embodied interaction of humans and dogs. Dogs appear again, even in the restated, less language-based version of the problem, as creatures whose guardians talk for them and define them, ignoring their canine contributions.

One is reminded of Vicki Hearne's ironic response to Wittgenstein's (1953) remark, "If a lion could talk we could not understand him." She commented to the effect that a talking lion would not be a lion, and therefore could not tell us what it meant to be a lion. So an actually speaking lion is of no interest. On the other hand, she goes on, "lions do talk . . . if largely not in words" (Hearne, 1994, p. 173). Hearne knows lion trainers who have conversations with their lions, citing Hubert Wells as a man with exceptional relationships in this regard. I believe that Hearne's closing lines to her chapter could well serve as a corrective to Sanders's basic proposition. She writes, "Wittgenstein has a lion of towering beauty who is not talking to us. I think that we court more than one kind of tragedy when we dismiss either the volubility of Wells's lions or the tremendous silence of the lion of the *Investigations*" (Hearne, 1994, p. 174). "Either" is a key word.[15]

To his credit, in his 1999 book Sanders moves away from this position about humans' and dogs' sharing symbols in order to communicate and organize activities. Because he is clearly the leading sociological ethnographer of dog-human interaction today, I am going to spend some space briefly reviewing his more recent formulation of human-dog interaction, in order to make clear the continuities and discontinuities between us.

One improvement in his 1999 book is that dogs are no longer presented as deficient language-users. That image is replaced with that of the dog as a communicator (see especially pages 133–34) that does not rely on symbols or symbolization to achieve interaction with humans. Dogs are instead sensitive readers of situations and actions, purveyors of "embodied messages" with the ability to comprehend human words to a limited degree. Sanders seems to distance himself from the Meadian part of symbolic interactionism, with respect to both human-dog interaction and human-human interaction. That must be appreciated as a deep intellectual reconsideration on his part.

Yet there are two other aspects of his work that differ significantly from the data, representations and analysis in this study. One has to do with the degree to which shared definitions of situations are required in order to have concerted action, and the other has to do with the ways in which those who staff interactions need (are required) to comprehend the experience of the other in order to achieve concerted and coordinated action together.

Consider the following paragraph:

> At its most elemental, social interaction involves conscious beings who are co-present. For successful interaction to take place, these actors must possess certain basic abilities and share fundamental understandings. The foundation of this exchange is the mutual definition of the situation in which the interaction is taking place. Central to this situational definition is a mutual understanding of who the actors are in the specific context and the purpose of the exchange—each actor is aware of his or her definition of the situation and goals and, in turn, estimates the understandings and goals of the other. Of key importance then is the ability of each actor to take the role of the other, to imaginatively see things from the other's point of view. (Sanders, 1999, p. 140)

This formulation echoes his earlier symbolic interactionist commitments and presents similar problems. The principal points of difference have to do with the way those interacting are represented as self-aware, cognizant of a shared definition of a situation, and acting with regard to an accurate appreciation of the other's point of view. These issues were discussed in the field notes about play with Katie, and above. From a praxiological perspective, "reality disjunctures" (Pollner, 1987) are those times when unshared definitions or features of the situation surface in specific circumstances and become *problematic for participants*. These remind us that in order to produce relatively and apparently coordinated interaction (what Garfinkel called coordinated action for all practical purposes), participants need not have been thinking along the same line, although they may be all along taking "thinking alike" to be the normal appearance of the case (as for example in conversation). Certainly, Sanders's use of the word "shared" needs to be examined very closely and cannot be naively accepted to mean "isomorphic" or "the same." Reciprocity of perspectives is a working assumption of the stock of practical knowledge at hand (Schutz, 1974). The data and representations of playing with Katie show that it is not an empirical requirement or prerequisite of concerted action.

"Imaginatively" (descriptively, I am not sure how to otherwise phrase this) taking Katie's role and understanding her experience, although not required in order to engage in the various forms of reported play, entered into play at times, especially when Katie's actions became problematic and did not provide for enjoyable or ongoing play. But shared (i.e., identical) comprehension certainly did not appear to serve as a foundation of our play together. Nor at times, as my autoethnographic notes report, did her behavior indicate even the slightest concern or appreciation of my perspective on the play. Thus sharing of perspectives is another requirement of Sanders's approach that needs to be looked at critically.

With regard to this issue of sharing the perspective of the Other, Sanders's discussion of the behavior of his companion dogs Emma and Isis on walks demonstrates the documentary nature of analysis. This is not a critique but an illustration of how documentary method works, and I could also supply the reader with examples from my own data. He writes, "If on the walk I stop and look in a particular direction, they will stop, glance at me, and gaze off in the direction I am looking. This seems a fairly clear indication of their elemental ability to put themselves into my perspective. In a literal sense they attempt to assume my point of view. If I look at something they conclude that it is probably something important" (Sanders, 1999, p. 144). The last statement is observationally grounded and appears true of dogs interacting with humans or other dogs. However, my own interpretation of similar events with my dogs would formulate this event slightly differently. I would say, one of the witnessable things that happen on walks is that humans and dogs can see each other looking or gazing in different directions. Sometimes such looking consists of a concentrated gaze in a certain direction. This kind of looking can be done for a variety of reasons, in various ways and under different circumstances. Dogs and humans can be observed to recognize *directed gaze* in each other and regularly do so.[16]

Most readers, certainly those who are not sociologists, would find great similarities between my work and that of Sanders. And they would be correct in that we both believe in accounting for social reality by examining the artful practices of social members in everyday life. We can clearly be grouped within a "social constructionist" school within sociology. But this basic similarity can mask important differences that exist between perspectives within this branch of sociology. In my discussion of his work I have emphasized these differences and perhaps have neglected to emphasize this basic similarity. This being said, I will attempt to characterize his work in relation to my own.

We need to be very careful about making too much, or too little, of what humans and dogs do together. The same can be said about what humans and humans do together. Traditional sociological thinking, EM and conversational analysis aside, has emphasized the role of language and symbolic thinking in structuring social activities. There has been reliance upon theories that, in my view, are based on inadequately grounded assumptions about social interaction and the social production of everyday life. Thus Sanders's interpretation is correct in acknowledging the competence of dogs (and humans) to recognize directed gaze, but it overextends the significance of such recognition as an indication of understanding the perspective of the other.

Shapiro's Empathic and Bodily Understanding of One's Dog

Kenneth Shapiro's ethnographic observations of his companion dog, Sabaka, have many similarities to my own. Shapiro is a psychologist who engages in a kind of psychosocial, Schutzian-style reflection on his relationship with his pet male dog, Sabaka. Consistent with a characterization of Schutz's work, Shapiro's 1990 essay is a result of critical but general reflection about his everyday experiences with his dog. As such it accurately portrays, as does Schutz's work, certain general features of these everyday experiences. In addition, Shapiro strongly historicizes the phenomenological project, as Schutz did, so that both the phenomenon of interest and the phenomenological reflection upon it are in their own ways subject to true historical particulars. These are strong points of his (and Schutz's) analysis. Less desirable, at least from an ethnomethodological perspective, and paralleling the same kinds of dissatisfaction found by ethnomethodologists with Schutz, is the writings' generality (i.e., it does not actually describe or demonstrate the *detailed practices* that underlie the processes he validly names). Also somewhat problematic is the focus upon the other's subjective experience of reality as the object of analysis. While sharing a certain basic orientation that Shapiro advocates in studying dogs, the current analysis does not invoke "understanding the subjective experience of the other" as the primary goal of analysis or glue of social interaction. This issue has been discussed at length in chapter 4.

There is a basic similarity between our approaches to reading the bodily movements of dogs using the capacity of human empathy, what he calls dwelling in the presence of an animal. Shapiro (1990, p. 184) writes that the idea of "dwelling in the presence" of an animal may be attributed to a poem by Denise Levertov, cited by Ursula LeGuin in 1987. Even earlier conceptions of this kind can be found in the works of theoretic-comparative biologists and psychologists such as Jacob von Uexkull. In his 1934 essay, "A Stroll through the Words of Animals and Men," von Uexkull discusses the idea of *a species-specific Umwelt* and of *Welt*. These terms are meant to sensitize the reader to the biologically given (*Umwelt*) and socially experientially defined (*Welt*) aspects of existence. In his fanciful and literary introduction, von Uexkull invites the reader to take a stroll in a field and encounter the worlds of insects and animals, each dwelling in its own bubble of reality, with biologically endowed receptor and effector mechanics to engage in that world. There can be no clearer example of an invitation to appreciate the evolutionary commonalities of interspecies biology as a way to account for experiential commonalities.

It is much to Shapiro's credit as a psychologist that he thinks sociologically. Psychologists generally do not have a critical grasp of the theoretical models of society. Thus I feel the strength of Shapiro's work is in his exploration of the subjectivity of his companion, and not as much in his characterization of their social relations. The sociology he employs utilizes some highly traditional and often critiqued sociological notions, for example, the idea of rules governing social interaction. However, it is to his credit that he at least acknowledges the importance of the social dimension. One can see some similarities in Shapiro's conception of interspecies interaction governed by "implicit rules and regulations" and my own account, which formulates our interaction in a more praxiological language; I also discuss rules and expectations in play, and when I do, I try to use these traditional concepts in a "respecified" way, ethnomethodologically (Button, 1991).

It is understandable that a psychologist focuses on understanding Sabaka's subjective experience, and that such a concern creates a host of problematics (see Lynch, 1997). Without denying the existence of "lively inner states" experienced and observed by people interacting with animals, the current data do not demonstrate participants' access to the subjective experience of the Other as a necessary condition to account for coordinated interaction. This is ground we have already covered. Indexical meanings, as opposed to lexical meanings, are observable *in situ*. In more radical versions of EM, even these indexical meanings may not demonstrably constitute intersubjectively shared meanings. Shared intersubjective meanings may not underlie normal interactions.[17]

The strength of Shapiro's reflection on his relationship with Sabaka is that he strongly captures general features of it, in the Schutzian style characterized above. The data are descriptively general characterizations—in fact, from an ethnographic or ethnomethodological perspective, there is very little "actual data" (i.e., attempts to directly describe or represent the details of observations made). This general but insightful reflection about things contrasts with the highly detailed accounts of my play with Katie and with the visual images presented to help the reader "see" what play actually consisted of for us at that time. Shapiro's reflections about his interaction with Sabaka represent an assemblage of relevant and important remarks about how he and his dog co-construct historically situated routine matters of daily existence. Many of these general insights are accurate and valuable—for example, how dog and man have moves with each other within given spaces that are not interpretable but *seeable as what they are in their immediacy* (Shapiro, 1990, p. 186). In this narrative, the dog is a center of potential action from within these situations. That is, Shapiro names many features observable in everyday human-dog interaction, and this is what makes Shapiro's analysis valuable and "reflecting of the actualities of particular instances."

Shapiro's empathic strategy of taking up a dog's posture is somewhat akin to my simulating deaf-blindness to understand children born deaf-blind. Such a strategy uses the phenomenological device of "imaginative variation." He claims that by taking up a dog's posture, a human can empathize with the embodied nature of the dog's moves. While one may in fact get some useful information doing this, the idea of entering another species's "reality bubble" (*Umwelt*) is epistemologically problematic. One gains some information from the attempt, as I did with my simulated deaf-blindness, but one may learn more about the limitations of the procedure than about the experience of reality by the Other (Goode, 1994a, pp. 24–25).

There are some interesting terminological differences. Sociologists tend to think of individuals and individual experience as primarily constituted by social relationships. Since the observations of the French "crowd psychologists" of the nineteenth century, it has been argued that the summation or aggregation of individual experiences do not constitute the totality of social phenomena, so much as they, the individual parts, are constituted by them. This is a thoroughly sociological view. I would not use the vocabulary of Shapiro, even though I understand that his is a psychosociological view of what I am describing. Katie participates in lived, everyday play. "Objects" do not "present themselves" to her. I present myself to her sometimes, and she to me. She gives me, and I give her, things with which to play. She participates in the play as a player, or, if we are to allow a more abstract vocabulary, "as a lived, mobile body."

On the other hand, if we utilize more abstract terminology, Shapiro's emphasis of the player as an embodied player of the game is commendable. In the language of Maurice Merleau-Ponty (1962, p. 137), "Consciousness is in the first not a matter of 'I think that' but of 'I can.'" Sabaka participates in a specific lived orderliness of play and other household activities, such orderlinesses themselves being constituted through individual and collective historical processes. By historical, I mean that Sabaka's and Shapiro's participation in these lived orderlinesses are subject to physical processes of aging, of increasing experience of each individual, and of having "grown old together" (Schutz, 1974).

If we were to view Shapiro's work through the lens of EM, what is specifically lacking is a sense of the routine grounds of everyday existence. Routines, understood in both the commonsensical vernacular and in a more technical sociological one (for example, see Garfinkel, 1967; Goode, 1994a, chapter 3), form the social bases for everyday existence, everyday practices and participants' awareness of and through them. Routines are just below the surface of Shapiro's writing. They are seen and named by him (see the following section on Sabaka's sense of space). His focus is instead on his own ability to empathize with and describe the individual dog's experience of things. This, again, is a disciplinary difference.

Shapiro concludes that Sabaka's experience is a form of sensorimotor judgment, that the dog does not have a deliberate way of intending to look, and is not reflective or meditative. These may be "accurate" characterizations of Sabaka at any particular time. As discussed above, scenes tolerate and even solicit multiple points of view in their analysis. However, witnessing Sabaka's unreflective behaviors occurs, in my opinion, within an unrecognized orderliness that makes them appear sensible and appropriate to Shapiro. In describing these states Shapiro demonstrates a somewhat paradigmatic bio-behavior view of his dog, that this is all his dog's experience ever could amount to. That view appears influenced by some of the texts he read during the study, to which he refers, and also, I think, to a sense of wanting to describe Sabaka's experience as something consistent with psychology. Given the face-to-face nature of this relationship, this "sensorimotor" viewpoint taken by Shapiro may be somewhat similar to that displayed by the "chimpers" in Wieder's article.

Based upon the data available to me, I cannot conclude that Katie is never reflective or meditative. I cannot say that she is not deliberate, perhaps even to the point of being devious and temporally projecting. Indeed, Sanders (1990) and others make much of the ability of dogs to be deceitful.[18] Other than acceding to the overall biological approach to dogs found in much of the professional literature, perhaps injected into the article by Shapiro at reviewers' requests (something I cannot know), Shapiro appears to describe a nonreflective animal who does not intend anything but simply finds him or herself in the immediate here and now of flux of experience and is only vaguely guided by some sort of bodily sense of things. That may capture an element of what dogs are about sometimes, but does not account for my own observations of Katie.

Sabaka's Sense of Space and Place

Shapiro writes a bit about how he thinks Sabaka experiences space. I find that text both instructive and misleading.

"My original plan for him to sleep outside had been derailed by Elkie's [his other dog] premature death, after which he slowly moved to sleeping arrangements close to us, in a shed attached to the main house" (Shapiro, 1990, p. 187). It is wonderful to read this text, since it acknowledges the historical project in which he, Sabaka and some other (an Other whom he mentions as ill but does not describe in any detail) were engaged. But the writing about this historically situated lived orderliness of the family is dense and summative of what was a long and detailed process in which Sabaka, *with forethought and cunning I would think*, indicated his desire to move closer to the sleeping humans, and achieved his project through a variety of ways of seeing and seizing into the world. Sabaka is eventually successful. Shapiro accurately names but glosses this mutual work. Somehow this does not strike me as a dog with only a sensorimotor level of awareness.

Shapiro provides a nice discussion of Sabaka's finding his place to sit and lie, reminiscent of Castaneda's (1972) discussion of "finding one's spot." That discussion degenerates, in my opinion, with the introduction of possible ethological explanations for Sabaka's movements. This is the move in method that Shapiro describes as "mixed," and takes one into speculation about the significance of behaviors within some theoretically reasoned evolutionary context. I have already discussed evolution as a reasonable but intellectually convenient kind of argument in chapter 2 (see also chapter 2, note 11, on Huizinga's work). In my own view, the relation of these behaviors to those of wild dogs in a lair is speculative and a theoretical distraction from understanding Sabaka as a companion dog living in a human home.

Although Shapiro's description of Sabaka moving within the home is not "direct description in detail," one feels that it captures a "sense" of Sabaka's actions. One gets a feel for his movements, again in a general, not particular, way. I find it interesting that Shapiro's reflections about Sabaka's sense and use of space could, with some few exceptions, have been written about a chimpanzee or even a human. This is again an example of how certain phenomenal features of humans and animals moving in everyday orderlinesses are treated by them as known in common, i.e, as intersubjective. As Husserl's reflection on the structure of intersubjectivity states, certain parts of existence are shared by all possible imaginable monads. All animals thus have "bodily experience [that] intends objects in a world as possible sites for inhabitation" (Shapiro, 1990, p. 188). Dogs and other animals conduct their bodies in ways that secure places to dwell. This can be done in a planned and knowing way, at least when the places are known places. When the spaces are not known, when they are ignorant of its phenomenal features, dogs secure spaces to dwell in ways appropriate to those spaces. That is, they comport themselves from within their inhabited space in ways respondent to and constitutive of the available features of that space (this writing seems convoluted). One can write this way about all animals, and such writing represents a summation of observations made about them.

Shapiro's discussion of Sabaka as a *primarily* spatial being is both instructive and misleading. It is clear, for example, from Sabaka's long-term project of sleeping closer to the family lair that he is a time-oriented being in some sense. Sabaka exhibited patience, practically speaking. Rather than saying that Sabaka "is radically ontologically place dependent," and that space, rather than time, grounds being for him, it would appear much more sensible to look extremely carefully at his projects (together with us or on his own) and to extend the very brief remark that Shapiro makes about Sabaka's undoubtedly having temporal structures in his experience. It might make sense to think about Sabaka's having a "lived temporality" in the very same way he has a "lived spatiality." Lived time emerges within historically evolving lived orderlinesses.[19]

Finally, I am not convinced by Shapiro's suggestion that his examples underwrite a functionalist or behaviorist frame in order to understand Sabaka. When I read Shapiro's brief narratives, they are about particular everyday events and how Sabaka participates in them. As argued throughout this text, any occurrence invites explanation from any number of theoretical frames of reference. I am sure that Sanders could explain these events through a symbolic interactionist perspective, Shapiro a behavioral one, and I from a praxiological one. Our differing descriptions represent disciplinary differences in how we see things.

Conclusion

In this chapter we examined the writings of Sanders and colleagues, and also of Kenneth Shapiro. Especially in Sanders's work, we found the use of symbolic interaction as the paradigm through which observations were organized. In Shapiro's research, we encounter a hybrid approach embracing, on the one hand, phenomenological psychology, and on the other behaviorism.

The analysis of Sanders's writings was used as an opportunity to demonstrate the differences between symbolic interaction and EM. Those differences have centrally to do with the role of language and symbols in organizing face-to-face interaction. Within the Meadian approach, taken up in various permutations by Blumer, Goffman and others, two central convictions about the explanation of coordinated human interaction were that it required: (1) the shared understanding of symbols, and (2) the ability of participants to validly comprehend the perspective of "the Other." EM critiques this view, de-emphasizing the symbolic, intersubjective requirements of everyday action. That is, EM criticizes symbolic interaction as an adequate model to explain human-human interaction.

These same requirements of the symbolic interaction approach become even more problematic when applied to dog-human interaction. This is because establishing shared understanding of symbols or valid understanding of the Other in dog-human interaction is even more difficult from a scientific stand-point. While it might occasionally make sense to think about people sharing the same meaning during the exchange of symbols, as well as understanding how the Other feels while uttering or signing symbols, this view is harder to maintain when the interaction involves one party that does not employ formal language.

It is important to appreciate that the EM critique of symbolic interaction is not that people do not or cannot understand the talk of others or the perspective of others. Such features are discoverable as scenic features of a lived order-liness. That is, it is possible to find such things, but they would not be understood as necessary preconditions for successful coordinated interaction. As described repeatedly in the text, human-human and dog-human interaction can proceed without such sharing.

When applying the symbolic interactionist approach to dog-human inter-action, one can find the phenomena described within symbolic interaction. Dogs do understand symbols, some even very many words and gestures, and there-fore sometimes dog-human interaction proceeds on the basis of shared spoken or manual symbols. This is observably the case. More often, however, interac-tion does not require or evidence shared *symbolic* frames (this is what the general model of intersubjectivity is trying to convey). Nor do its practices evidence a necessary or valid comprehension of the perspective of the Other. When sym-bolic interaction is employed in a paradigmatic fashion, it becomes seriously misleading about the way interaction is organized. It makes those who utilize this frame see the world in its terms, even when the observable details of events may suggest otherwise. I tried to use some examples from Sanders's work to convey the differences in interpretation between EM and symbolic interaction.

Another area of difference between the ethnographer who uses symbolic interaction as a theory and the ethnomethodologist has to do with the relation-ship between scientific description and, to paraphrase Sanders, "folk ethology." I tried to illustrate this in the section that dealt with the assertion that dogs are people. While EM would not dismiss any regularly observable feature of the thing being investigated, for example in this case the repetitive use of variants of the utterance that the companion dog is "a person," it would not construe that utterance as either a necessarily valid indicator of expected features of the dog-human interaction being studied, or as a valid general characterization of actual practices in dog-human interaction. For EM such utterances would be comprehended as indexical, i.e., as performing immediate work in the exchange in which the utterance is being produced. Indeed, it would be interesting to study when and how such utterances are made, with what apparent purpose and whether the sentiments conveyed characterize the relationship being described in any observable way.

Symbolic interaction and EM are often thought of as belonging to the same parts of sociology: qualitative sociology and social constructionism. It is true that these two approaches share certain emphases and methods. In this chapter, however, I have tried to make clear some substantive differences in how these two sociologies would make sense of dog-human interaction. In doing so, I have perhaps overemphasized differences at the expense of similarities.

In some ways this is also true of the treatment of Kenneth Shapiro's work. While we share certain beliefs about how to understand dogs, I concentrated more on our differences than commonalities. I accounted for at least some of these differences via disciplinary training and interest. It is reasonable that a psychologist would turn to phenomenological method to make sense of another individual's viewpoint and experience. In a way pointing out the problematic character of this enterprise is like criticizing Shapiro for being a psychologist. And I admit that my reading of Shapiro's work sociologized it. That is, I took his basically psychological project of understanding Sabaka and saw it more in terms of an interactional system between the humans in the household and the dog. When it was viewed this way, I felt that the writing was informing. When it was viewed as accurate reportage about Sabaka's subjective states, I found it to be possibly misleading.

I am not sure why Shapiro concludes that Sabaka's experience must be understood as a form of sensorimotor judgment and that the dog is completely dominated by the present. These conclusions seem to me to be unwarranted from the data he presents. I am also uneasy with the invocation of evolutionary theory to explain interactional regularities with Sabaka. It is not that I do not believe in evolution. It makes sense as a theory. The problem I have with the use of evolution as an explanatory device is when it is invoked in a general and paradigmatic way to explain something, for example dog-human play, before the thing has been "adequately described" in its own right. When evolution is used this way it can make it seem that things have been explained and no further analysis or description is necessary. Then the use of evolutionary theory becomes antithetical to the goal of (EM) analysis. Asserting that dogs play the way they do because they have a play instinct that has evolved over time may be in some sense accurate. That is, something about dogs' make-up, call it instinct or whatever, is sufficient to allow the behaviors of play and must have evolved over time. However, what those inborn characteristics/proclivities are, or how they work, or what role they play in structuring play with humans is not explicated in any way by simply asserting evolutionary theory. Moreover, these evolutionary inborn characteristics are inferentially there, not directly observable. What is directly observable are the practices of play between the dog and the person. Thus, when evolution is invoked in a facile way to explain dog-human interactional patterns, it can serve as "an admission of helplessness before the problem of reality" (see chapter 2, note 11, on Huizinga).

Arluke, Sanders, Shapiro, Sigman and I are members of a relatively small number of scientists who observe dog-human interaction in a naturalistic fashion. Because of our different intellectual training, it can often seem as if we are like the blind men in the joke about the blind men and the elephant—as if we are all feeling the animal in a different place, or in a different way, and coming up with very divergent conclusions. And like those blind men, each of us probably maintains a conviction that our version of the elephant is accurate, if not the best. In a way one can look at this book is an attempt to make clearer EM's version of the elephant.

7

What We Learned

There are no "conclusions" to this book, if we mean by this term end points of inquiry. The analysis is a first attempt to ethnomethodologically examine one important aspect of companion dog-human relationships—playing together. Its claims and notations should be viewed as initial reports and demonstrations of the everyday production of this phenomenon. As a detailed single case study, this research does not address "distributional" issues. It makes no empirical claims about how other companion dogs and guardians play. On the other hand, the punctilious praxiological description of playing with Katie as an observable, everyday affair discloses features of play and ways of thinking about and actually doing play that, as Mitchell and colleagues' work demonstrates, exist in the play of other dog-human players. Disclosing the general through intense microscopic examination of the particular was discussed above.

Let us review what we did and what we might have learned through the collection and analysis of data. The research was introduced in two ways: as a contribution to EM and to animal studies.

As part of EM studies, we began by reconsidering EM's proposal about the nature of social order. This study was designed to be an exemplar of ethnomethodological research. It attempted to display and analyze an observable, everyday social order—David Playing With Katie. In accordance with the policy of ethnomethodological indifference, the display was done, as much as practically possible, without recourse to analytic devices of formal theorizing, or by relying on the canonical (i.e., accepted established truths) status of existing relevant literatures, or in consultation with other resources extrinsic to the playing. In this sense the account was to be "local," relying upon only what was observably available to players doing the playing. Through four types of data—autoethnography, ethnography, sequenced video images, and video images—the phenomenon was described, represented, and analyzed in terms suggested from within the playing itself (in its "primary quality"). This was the attempt, and the reader can consider in what ways it succeeded or failed.

At the end of the ethnomethodological introduction I requested the reader do two exercises. One was imaginative variation—to imagine a description of what an instance of Katie's and my playing together might look like. The other was a simulation of this research by writing down and videotaping what one does when one actually plays with a dog. The former exercise was intended to illustrate that social facts are only witnessable and not imaginable. If you pick up that description now and read it, the text may help you evaluate the success of this work in delivering news about the details of play with a companion dog. Consider your description in relationship to the data I provided about the phenomenon as it actually happens. What is the message? Did you get any of the general features as you might have imagined them to be? Did you imagine the practices of which play consists in any actual doing of it? You may have been able to get the basic idea, like throw the ball, but it is not likely that you could get much further than that. It is absolutely not the point of the exercise to make a fool of the reader. In fact, those who actually did it are thanked and acknowledged as notably dedicated and serious readers. The point of the imagining exercise is to realize the "goofiness" of normal science's attempts to specify features of any phenomenon of social order before engaging with it directly and critically.

For those (I assume very few) readers who actually attempted to play with a dog and record the event, reading this text has been a qualitatively different experience. Reading is like looking into a magic mirror. While Nietzsche's original reference is that when apes look in, saints won't look back, the importance of his recommendation is that the text is not a docile object that is independent of its reading by a particular reader. Noticed textual features inescapably reflect "the readiness to learn" of the reader. Thus the reader who has actually attempted to do what I tried will have had the benefit of reading with some version of real embodied experience of the various phenomena and conundrums that I have described. He or she will know what I meant in a way that those who have not made this attempt cannot. For that reader, looking at his or her notes or tapes at this time should illustrate this. I would imagine that doing this would reveal certain areas that this research pointed to, perhaps praxiological, perhaps analytic. These similarities would be a result of doing the actual activities of recording and analyzing dog-human play as a local production.

The discussions in this book do not easily articulate with EM's various established literatures, such as the sociology of science, conversational analysis, or gender studies. As an examination of everyday practice and issues related to the nature of social order, embodied interaction, intersubjectivity, and communication, it addresses some central concerns in sociology and ethnomethodology, in the same way Sudnow's work does, without being easily slotted into one of the developing EM literatures.

I also introduced this study as a contribution to animal studies, particularly to an understanding of dog-human interaction. From this perspective, major issues identified were (1) defining the nature of play; (2) defining the nature of animal (dog) behaviors during play; and (3) describing the motives, intentions, and subjective states of other players during play, especially with regard to the anthropomorphic ascription of human subjective states to dogs. The written data and analytic discussions pointed to all these issues and made some central observations:

1. Behavioral or atomistic conceptions of dog-human play do not appear to be adequate for its description or understanding. Instead, an interactional model that accounts for "intentionality" of other players needs to be adopted.

2. Dog-human play is a complex activity, with many aspects and levels, and without objective or simple description. Descriptions and analyses need to be based, at least in the first instance, upon observable, local practice and not upon extrinsic theoretical frameworks.

3. Much dog-human play appears to be autotelic, i.e., done for its own sake and in this sense not goal-directed or instrumental. While playing may help develop abilities in other aspects of life, there is no observational basis to conclude that play is an activity done intentionally by animals as practice for real life.

4. People read the actions of dogs in play indexically, that is, as meaningful forms of participation geared to the specific history and content of the interaction. Some of these indexical communications appear to be very generally known and require only minimal knowledge of the event (for example, Katie's offering a stick to play), while others appear to be particular to relationships (for example, my recognition of a slight hesitation in Katie's pursuit because I have been poor in performance that day).

5. Actions and expressions of players are understood within specific occasions of play, which are subject to many contingencies and variations of player and circumstance. Consequently, any particular occasion of play cannot be adequately described or comprehended by a general model or description.

6. Dog-human players who play regularly, such as companion dogs and their guardians, have a specific history of play together that influences how play actions are understood as practical matters. This is why playing with Katie is not entirely observable by an outsider. Because of the biology of mammals, such play's history and organization is subject to the properties of bodily aging ("growing old together").

7. It is fruitful to characterize playing with Katie in terms employed by

animal studies. Thus in Mitchell's nomenclature, Katie and I were experts in creating variations in fakeout, avoid fakeout, and hide object, employing the devices of manipulation and self-handicap. These were the play motifs that Katie and I elaborated upon, while other forms, present in the play of other dog-human players, were entirely absent from ours.

8. Human players understand and describe the psychological states of dog players using anthropomorphic terms that are anecdotally embedded. This was true in the data presented about playing with Katie, as well as a finding of Mitchell and his colleagues. In this sense, anthropomorphizing is a positive sociological phenomenon, i.e., it is an observable practice of everyday life.

9. In the course of play human players believe their interpretations of dog players' motives, experience, feelings, etc. are accurate unless something occurs to show otherwise (EM also notes this to be true with human-human interaction).

10. Anthropomorphism occurs in different forms, and accuracy or inaccuracy is not always easy to determine. Understandings between dogs and human players are practical, just as they are between human players. This is not to say that understandings between players do not occur in play, or that players cannot be accurate in their anthropomorphizing, although determining "accuracy" may be problematic.

11. The intersubjective orderliness of play can be accounted for in terms other than mutually shared symbols. Most dogs understand some few human words, and words dogs do comprehend can enter into play. Language also organizes dog-human play through the human players' participation in language. The guardian's cultural understandings of play with dogs are based upon the language and culture he or she has learned. For this reason and in just this way, the language "structures" his or her play. However, formal or informal symbol systems, spoken or gestured, do not otherwise appear to play a central role in the detailed practices involved in naturally occurring dog-human play.

12. There are certain features that are common to communication with dogs and with people who lack formal language. Such similarities are probably due to the fact that in each case a person who uses language is in communication with an intelligent Other who does not. There is nothing scientifically or ethically incorrect about acknowledging such commonalities. However, these commonalities should not be used to equate in any overall way these two kinds of social situations or those within them. In social science, common features of very different kinds of everyday orders are allowed to stand on behalf of a more full descrip-

tion of events and then these features are equated with the entirety of the event, including the processes and actors in them. This common analytic device is scientifically misleading. The embodied practices of communicating with a child born deaf-blind, for example, are remarkably different from those of communicating with a dog.

There are some basic differences between this research and much of what is found in most of animal studies. The first is in the type of method used. I engaged in a microscopic, in-depth, single case study in order to deconstruct and display the history and practice of play between a companion dog and her guardian in the long run. This form of research is not common in animal studies because of the belief that individual cases are limited in generalizability, an issue discussed at several points in this book. In animal studies, researchers tend to be interested in making generalizations about "average" play, across many cases and in the short run. There are things to be gained and lost from utilizing either approach, each representing a different way of looking at dog-human play, and each resulting in different kinds of knowledge about it.

A second difference has to do with the behavioral formulation of play that seems to dominate the animal studies literature. This is not a perspective particularly useful to this research's objective. Even the social-psychological formulation of play as found in the work of Mitchell and colleagues is somewhat different from what is advanced here, i.e., an ethnomethodological or praxiological approach. I have tried to make these differences clear in the discussion of "projects in play" in chapter 3. The differences are a result of different paradigms of play. EM advances descriptions of events in which the event's practices and structures provide for the psychology of participants. Psychology, generally speaking, conceptualizes play additively, where individuals' projects and impulses taken together constitute collective events. It is not a case of which view is "correct." This book is a contribution because few studies take this praxiological approach.

Chapter 4 explored the epistemological commitments made by people in describing interaction with animals. Here we followed the work of Crist and her reinterpretation of Darwin's writings. We contrasted two views of anthropomorphism: first, the interpretation of anthropomorphism as projecting human qualities onto animals, and second, anthropomorphism seen as the use of conventional, natural language terms to describe observable aspects of animal behaviors as they naturally unfold in the course of interaction. This latter view resonates very much with the idea of witnessable details of orderliness about which ethnomethodologists write, and was relied upon in the production of written data in this book. Anthropomorphism is an observable sociological phenomenon. Production of anthropomorphic characterizations of animal behavior can and should be studied in their own right, preferably in naturally occurring, nonexperimental situations. They can be described and analyzed from within the situations in which they are produced without asking whether they "really" reflect the inner state of the animal.

As Hearne noted, any written inquiry about animals is also one into the nature of language. In this book we learned at least this about language:

1. Studying playing with Katie turns research into a reflexive analysis of ordinarily assumed linguistic matters (Hearne's observation);

2. All languages and language uses are anthropocentric in that they are humanly authored and staffed, thus reflecting particularly human ideas, practices and values;

3. All languages are relative; they formulate worldly features in substantially different ways that cannot be "resolved." One does not ask who is right or wrong about their description of trees, New Yorkers or Bambudi pygmies, or who describes snow correctly, the Sami or Italians;

4. Formal definitions (such as that provided by Huizinga) will collect some relevant matters related to the topic being investigated but will be specifically misleading and inadequate in the examination of an everyday orderliness *in any particular instance;*

5. My own research about playing with Katie as an everyday orderliness is necessarily the study of the reality-structuring commitments of mid- to late-twentieth-century American vernacular regarding playing with dogs; and

6. It would be possible to vary players' natural languages as a condition of dog-human play in order to research language's commitments, and to display culturally and linguistically relative features of playing with a dog.

Mitchell and his colleagues' discussion of anthropomorphism resonated with the perspective taken in this research. This is partly because he acknowledges that all forms of description of animals rest upon the knowledge and presumptions of the observer and that in the absence of any amorphic or transcendental view, determining the validity and appropriateness of anthropomorphic thinking may not be easy. Mitchell treats anthropomorphism as an empirical phenomenon. He analyzes its various conceptions—global, categorical, subjective, and situational—showing that in some cases it is not a matter of "accurate" usage in the scientific sense (i.e., cars can't "really" be angry with you) but more a matter of conventional language usage (in which such a statement is perfectly acceptable).

In Mitchell's definition, anthropomorphism refers to the extrapolation of human characteristics to nonhumans. It is important to note that he does not mean the inappropriate extrapolation, only that the device of describing animal behaviors with human terms is being used. In writing about situational anthropomorphism, Mitchell notes that when observers engage in anthropomorphic description, they usually do so from within a narrative format. They tell a story in which the anthropomorphic movements and states of the animal make sense. That is the method of anthropomorphism according to Mitchell.

As mentioned above, that is also the method employed in constructing the written account of my play with Katie. Insofar as the digitalized videotapes and sequenced captured video images are seen by the reader as instructed by the text, this method also extends to the visual data. The visual data were offered strictly as illustrative of matters written in the data. One can ask of such a method, "How do you know that Katie is feeling or doing x or y at this point?" or "How do you know if you are wrong or right about your description of Katie doing x or y?" Mitchell posed both such questions about my data. The first is a very good question and would lead to a highly punctilious analysis of body movements, facial expressivity, rationales for interpretation, and eventually perhaps theoretical justifications.

The latter is more difficult. One converses or drives without an adequate account of how. In the data I clearly wrote as if knew "that," but I rarely address "how." Obviously it is possible to be "inaccurate" when engaging anthropomorphic devices in any instance. Mitchell felt, for example, that I was giving Katie a bit too much credit to say that she understood the "aesthetic" quality of a ball caught in stride or a particularly agile block of a kick. It could be that I was guilty of "categorical" anthropomorphism at that time. Or could I have been wrong about Katie's showing off—that she was not showing off at all, but just reacting excitedly to the offers of others to throw the stick? Could I have been guilty of situational anthropomorphism? Of course the answer to both questions is yes. I *could* have been wrong. I don't think I was wrong in these instances, but it is possible, since it would be difficult to prove one way or the other. The fact that methods can lead to spurious or incorrect conclusions, sometimes with consequence and sometimes without, is part of everyday life. Methods and techniques employed on an everyday basis in an electron microscopy lab lead to spurious or incorrect (from a scientific standard) conclusions. The methods of the lab can be (and have been) so described as positive sociological phenomena (Lynch, 1993). In this same way, the orderliness of methods describing dog-human play need to be described as positive sociological phenomena, their accuracy with respect to some criterion or lack thereof being a secondary matter to such description.

Mitchell takes the view that when you describe an animal anthropomorphically, you do not commit yourself to an introspection of that animal's experience or, for that matter, your own. Using terms like "sad," "angry," "jealous," "showing off," "excited," etc., to describe Katie does not mean that I know what the experience of these things is for her (hence the brief discussion of Katie's being dog-happy, dog-angry, etc.). It means that I have been taught through convention to associate certain words with certain expressions (growling, bark-ing and snarling with anger, for example), and that when I see Katie do such things in a situation that would warrant it, I say she is angry. In this view, it is not my projection onto Katie that she is angry or a statement that I understand exactly what she is feeling. It is a linguistic ("mother tongue") formulation of her expressions as meaningfully embedded in a course of events.

This formulation is part of an unfolding series of events that gets told as a story or an anecdote. Mitchell critically analyzes anecdotes and properly con-cludes that they cannot be naively accepted as truth. There are features of the storytelling per se that can powerfully influence whether various propositions embedded in the story are accepted as true or not. Thus, in Mitchell's view, subjective anthropomorphism is not a method one can accept uncritically as reliable. Of course this is true. No method can be accepted uncritically, and no method is completely reliable.

Yet Mitchell's conclusion, like some scientists', is not to therefore abandon anthropomorphism. Aside from the fact that such a suggestion would only be heard by academics and that millions of people with companion dogs would still go on their daily business anthropomorphizing in their interpretation of their animal companions' behaviors, neither of us believe that the anthropomorphic method is in any sense inherently or theoretically right or wrong. It is just that for those of us interested in the scientific study of dog-human play, it needs to be employed in a careful and self-critical manner.

Throughout this text there has been insistence on not treating the data as docile. The ethnomethodological basis for this was presented at the beginning of the book and entertained in some detail. As described in note 12 of the intro-duction, videography reflects a very long tradition in visual social-scientific analysis, preceding the particular technology available to videographers today. The epis-temology of that earlier tradition stands in contradistinction to current ways of thinking about video data. The former treated video as capturing objective, sometimes hidden to the naked eye, features of [whatever], while the latter sees video as constructed-in-use and interpreted-in-viewing, not so clearly or obvi-ously related to an objective [whatever]. This, I argue, refers to both the mean-ing (semantic features) that viewers find "on the tape," and also the audiovisual particulars (syntactic features). Even sights and sounds on tape may be only instructably observable, and sometimes they are not even that. That is, viewers can fail to see the instructed actions and meanings.

This may have indeed been the case with some of the data the reader was asked to read and watch. It may have been difficult to find in the video-captured sequences, or in the video portion of the videotape, the details of things to which the description in the text alerted you. These may have been particularly hard to see in the sequenced images, partially due to the quality of the images on the tape. All sequenced video-captured images and videotape data were sub-optimal in that the camera was unmanned. The unmanned camera structured our play profoundly (for example, caused me to remain in the lens's view and to play for the camera) and affected the research utility of the videotape data themselves. These data fail to capture many of the game events I would have liked to display. Even when the event is on the screen or page, what the reader can see sometimes does a fair to poor job in capturing and displaying the desired feature or process to the reader. This unfortunate quality is an artifact of the unmanned camera. There is no question that the data would have better illustrated the details of play if I had had a cameraperson to work with during data collection.

Another interesting technical reason why the video-captured images lose the phenomenon has to do with time. The particular hardware and software used to capture images allowed only for prespecified time interval sampling of the tape; these could be no shorter than one second. This technical limitation essentially applied a device of "chronological time" to the "lived or played time" of the playing. Often perspicuous details of the events as experienced as a player did not at all match up with the time sampling interval built into the image capturing system. A marked improvement would have been a video-capture technology that allowed me to capture images according to "played time." While such capability exists, it was fiscally unavailable. Thus, in my video-captured images the phenomena of play could be lost technologically.

I acknowledge these and other limitations of the data to display the phenomenon. At the same time I propose to the reader that the techniques used in this research are useful tools to explore the practices involved in play with dogs (there has been much technological progress since beginning this research). While the reader can and should ask him- or herself about the strengths and weaknesses of this approach, these may be hard to assess given lack of independent and direct access to the phenomenon. Nonetheless, it will be difficult for the reader to stop him- or herself from asking questions about the adequacy of the study. In what ways did the written and visual data display, or perhaps fail to display, the "haecceities" of this lived orderliness? Did you find the general done in detail that EM seeks? Do you think that the play as displayed in this book would be the play that you would observe if you visited my home (imagine you could have done it six years ago when I was collecting data)? Was there any progress made in Sacks's quest "to see whether actual single events are studiable and how they might be studiable, and then what an explanation of them would look like?" *Any* progress would be noteworthy, and I think there has been at least some.

The answers are important. I do not want to make too much or too little of that importance, to either inflate or minimize what I found when I looked at my play with Katie, or to make too much or too little of the reader's position to judge the findings. As the folks on Ethno Hotline reminded me when I announced the project, whatever I found would not likely be anything that would help improve either humanity's or dogs' lot or earn many colleagues' recognition and esteem.[1] Nonetheless, what I described and displayed is sociologically important. If there is order "at all points," then the study of any instance will reveal that order. What I hope I found, what I tried to display, was the order in and of Katie's and my play together. What I wanted to do was show the observable, intrinsic events of play as they appeared to and were done by Katie and me. If I have been in any way successful, this would be a notable achievement for EM and a unique contribution to animal studies.

This book is an attempt to display in detail a guardian playing with his dog, an instance of *just that*. That people play with dogs is in itself, in its own right, a "miracle of everyday society." It does not exist to be a matter for professional sociological inquiry. You do not need to write a book or know anything about Darwin, Durkheim, Garfinkel, sociology, animal studies, EM or any academic matter to find playing with a dog captivating, amazing, humorous, boring, complicated, etc., or to experience a certain deep, even "monumental" appreciation seeing dogs and humans at play. By this I am not saying that play between companion dogs and their guardians is (or is not) socially or politically important or consequential. It is more like when Sacks watched and meticulously analyzed a videotape of a couple greeting each other at the door. He was not doing so to advance a political agenda—to change how people greet each other at doors, for example. He did it to discover and appreciate the incredible details in and of the simplest things we do, and that is what this book is about.

Postscript

It is July, 2004, almost eight years since I began the research project reported in this book. Katie will be twelve years old in September. We have "grown old together," and the phenomenon of our play as described and displayed in these pages has been irretrievably lost to the biological properties of aging. The play that appears on these pages and that I videotaped cannot be found any longer. In this sense what we did was not like lining up for coffee or driving the 495 freeway. Human-dog play may be "immortal" in Garfinkel's terms, but it is also a kind of thing that ages biologically and specific to particular cohorts. At a dog age corresponding to a human age of 70 (or so), Katie is not the agile, capable player she used to be, although still willing and sometimes wildly enthusiastic. I have aged too, and moved on in my dog-playing career with a new canine friend and player, Jack. That is entirely, and actually richly, another story.

I could continue to write about growing old together, the biological properties of human and canine aging, and their structuring of human-dog play. Producing and examining additional data would, I am sure, prove beneficial to our inquiry. Given what we have learned it would be interesting to read and watch David Playing With Katie when she is fifteen and I sixty. I imagine I would find many discoverable topics that would be worth exploring as endogenous features of play. Instead, we will stop for now.

Second Postscript

Very shortly after writing the above postscript, Katie was diagnosed with melanoma of the eye. I took her to the best animal hospital in the New York area, where she was assessed as having "benign melanoma" of the eye, meaning that it had not spread to her lungs and head, which had been x-rayed. She was given a good chance for recovery—if her left eye was enucleated. We elected that option. It turned out to be a very traumatic one for Katie, especially in the immediate postoperative period. She suffered greatly and without cognizance. Eventually she recovered much of her strength and learned to adapt to the loss of her eye. She never was quite the same, either physically or psychologically, after that operation.

A couple of months later our French cousin came to stay with us for two weeks. Katie loved Henri and she spent those two weeks showing off to him and sometimes sleeping on the floor next to him. She had a wonderful time with him. The day he was scheduled to fly back to Paris we all went on a long, early-morning walk in the park. Katie took the lead; she was sprightly and acted almost like she did when she was a puppy. I did not know at that time that this was her swan song. In the evening, after Henri's departure, she became noticeably ill. She was unable or unwilling to climb the stairs to our bedroom and had to be carried. The next morning, when I went to check on her, she had wet her pillow. It was that moment that I knew she was terribly sick.

I won't go into the specifics of the next few hours. By four o'clock, after a battery of tests indicating massively metastasized cancer, Katie was dead. I elected to euthanize her and not to bring her home to die "naturally." This is a decision that I will have to live with, made worse by her reactions during the procedure, the details of which will always remain with me. Both Diane and I grieved deeply. Ironically, the next day I received confirmation of the publication of this book by Purdue University Press. I was profoundly ambivalent at the news.

As with anyone you love who dies, sadness never really ends. It changes over time, becomes less intense in some respects, but the memory of the loved one and her loss does not go away. Katie's cremated remains and her collar are in my office at home, only a few feet from where I sit as I write this second, and final, postscript. I admit without any embarrassment that I speak to her regularly and still miss her terribly. I wish I could stroke her head again, just one more time.

We have another dog living with us now. Her name is Daisy, a small poodle mix rescued from the streets of Philadelphia whom we love. She is a companion to Jack and to us, but she was not intended as a replacement for Katie, who, like all dogs, was a unique, completely unreplaceable creature. The reader is aware of how much I learned from her, and perhaps as well how much I failed to learn from her. She was a privilege to have known and shared twelve years of life with.

I had a fantasy while completing the first draft of this book. It was about Katie and me promoting it on television together. I would be interviewed about the work and explain it brilliantly. Then, in a shot coordinated with the production crew, I would throw the ball for her and Katie would pursue and capture beautifully. At that point in my fantasy millions of viewers would go nuts. After I had her eye removed, the dream changed to one-eyed Katie and me appearing on television, which, as a disability advocate, was also a great fantasy. Sadly, neither version came to be. This would have been disappointing to Katie because, as the reader already knows, she was a quite a show-off (written with appropriate pride), and there is no doubt in my mind she would have adored all the attention.

Appendix A: Descriptions of Sequenced and Video-Captured Images

1. CONTROL: 27 sequenced JPEG images (CONTROL-01–27). This sequence shows Katie holding a ball at the top of the driveway. Each image looks much the same, except that towards the end of the sequence I walk toward Katie on the right side of the frame. Although invisible in the images, as I approach her I am coaxing her to release the ball to me (see source video file CONTROL.AVI).

2. SOCCERA: 15 sequenced JPEG images (SOCCERA-01–15). The field is covered with leaves. In this sequence I am standing playing doggie soccer with Katie. In the first 13 images she shadows my movements as I feign kicking the ball. In the next to last image she pursues the real kick, and in the last image I admire her pursuit. These images are printed on pages 167–171.

3. SOCCERB: 13 sequenced JPEG images (SOCCERB-01–13). The field is clean. First images show Katie at my feet watching my feigning moves by watching my body (not the ball). She is shadowing me. In images 05–10 she is intensely shadowing my movements, radically shifting her body position with respect to my own movements. In image 11 she begins to release on the real kick. In image 12 she can be seen at the extreme left of the frame pursuing the kicked ball. In the last image I am admiring her good pursuit.

4. FACE: 4 single JPEG images showing Katie's face during play. FACE-01.JPG shows Katie full face with the ball, resting after intense play; FACE-02.JPG shows Katie full face with the ball, resting after intense play; FACE-03.JPG shows Katie concentrated during seated play; and FACE-04.JPG shows Katie concentrated on the ball during seated play. These images are printed on pages 172–173.

5. FIELD: 3 single JPEG images showing field conditions. FIELD-01.JPG shows a clear field with few leaves and branches; FIELD-02.JPG shows a wet field, with few leaves; and FIELD-03. JPG shows a brand-new surface one day after resurfacing.

6. FOOTBALL: 11 sequenced JPEG images (FOOTBALL-01–11.) This sequence shows Katie in football receiver role (i.e., she will release to catch the ball before I have thrown it, as a passer in football runs his/her pattern before the ball is thrown). The ball is raised to a throwing position in 06, and I feign throwing the ball until 08. In 07 Katie is beginning to release before the ball is thrown.

7. FREEKICK: 2 single JPEG images. These images show Katie waiting for a "free kick."

8. MISSED: 8 sequenced JPEG images (MISSED-01–08). This sequence shows Katie pursuing and missing a ball, seen most clearly in 06.

9. PURSUIT: 19 sequenced JPEG images (PURSUIT-01–19). This contains two sequences of Katie pursuing and capturing thrown balls. The ball and the capture are evident in both sequences. Following the captures is a series of images showing Katie returning the captured ball to me.

10. SHADOWINGA: 10 JPEG images (SHADOWINGA-01–10). A fine sequence illustrating Katie's intense bodily shadowing of my movements during my soccer play with her. After very many fakes and movements, finally in 08 I begin my movement to kick in earnest and Katie releases to pursue. In 09–10 I admire Katie's spirited pursuit. These images are printed on pages 174–177.

11. SHADOWINGB: 17 sequenced JPEG images (SHADOWINGB-01–17). Katie presents the ball between my knees (01–03) and shadows me while watching my waist (not the ball). In 15, I begin a kick in earnest and Katie releases.

12. SWITCHING: 29 JPEG images (SWITCHING-1–29). This sequence shows me switching game motifs. The beginning sequence shows Katie shadowing me during football play, a kick, her release and retrieve. In 20–22, I switch the game motif to standing throw. In image 29, Katie is shown at the moment of capture of a throw.

13. THROWINGA: 6 JPEG images (THROWINGA-01–06). This sequence shows Katie releasing for a football-style throw (i.e. turning to get ball before it has been released from my hand [THROWINGA-04]). The beginning sequence shows her guarding me during seated play. These images are printed on pages 178–179.

14. THROWINGB: 16 JPEG images (THROWINGB-01–16). During seated play Katie "guards" me while I am sitting. The sequence shows me pick up the ball very slowly into throw position and fake several throws, with Katie watching the ball intensely. In 15 Katie has released to pursue the ball after it has been thrown.

15. WALL: 9 JPEG images (WALL-01–9). This sequence shows Katie pur-

suing the ball onto the playing field boundary (the wall to my right). It does not capture the fact that I bounced the ball off of the opposing wall to my right (indicating use of the properties of play boundaries during play).

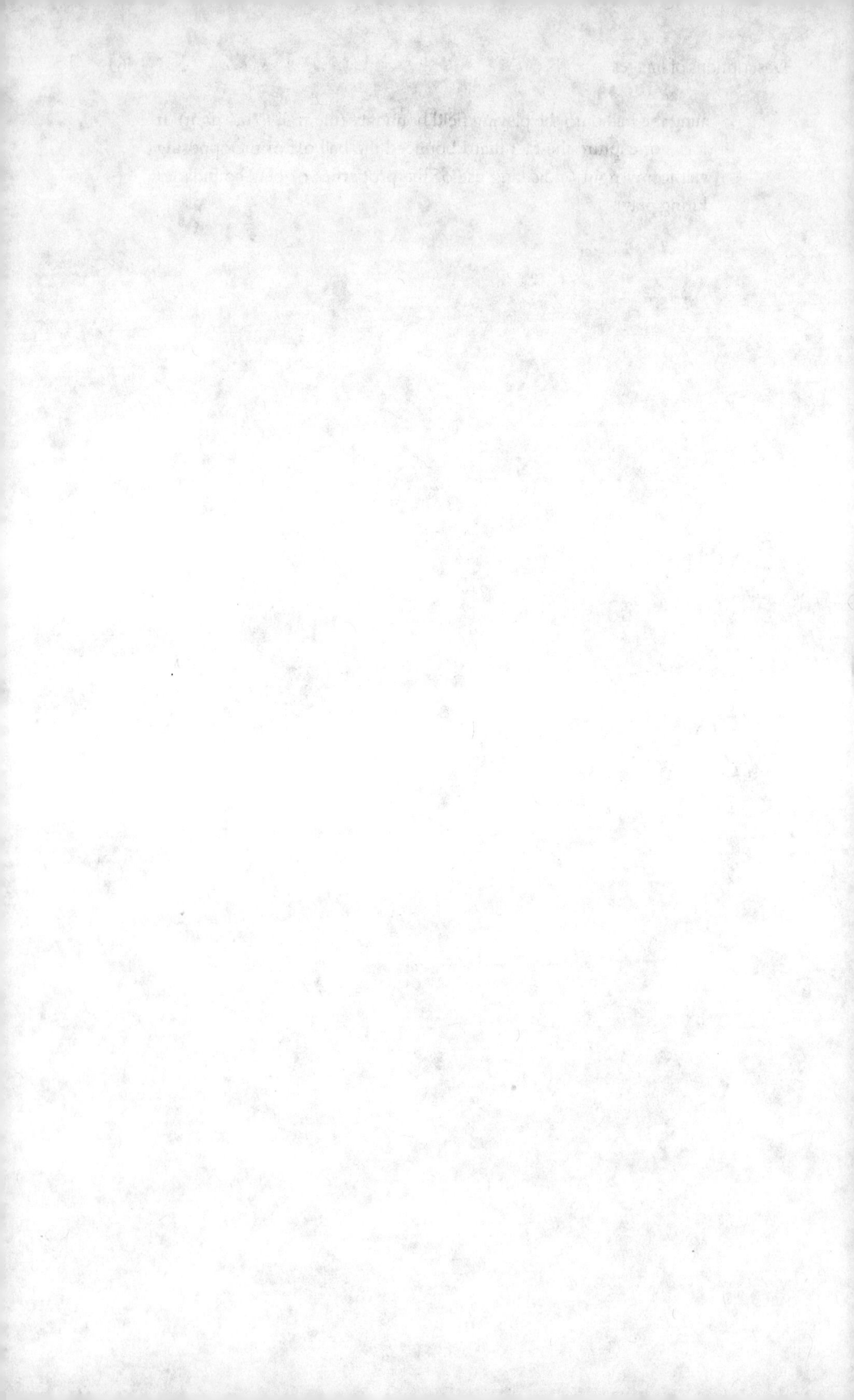

Appendix B: Images

I. Dürer's Corgi

An image of a corgi-style dog taken from an early-sixteenth-century woodcut by Albrecht Dürer, who had visited the Netherlands some years before.

II. Peter's Picture of Katie

A drawing made by my son when Katie was about age 4, at the height of her ball playing. The picture captures the frenetic, intense and preoccupied nature of her relation to playing ball and stick retrieve.

III. SOCCERA-01–03

Doggie Soccer 1

Doggie Soccer 1

Doggie Soccer 1

SOCCERA-04–06

Doggie Soccer 1

Doggie Soccer 1

Doggie Soccer 1

SOCCERA-07–09

SOCCERA-10–12

SOCCERA-I3–I5

Doggie Soccer 1

Doggie Soccer 1

Doggie Soccer 1

IV. FACE-01–03

FACE-04

V. SHADOWINGA-0I–03

SHADOWINGA-04–06

SHADOWINGA-07–09

SHADOWINGA-10

THROWINGA-0I–03

THROWINGA-04–06

Appendix C: Ethomethodology

This appendix was originally the introduction to this book. It is an introduction aimed at readers interested in ethnomethodology (EM). As the book evolved into one aimed at a more inclusive audience, this ethnomethodological introduction was jettisoned for the present three-part one. I have retained this more technical and up-to-date version of how this research relates to EM's program for those more interested in the ethnomethodology of this enterprise.

> The specific aim [of sociological analysis] is, in the first instance, to see whether actual single events are studiable and how they might be studiable, and then what an explanation of them would look like. (Sacks, lecture, fall 1967, intro)

The current analysis partakes of Sacks's vision of sociology and is intended as an exemplar of ethnomethodological analysis.

EM, a form of sociology invented in the 1950s and 1960s by Harold Garfinkel and a group of colleagues, is today largely ignored and considered to be out of the main thrust of sociology. Its creation was based upon an insight about social relations and social order that contrasted with that of mainstream professional sociological work, work that employed what Garfinkel called the methods of formal constructive analysis. Most sociologists theorized about events and then methodically examined them to prove or disprove their theories. As an alternative, EM examined the possibility of sociology's becoming "a natural observational science" (Sacks, n.d., n.p.). Sacks and Garfinkel contrasted their own interests with that of mainstream or constructive analytic sociology, which was often characterized, at least in early EM, in unflattering terms as being "goofy" or "hopeless" (this in the sense of being hopelessly theory-laden and driven, or hopelessly common-sense). When I studied with him in the 1970s, Garfinkel employed a shibboleth that went, "The problem with sociologists is not that they don't know enough; the problem is that they know too much." The same exact sentiment can be found in Sacks, Sudnow, Cicourel and others of that founding EM group. Formal academic sociology required that practitioners know beforehand what could be learned before research can begin (or at least what the relevant matters are before research begins).

Garfinkel and his colleagues found this a notable form of analysis and not without victories. Yet the victories were Pyrrhic, with unacceptable analytic costs. One of these was the theoretical elimination of instances of mundane, everyday human life as important and worthy of research. A lexicon of terms and concepts—institutions, norms, "internalization," "socialization," etc.—that were arrived at through theoretical reflection were "applied" to a real world. They had become the required, reasoned basis for producing sociology's orderly accounts of social relations, ordering its observations through what Garfinkel (2002) calls generic representational theorizing. In contrast, ethnomethodologists did not have a need for sociological theory to find order in everyday society. In fact, theories found in sociological writings were specifically impediments to this task (see, for example, Garfinkel's discussion of Sacks's gloss, 2002, p. 182). They proposed, and continue to propose, something quite different.

First they claimed that there are orders (orderlinesses, lived orderliness) inherent in all mundane activities and that these activities are methodic. While these orders or methods could be observed, most commonly they are simultaneously "depended upon and ignored" by the populations doing them, and by the conventional sociologists who study them.

> The search for good problems by reference to known big issues will have large scale, massive institutions as the apparatus by which order is generated and by a study of which order will be found. If, on the other hand, we figure or guess or decide that whatever humans do, they are just another animal after all, maybe more complicated than others but perhaps not noticeably so, then whatever humans do can be examined to discover some way they do it, and they will be stably describable. That is, *we may alternatively take it that there is order at all points.* (Sacks, n.d., p. 2 ; italics mine)

This insight, traceable to the work of Aaron Gurwitsch through Garfinkel's reinterpretation of it, is one of the basic tenets of EM. The ubiquitous, massive presence of orderlinesses in everyday, mundane activities and the ways these are accomplished by societal members are EM's objects of sociological analysis as a natural observational science. These objects could not be found or understood by armchair theorizing. They are to be explicated through a "close looking at the world."

> We will be using observation as a basis for theorizing. Thus we can start with things that are not currently imaginable, by showing that they happened. We can then come to see that a base for using close looking at the world for theorizing about it is that from close looking at the world we can find things that we could not, by imagination, assert were there. We would not know they were typical. (Sacks, Lecture 1, fall 1971)

> Indeed, we might not have noticed that they happen. (Sacks, n.d., p. 25)

Sacks turned to conversations and utilized their audio recordings to achieve an analysis of an everyday social orderliness—conversation. The decision was somewhat incidental in the sense that he chose conversations and tape recordings of them because conversations were easily found and recorded. The existence and structure of ordinary conversations, like other everyday orders, were depended upon and ignored by conventional social sciences. Sacks made very limited claims about the tapes, whose basic virtue was simply that they could be transcribed and consulted an indefinite number of times. The recordings of conversations were seen as preserving at least some features of conversation (i.e., its sequential, aural features), even if severely limited in terms of capturing other things that may have happened. He makes a comment that "at least what was on the tape had happened," perhaps indicating in this remark a somewhat naive treatment of the tapes as docile records (see Garfinkel's device below). For Sacks, they were a "good enough" record of what happened conversationally to permit analysis of this everyday orderliness of society. They continue to be consulted in this way by conversational analysts.

Sacks thought sociology would not be a science until it could

handle the details of actual events, handle them formally, and in the first instance be informative about them in the ways primitive sciences tend to be informative—that is, that anyone else can go and see whether what was said was so. And that is a tremendous control on seeing whether one is learning anything. (n.d., p. 26)

Thus important properties of the tapes for Sacks were that they captured at least some details of actual events, they could be consulted multiply and inspected for detail, and they could be studied by others in order to determine if what was said about them was so. Their usage was to examine whether "actual single events are studiable and how they might be studiable, and then what an explanation of them would look like."

Many of the ideas that Sacks put forth emerged in exchanges with Garfinkel and were specifically documented by Garfinkel (2002, pp. 84–86). While Garfinkel is clearly the originator of EM and its foremost intellectual representative, my task is not to sort out EM's specific debt to either. Sacks's untimely death prevents us from seeing how he would have developed the line of argument, which all ethnomethodologists deeply regret. EM was squarely placed in the hands of Garfinkel, his colleagues, and his students.

Garfinkel's Device

As stated above, EM is predicated on direct and close looking at the world; but it would be misleading to think that close looking is a simple or programmatic affair. Its basic requirement, that of being in the presence of the object in-itself, can take many forms and result in many kinds of analyses. Importantly, the relationship of the data produced by the analyst to observable features of the social order is never simple or isomorphic. The key word here is "produced." Features of social order always require the use of an analytic device whose concrete application results in the production of data. For the social scientist engaged in analysis, data in written accounts or recorded videotapes (or what have you) represent, or stand on behalf of, actual features of the observed orderliness. The nature of any research process requires that data, not the events themselves, become the analyst's objects of interest. This is true for all forms of scientific research.

Garfinkel's device (see Garfinkel, 2002; Garfinkel & Wieder, 1993; Goode, 1994a, pp. 127–146 for a fuller explanation) is a way to clarify epistemological relationships in the methodology of social research. It is a generic device that can be used to describe virtually any research. Its use makes clearer the relationship between mundane, observable, everyday actions and analytic procedures employed to describe/display and explicate them. See figure 1, p. 15, which applies Garfinkel's device to the current analysis.

The figure names the methodologies used, the logics of the empirical inquiry, in making play with Katie a researchable object. The reader will note that four "types" of empirical data are utilized in different ways in order to "collectively represent" (for want of a better phrase) observable details of our play. The data are produced through "methodic procedures," i.e., any systematic, rationally conceived set of data-gathering activities that are reasoned to encode, record, capture or reflect real features of phenomena under investigation. Through their actual administration, such procedures produce "data," i.e., concrete results of the methodic procedures in the form of accounts, measurements, descriptions, representations, etc. In the research process, the data come to "stand for" or "stand on behalf of" the lived orderliness, and the data's competent manipulation becomes the basis for defensible claims about what can or cannot be stated as having been established, i.e., as really being the case. Data are typically subject to techniques of formal analysis, by which Garfinkel means cleaning and graphical representation of data, diagramming, sequencing, modeling, statistical manipulation, content analysis, and so on. Scientific conclusions are based upon what is demonstrable through competently performed, discipline-based, carefully described and professionally sanctioned analytic techniques.

Garfinkel's device illustrates the constructed relationship between data produced by methodical procedures and the details of the organization of everyday orderliness. The relationship is not isomorphic or "objectively" determinable. That is to say, no matter how many methods or kinds of data, or the particular capability of these methods to recover this or that feature of the detailed organization of everyday life, there will always be an interpretive dimension to scientific data, both in its construction and subsequent explication. There is no way out of this, no objective space, that ultimately allows researchers to write as if they had direct access to transcendental knowledge. This should not be interpreted to mean that all analyses are equally off base or hopelessly interpretive.

One clear implication of Garfinkel's deconstruction of sociological methodology is that its findings must be appreciated as the constructed matters that they are. All data and their analyses are constructed. Acknowledging and detailing this in my own work is not an attempt to weaken its claims. I will not be equivocal in recommending that this current analysis of human-dog interaction has advantages over previous ones. Some of these advantages consist in making clear the problematic, assumed, and unrecognized epistemological commitments of previous studies.

Autoethnographic notes, ethnographic field notes, sequenced captured video images and video sequences are ways of looking closely at playing with my dog. Like the audiotapes Sacks used, they do not capture everything that goes on, but for the time being we will treat them in Sacks's fashion—that is, that at least what is on or in them went on. For all practical purposes, they can be used to "handle," to "display," certain features of the thing. But as indicated in previous writings and again in chapter 5, with video recordings the situation is more complicated than this. Videos and other forms of visual data are objects that are constructed in use, but they do not necessarily display the conventions of their construction and they do not come with "built-in," self-explicating interpretations. The "same" everyday event can result in audiovisual data that can be constructed to be, and later made to mean, many different things.

Garfinkel's device is offered to deepen understanding of how I displayed/ analyzed my playing with Katie. It is not meant to make ironic my or any other sociological research (it is not intended by him as an ironic device). By pointing out that assuming a correspondence theory between audiovisual data/autoethnographic data and everyday events as they might be observable to participants and outsiders is problematic, I am not saying that audiovisual or ethnographic data are hopelessly subjective or wrongly distorting of these events. In fact in some ways it is their very capability to "distort" everyday reality that makes them scientifically interesting and valuable in the first place. Audiovisual data can be, despite limitations, a very strong way of representing observable details of actual interaction *in situ*. Carefully used, such forms of data can be consulted to locate and display the social practices involved in the production of the orderlinesses of everyday events.

Garfinkel's device serves as a strong reminder that there is no sociological way to talk about or represent a real world, in this case my play with Katie, that does not partake of social conventions. At the same time it acknowledges the relative strengths of different forms of data to capture, represent or dismiss aspects of everyday social order. The device reminds us that videotape or any other form of data cannot be treated as mere reflections of what happened, and that "what happened" can never be contained fully in any set of data.

What Animal Are We After?

Why can't the data be treated as docile? I want to spend some time answering this question, briefly summarizing Garfinkel's most recent statement about EM, and then locating this current analysis with regard to that vision. By doing this, the reader will have been further instructed to read the notes and view the images and tapes in a certain manner.

In the thirty years that I have known Garfinkel, he has consistently maintained that his work is an attempt to reinterpret Durkheim's famous aphorism, "The objective reality of social facts is sociology's fundamental principle" (Durkheim, 1938). In his book with Ann Rawls, *Ethnomethodology's Program*, he summarizes this idea through this respecification: "The objective reality of social facts is sociology's fundamental phenomenon" (Garfinkel, 2002). By substituting the word "phenomenon" for "principle," he alerts us to EM's rediscovery of what Durkheim meant, or ought to have meant "really," by the aphorism, as well as to professional sociology's neglect of that intent. This Garfinkel and Rawls refer to as Durkheim's neglected legacy. First and foremost, this work and all ethnomethodological studies are attempts to describe, display and analyze what Durkheim called "social facts."

Displays and explications of social facts, the "work" of everyday society, are carried out under, and with observance of, what Garfinkel calls "ethnomethodological indifference," which requires that the analyst remain indifferent to the methods, procedures and findings of constructive analysis.

> For this time being we'll carry out the tasks of our research while abstaining from the use of the classic corpus of findings, policies, methods, and the rest. . . . It is a research practice. One does it as an observance. Something like driving in traffic effectively and correctly, one learns to observe it as a skill . . . to pay no ontical judgmental attention to the established corpus of social science. Not to decide in advance what the phenomenon consists of on the basis of prior formal analytic studies. . . . The policy requires that the tasks of inquiry and argument provide for the practical objectivity and practical observability of structures of practical action and practical reason, in and as of ordinary activities, while exercising an indifference to the poli-

cies of natural theorizing, withholding the corpus status of formal analytic descriptive facts, avoiding the design and administration of generic representations and their methodolized dopes, and in related ways making no use of the methods of constructive analysis. (Garfinkel, 2002, p. 171)

Indifference to constructive, formal analysis and its literatures is something ethnomethodologists specifically try to achieve as a craft, with varied degrees of success—but why? Why would Garfinkel recommend that we study everyday social life without access to these methods? Why would one want to practice such a craft?

This brings us to the crux of EM's vision of society, of its reinterpretation of Durkheim. While disciplinary sociology took the aphorism as an occasion to develop and administer to everyday life the various forms of generic representational theorizing, EM took Durkheim's insight to mean that everyday social objects need to be studied as given phenomena in their own terms, a-theoretically, and observationally. Failing to do so, Garfinkel argues, disciplinary sociology has neglected to address a massive domain of social phenomena. Describing and displaying these "missed" (seen but unnoticed, relied upon but not reflected upon) everyday phenomena is what EM is about.

The way that this is done is a reflection of EM's vision of how society works. Specifically, it is based upon the insight that "there is order at all points." Better, there are orders or orderlinesses in the observable details of everyday life events; these everyday events are done methodically, and these methods can be described and demonstrated endogenously, i.e., in their own terms. By not paying attention to these everyday social orders in their own terms, through careful administration of the policies and procedures of constructive analysis, disciplinary sociology provides for their "escape" from analysis. Garfinkel has various glosses for this:

> More, and certainly, orderlinesses in and as the plenum do not depend for production, observability, witnessability, recognition, and elucidation upon the mastery of generically theorized societies; or upon assurances of lineages of essential philosophy; or of phenomenological philosophy; or of idealist or empiricist specifications of real worldliness—and now comes a Borgesian library of technical occupations in social sciences, philosophy, and intellectual history exhibiting the escape from accountability of the phenomena they describe, lost with the methods that are so carefully used to describe them. (Garfinkel, 2002, p. 137)

Described here are the misleading possibilities of generic, constructive, analytic theorizing and its knowledge when consulted to understand everyday society. In sociology, it is the careful employment of various forms of constructive analysis that allows everyday society to escape. Exactly what is escaping and how is EM going to capture it? What is the animal that we are after?

In selecting an ordinary and massively available thing such as playing with a companion dog, we are after a social order as it is given in its immediacy, as a most ordinary affair of everyday life. As an ordinary affair, it is naturally achieved and available to players as orderly, without reference to anything extrinsic to itself. Players of a game need to know nothing outside of the immediate doing of it. Garfinkel crystallizes this in the statement, "Nothing needs to be introduced to the production and accountability of social facts" (Garfinkel, 2002, p. 191). He means that the importation of concerns, ideas, theories, etc. that are not witnessable as interior or endogenous to the social fact and its staffing will distort or even miss the social fact entirely. What is required to produce an adequate account of any social fact is entirely endogenous to the setting of its production. We do not need to know anything more or less than Katie and I do in order to account for our playing together; this is almost tautological.

Garfinkel uses the words "naturally accountable orderlinesses" to describe what can be witnessable in, and as a matter of, social facts. Intrinsic to the setting and "vulgarly" available to the parties involved in the production of social facts, are "orderlinesses of details," "details of structures," "coherence of figural contexture," "right looking adumbrational passing of things," and "the coherence in figurational contextures of endless assemblages of phenomenal field properties of things," to list a few of the names he gives to this property. The property is the apparent, exhibited, processional order of everyday phenomena. EM's focus on this observable orderliness of everyday social facts is due in part to the influence of Aaron Gurwitsch on Garfinkel's thinking, what Garfinkel calls his deliberate misreading of Gurwitsch's work on the Gestalt properties of phenomena. The reinterpretation of Gurwitsch was based upon Garfinkel's insight that the coherence and orderliness of the details of objects were things that needed to be found, not in the psychology laboratory experiment, but in everyday "work" sites of ordinary society. EM's program of research demonstrates that they can be found through natural and other forms of close observation.

In this research we are primarily interested in a description/demonstration of the intrinsically orderly features of my playing with Katie, as given to us directly and without need to add anything from outside. We want a description/display of what we are doing without using the devices of generic representational theorizing. We want to find the orderliness of our play "in the look of things."

An ethnomethodological appreciation of everyday social order gives full cognizance to its contingent, historically specific, processional features (that every witnessed occasion of social order has an "event biography," so to speak). Yet the "kind" of order that is revealed through ethnomethodological description/demonstration is not satisfactory to sociologists who practice formal, constructive analyses of social phenomena. Garfinkel glosses the kind of order he is getting at by use of the term "haecceities":

> EM studies were not looking for quiddities [i.e., "essential details of practices"]. They were looking for haecceities—just-thisness; just here, just now, with just what is at hand, with just who is here, in just the time we need, and therein, in, about, as, and over the course of the in vivo work . . . (Garfinkel, 2002, p. 99, n.16)

This is a critical and yet difficult point. Garfinkel is not saying that because order is produced in an existential situation that it is hopelessly situated and entirely idiosyncratic to that particular situation. Everyday activities are only done in particular situations and are uniquely suited to just those situations, but they are not idiosyncratic to them. Whatever "social order" could mean, or be taken to mean, must be findable within everyday social situations. That social order consists of this: the just-thisness of witnessed things are organized, and their organization reflects collectively recognized generalities, what is known in the society, through its language, embedded in local culture, about whatever the fact of the matter is that the local cohort is recognizably and observably doing. If this were not the case, then the endless occasions of supermarket lines, traffic jams, flirting, playing with your pet, or whatever could not be possible. Garfinkel has various glosses for this—for example, "lived order."

Garfinkel characterizes what makes ethnomethodological studies particularly ethnomethodological:

> It is ethnomethodological about EM studies that they show for ordinary society's substantive elements, in material contents, just and only in any actual case, that and just how vulgarly competent members concert their activities to produce, show, exhibit, make observably the case*, demonstrate, etc., coherence, cogency, analysis, detail, structure, consistency, order, meaning, mistakes, errors, coincidence, facticity, reason, methods—locally, reflexively, naturally accountable phenomena—in and as of the haecceities of their ordinary lives together. (Garfinkel, 2002, p. 168)

If that is not clear it is not surprising, unless you happen to be a student of EM. Admittedly Garfinkel's is a dense text—what Castaneda called "the sorcerer's description"—and probably not much use to an initiate or outsider. EM is complicated, and more will be fleshed out as we go along. I am trying to give the reader enough of a sense of what the ethnomethodological project is about to appreciate how this research is a contribution to it.

Playing with Katie as Part of EM Studies

There are some remarkable features of this study when appreciated as part of the ethnomethodological corpus. EM went through two phases of development. Early studies were concerned with accomplishments that were described as members' interpretive and documentary work of ordinary fact-finding. The latter studies, begun in the early 1970s, "examined locally produced, endogenously achieved, naturally accountable coherent haecceities that compose as coherent constructed actions the phenomenal fields of ordinary human 'jobs'" (Garfinkel, 2002, p. 106). Notable in later studies is their emphasis on congregational work of members. This Garfinkel calls "the shop floor problem":

> The shop floor, a natural metaphor, is indispensable in that search [i.e., the search for endogenously produced social facts]. The metaphor is indispensable because it is ubiquitously used in the most diverse jobs and work settings by bench practitioners to make congregationally recognized accountable provision for work's particular haecceities in and as of work's particular places, and particular bodies, with these instruments and with just this equipment, in just this territory. (Garfinkel, 2002, pp. 248–49)

Most of the studies that are part of EM's corpus of findings can be described via the shop floor metaphor. The shop floor is a congregational phenomenon, that is, it is the production of work administered by local endogenous populations of "members" who do so in detail, concertedly, recognizably and accountably, with and for one another. The shop floor provides for "workplace practices in congregationally embodied and congregationally witnessable coherent field properties of making and exhibiting accountable things" (Garfinkel, 2002, p. 109). In the ethnomethodological corpus, even when the work being described involves "individual" practice (i.e., jazz improvisation at the piano), it is, in some describable fashion or another, congregationally embedded. That is, the practices are ultimately done for oneself and for others in recognizably mutually accountable ways.

The shop floor metaphor cannot be used quite this way in this current analysis. It also could not be easily used in the analysis of materials contained in *A World without Words* (WWW), especially with regard to the interaction between Christina and me. Both cases of research are perspicuously not matters observed and discussed on the shop floor. Both involve the smallest possible social unit, the dyad, and in both dyads one of the participants is not a member. With "member," I mean to call up Garfinkel's adaptation from Parsons's "collectivity member." To be a member of a collectivity entails certain vulgar competences of language, perception, action, culture, etc. In *Studies in Ethnomethodology*, Garfinkel sometimes writes about "any adult member" as an index to the phenomenon that members of collectivities treat each other as having certain competences and depend upon them in the production and recognition of their work together. Neither Katie nor Christina can be described as a "member" in Parsons's terms. The interactions that were studied were conducted almost exclusively dyadically, with no one else to whom we were practically accountable. Playing with Katie was done in front of my house in the morning or in the park, in the absence of human observers. In the case of the play examined here, a mechanical observer was present (video camera), whose effect in structuring play will be discussed, but with which no shop floor talk was possible. What we have is a study of a kind of a group that is not easy to even name sociologically, a group about which there is no assumption of membership, done singularly, i.e., not on the shop floor. I believe that both this research and WWW are somewhat unique cases in EM. They are troublesome for ethnomethodological studies.

Garfinkel has his own definition of troublemakers:

> Another subject is familiar and prevalent in the analytic literatures: the accomplished transparency and specifically unremarkable smoothness of concerted skills of "equipmentally affiliated" shop work and shoptalk. These are respecified with "Heideggerian uses" of handicaps, illnesses, disabilities, their equipmentally affiliated "aids to independent living," as well as with inverting lenses and other bodily, characterological, organizational and procedural "troublemakers." With these "troublemakers" work's incarnate social organizational details are revealed by overcoming their transparency in their topically ordinary concerted recurrences of ongoingly developing phenomenal fields of ordered details of generality, uniformity, interchangeable populations, and the rest, i.e., in ordered details of structures. (Garfinkel, 2002, pp. 125–26)

Researching playing with Katie, or how I interact with Christina, is trouble for EM in the sense that it cannot utilize two of its most common ways of looking (congregationally, and with the assumptions of the commonalities of local population "membership"). Both of these studies cannot involve these ways of looking in the same way we use them to look at lining up for coffee or driving to work.

This has certain implications—for example, with regard to the role of language. In play our dyad is producing events of play *without reflection*, immediately seeable and *without reflection* doable for one another. Given this observation, language is involved in play in several ways because one of the players is a user of a natural language. This, as the reader will see, is true even though language is not the primary commonly shared vehicle for our communication and actions during play, as it is in most human interactions. Without the assumption of membership, the ability of language to name features of social order is made

problematic and thereby notable. This was addressed as such in WWW and is a
salient issue in the current analysis.

Another concept in EM relevant to the current analysis has to do with the
way Katie and I are seen as "staffing," i.e., concertedly producing, the events of
play. Garfinkel explains what he means by an endogenous population or populational cohort.

> We are an "endogenous population."
>
> EM specifies the local order production staff in its exhibited work
> properties as a reincarnation of the demographic populational cohort, an
> endogenous populational cohort, the congregational populational cohort
> of us, of the local just these of us, in this actual case, doing what we are
> accountably doing, and doing just that accountable social fact, that thing, in
> just accountably this case, doing just what we are accountably doing, and
> doing just that accountable social fact, that thing, in just accountably this
> case and therein just in any actual case observably and evidently. (Garfinkel,
> 2002, p. 183)

And, with the further implication, as characterized by Rawls,

> . . . [T]he populational cohort has its character as a cohort or congregation
> by virtue of being engaged in doing just this thing. Whereas social science
> tends to treat individuals as moving in and out of situations, Garfinkel
> talks of congregations and populational cohorts that provide for the ap-
> pearance of individuals and particular persons. (Garfinkel, 2002, p. 245,
> n.1)

This means that "social facts provide for the individuals who do them."
That is, the production of the activity in its details provides for what the individuals who do it do, and not the reverse. That reverse is the logic of traditional
sociology, which explains social life in terms of individuals coming together to
additively produce social facts. To state the case in overly dichotomous terms, in
traditional sociology social facts owe their existence to individuals, and in EM
individuals owe their existence to social facts.

Katie and I constitute a populational cohort. In some ways we embody in
our doings what playing ball could be when a human and dog do it together. It,
the playing with the ball, provides for our possible actions and experiences as
players. I think that characterization makes sense, as is evidenced in the details
of the notes on our play. We "inhabit" the kinds of things that a person, dog and
ball can do together. We "embody" the details of these doings. At the same time,
playing with one's companion dog is, of course, a thoroughly social object, a
social fact. It is not *just* a matter of body and ball dynamics.

That we are an "immortal" populational cohort does not appear to characterize Katie and me. As Garfinkel notes, in the concerted actions of everyday

society, in events such as driving, lining up, having a conversation, hearing a lecture, i.e., for most congregational events, the congregational cohort displays as a matter of course, in the observable features of the social fact, that it is interchangeably replaceable by any next cohort.

> Immortal is used to speak of human jobs as of which local members, being in the midst of organizational things, know, just of these organizational things that they are in the midst of, that preceded them and will be there after they leave it. Immortal is a metaphor for the great recurrences of ordinary society, staffed, provided for, produced, observable, locally and naturally accountable in and as of an "assemblage of haecceities." (Garfinkel, 2002, p. 92, n.1)

Unlike the way freeway drivers drive, no others would make play in just the way Katie and I do; and there is no organizational thing that preceded us that was constraining or demonstrative of playing. Nor will there be an activity left after we cease playing. There will be no thing remaining to be staffed by whatever next cohort. Our particular efforts, unlike speaking, driving, lining up, etc., will not be there after we leave it. At the same time, playing with Katie is a part of "immortal" society in the sense that it partakes of cultural knowledge available to me, and asymmetrically to Katie, that characterizes human-dog play in our society. Unlike drivers in traffic, no players can or will reproduce just our play together, but innumerable other players will follow us in partaking of that cultural knowledge.

I could go on, but I will not. That is because any summary of EM's program will not enable the reader to achieve an embodied understanding of what (David Playing With Katie) consists of as an order of details of structure. The notes and the visual forms of data need to be seen as praxiological descriptions, "available as revealed details of a witnessable demonstration" (Garfinkel, 2002, p. 185). "Witnessable" is the key word. Access to the actual phenomenon is direct, exclusively and thoroughly just that. If one is able to do it in detail, one can claim to know it in detail. This is what I described in the introduction and what Garfinkel calls "unique adequacy." Only cohorts of the thing done can knowledgeably speak of its phenomenal details.

In lieu of that possibility, as the reader cannot become a practitioner of the thing being displayed and analyzed, let me make some methodological suggestions.

Dissatisfactions with the ability of ethnographic texts to capture the details of any experienced thing are notorious. Written descriptions are "just stories," "thoroughly literary enterprises," and "snapshots" taken with the lens of language (to use a Wittgensteinian metaphor). Writings based upon observation "language-ifies" the thing under consideration. It interprets the event into text, and thereby the event can become disembodied and not reflective of its audio-visual-somatic details, *in vivo*. In descriptions of events, their lived details are not easily captured. Visual images, the sequenced captured video images and the videotape, while obviously displaying bodies at work, transform the thing being taped into recorded representations. This is what Garfinkel points out in the device presented in figure 1. So you cannot read or see either form of data in a naïve fashion. They are practical representations of recordable (either in writing or on video) matters of David Playing Ball With Katie. They display, at best, a sense of the details of the embodied work, and need to be read and seen in that light.

Notes

Notes to Chapter 1

1. The term "amorphic" comes from the work of Cenami Spada, as cited by Mitchell (1997b, p. 411). Her usage is similar to the way ethnomethodology and phenomenological sociology employ the term "transcendental perspective."
2. With regard to these internal states, it is interesting that the data employ, without restraint or reflection, anthropomorphic terms to describe Katie's and my psychology during play. Part of this usage had to do with my ignorance of the animal studies literature surrounding this issue. During the writing it never occurred to me that Katie and I shared the same experience or perception of play events, since that proposition makes little common sense. More reasonable, and is argued in chapter 4, is the idea that as mammals we share certain similarities in our experiences of play (in this case). Dogs and humans feel "anger," but there is no way to establish that this feeling is the same for the two species, or for individuals within these species. It is more descriptively accurate to say that people feel "people anger" and dogs "dog anger," but that each is naturally recognizable to the other.
3. Because anecdotes can be erroneous, some researchers have advocated that they be abandoned entirely. This is an absurd position. On this basis, all methods would need to be abandoned entirely because in actual use they can lead to error. This can be true of the most rigorously conducted experiment. Error is built in to many forms of methods that employ probability theory to calculate the amount of acceptable error (i.e., descriptive and inferential statistics). A more reasonable position in animal studies can be found in the writings of Mitchell, Rollin, Shapiro and others, who see anecdotes as acceptable sources of information dependent on common sense and background knowledge.
4. In the original manuscript there was a somewhat technical introduction to ethnomethodology and its relationship to this research. As a result of the editing process, that introduction now appears in Appendix C: Ethnomethodology and is intended for those readers who are particularly interested in ethnomethodology.
5. For a fuller appreciation of the relationship of this view of social order with others available in sociology, see *Ethnomethodology's Program* (Garfinkel, 2002), which traces the lineage of ethnomethodology to the sociology of Emile Durkheim.
6. In Garfinkel's view social action is conceptualized as a local achievement or accomplishment. That is to say, whatever general rules, procedures, norms or guidelines governing everyday life, these must be enacted and made to fit on the specific occasion and in concrete circumstances, by a local cohort and in a concerted way.
7. Of course, this does not mean that the results of EM studies are not related to theoretical formulations of whatever is being studied. EM was not formulated in ignorance of social

theory, but it does eschew formal, grand-scale sociological theorizing as a way to shed light on everyday society. On the one hand, there is no limit, other than human imagination, to the theories that can be applied to dog-human interaction, everyday conversation, or what have you. However, both dogs and humans engage in these activities without any knowledge of such theories. They don't need to know any theory to engage in them. EM asks what it is that they need to know and do in order to achieve that concerted activity together. In this view, a priori formal theorizing about everyday life is an impediment to understanding it.

8. "Immersion" and "distancing" are parallel to the anthropological terms "emic" and "etic." The anthropologist distinguishes between native knowledge of events (emic knowledge) and his or her outside knowledge of these same events (etic knowledge). Field anthropology involves an immersion into the affairs of the natives, and a distancing from these same affairs through analysis and reflection.

9. This will be discussed in some detail when considering the relationship of this study to others in the animal studies literature. At this juncture it should be said that I am not maintaining that individual characteristics or biographical histories of players are unimportant to understanding actual instances of dog-human play.

10. This is an insight shared by both animal studies and EM. The practice of using mental terms to describe the activities of others without any knowledge of their interior experiences is well-described by Jeff Coulter (1983). Demonstrations of the problematic aspects of the assumption of mutual understanding abound in Garfinkel's *Studies in Ethnomethodology* (1967), and are also found in conversational analysis, whose conception of conversation does not involve a commitment to words as conveyers of lexical meanings. In a student exercise for Garfinkel, I recorded some conversation at an informal evening gathering at my home. I played back part of that conversation, a short sexual joke, and asked those present to comment about what they thought the speaker said when he or she said what he or she did. The results of that procedure indicated that there was actually little agreement about the interpretation of the utterance, especially in terms of its signification within the situation. Agreement was more about form (it's a joke) rather than meaning (what was funny). People can have conversations without understanding each other, but in having conversations they take it that what they understand was what the other intended, unless evidence indicates otherwise.

11. There are some differences between this version of the exercise and that described by Garfinkel and Wieder (1993) and Garfinkel (2002). This particular interpretation is of the work he conducted while I was his teaching assistant (UCLA, Department of Sociology, 1978). I was not privy to subsequent revisions and refinements. I also made some minor modifications for teaching purposes.

12. The first version of this manuscript also contained a long appendix documenting the history of the use of visual images in social science. That lengthy appendix was deleted from the final version of the book in order to make for a more focused and succinct text. Some essential ideas relevant to videography are presented briefly in this note.

    The history of visual images in social science can be traced well back before the invention of video—initially to the nineteenth-century sequenced photographic images of Jules Etienne-Marey, and Eadweard Muybridge (although there was a critical difference between the two—see Marta Braun's *Picturing Time*). The appendix's version of this history compared the early, naive use of images—that saw them as objective indicators of reality, having a simple one-to-one correspondence to the thing itself—and a modern view that appreciates the way in which images are both constructed to be used for specific purposes and require interpretation both in their making and viewing (see particularly Green's 1986 treatment of the use of photography in eugenics for an excellent discussion of the pre- and post-modern attitudes towards photographic data in social science).

In chapter 5 of *A World without Words* I explored the ways in which videotapes of events are not objective records of those events. I used the term "video sorcery" to indicate the ways in which both the perceived audiovisual details and meanings of events 'on the tapes' can be manipulated by the social context within which the tapes are presented. In that discussion I showed how the syntactics of videotaped events (visual details of who does what and what they are doing) and the semantics of videotaped events (what is the meaning of the things being done) can be affected by how the scientist introduces the tapes to the viewers. In the original appendix on videography I took this same position with regard to tapes of play with Katie. What I wanted to do was make clear to the reader that by using videotapes of my play, I am not intending them naively as objective records of play events. I am not claiming that the written data and interpretations of our play presented in the text are not powerful ways to conjure up the phenomena for which the videos are provided as evidence. Quite the reverse. Generally speaking, EM studies acknowledge that one needs to be reflexive about the methodology employed, and to appreciate that all data are socially constructed for a purpose. In the current research, as the text will make quite clear, the video data do not function independently as records of objective reality. Instead, they are documentary in nature—offered as evidence of the existence of the phenomena described in the text. Readers wanting to see the original appendix on videography can address inquiries to: David Goode, Deputy Chair, SAS Department, College of Staten Island (4S-236), 2800 Victory Boulevard, Staten Island, New York 10314.

13. Even the naive anthropomorphic language found in common writing and speaking about dog-human play imports terms and ideas that originate extrinsically to the thing being studied. Language is usually learned before one actually plays with dogs. This is not true for dogs, babies or humans without formal language who play with dogs. But for most of us, the human player comes to the play armed with a mother tongue, a natural lexicon of terms and formulations related to play with dogs. The language and its usage create what we see while we play, and also what we do while we play (see EM's idea of accountability). In this sense, no linguistic account of play is unprejudiced, whether it be an ethnomethodological one or one based upon formal theorizing.

14. A short note about terminology: the words "companion dog" will be used in the text in place of the terms "pet dog," which at this date is more common in everyday talk about dogs. Companion dog implies a relationship that is more egalitarian than "having a pet." Similarly, the word "owner," which is also commonly employed in everyday conversation, has been replaced with the word "guardian," and for the same reason. It is important to note that the use of these terms does not imply that most persons in everyday life describe their relationship with dogs in this way. Also, it is important to note that in contemporary American society companion dogs are only one kind of dog. Each category has a corresponding human one (guide dog user, trainer, guard dog owner, shepherd dog trainer and owner, etc). Some differences between these types of dog-human relation-

ships are explored in chapter 5. For now it should be understood that "guardian-companion dog" is used to refer to that relationship in which a dog and human live together in a residential setting, but that the relationship involves primarily the routine, mundane activities of daily life and does not include formal training to achieve some practical social function such as guiding, competing, hunting, assisting, etc. The relationship often centers around mutual affection.

15. This is probably similar to what motivated the philosopher Immanuel Kant to write about the antimonies of reason, which involved his conviction that what seemed reasonable and entirely clear should be questioned for this very reason. In this case, in addition, a kind of "so-whatness," "obvious irrelevance to anything important," and "lack of any significance to sociology," was felt by me at the time I selected the project, and was confirmed by reactions of ethnomethodologists and other social scientists when I initially announced the study on the Internet (see chapter 7, note 1).

16. I described praktognosic ways of knowing in *A World without Words* (Goode, 1994a). In its original use in neurology it referred to a bodily form of knowing that was only available in the doing. The concept bears some similarity to that of "tacit knowledge" as written about by Michael Polanyi. Garfinkel characterized these variants of the same idea as "cognate versions of a praxiological conception of social action" (personal communication, Department of Sociology, UCLA, 1978). In the current writing "praktognosic" is taken to refer to embodied knowledge, mental states and movements involved in the production of ordinary activity of which the person is normally unaware and cannot be formulated in so many words. For example, most members of adult society, except those with certain forms of disability, can participate in a conversation. But as revealed by the work of conversational analysts, while the practices of conversation are entirely known to them in the doing, they are entirely absent as matters that can be formulated in language. Simply put, people have conversations without in any way consciously knowing what they are doing when they are doing it. The practices and knowledge required for conversation are, in my terminology, praktognosic.

Notes to Chapter 2

1. Appendix B-I is a woodcut by Albrecht Dürer from the beginning of the sixteenth century. In it we find a remarkably corgi-like dog. This actually makes some historical sense in that Dürer visited Holland, where he may have seen such dogs. With a dog such as Katie, whose origin is reputed to be very old, there are many problems in interpreting the information. Another set of issues exists regarding current breeding and selling practices. According to Deborah Harper's 1994 update of her handbook (*The New Complete Welsh Corgi*), there are three separate theories about the origin of the corgi breed. All attribute an early origin, approximately 1000 A.D. or soon thereafter. Two involve Scandinavian influences (the Valhund or the Lundehund), and one the influence of Flemish weavers who immigrated to Wales and brought spitz (Pembroke) and Tekkel (Cardigan) class dogs. These dogs may have interbred with local farm dogs. While there is clear evidence of dogs in Wales at this time, the relationship between these dogs and the present-day Pembroke corgi is entirely speculative. It is not until the end of the nineteenth century that we find any reliable information about the breeding of corgis.

When one examines photos of corgis who were champions in the early twentieth century and compares them with corgis of today, there are remarkable differences in both temperament and bodily form. Interesting, these early-twentieth-century examples of Pembrokes resemble much more a shepherd style (perhaps Valhund-based) than the Pembrokes of today.

2. For a discussion of Katie's intensity and compulsiveness during play, see the sections "The Meaning of Play for Katie" and "Lively Inner States During Play." Also see sequence 4: Face-01–03 (printed on pages 172–173) for images of Katie's face during play.

3. The nomenclature employed in the text is as follows. The sequence number is followed by the sequence name. The disk accompanying this book contains JPEG images that were taken from the original video files (AVI files). The appendices printed in this book contain all the images of sequences 2, 4, 10, and 13. All images, unless otherwise specified, were produced through the following procedure. Initial videotaping was done via a tripod mounted video camera (Panasonic AG-450 S-VHS with a 10:1 power zoom and built in microphone. The camera was set up, usually in the garage, prior to play sessions and was not manned during play. The video images captured on tape were then processed via a video-capture software, digitalized, and then recorded onto disk as .JPEG files. Video-capture was done on a Dell Optiplex GX1 computer with a Pentium III 450MgHz processor. This computer had a Winnov AV PCI capture card, version 2.92a, copyright Winnov, 1998. The complete set of images for each sequence is available on the accompanying disk. They are in the form of .JPEG files that were compressed (WNVI). They may be viewed by using ACDsee 32V.2.4., Imaging for Windows, Windows Media Player, MS Paint or similar software. Video files of the original sequences of play from which images were captured are available on the accompanying disk *but without sound.* The files on the disk are referred to in the text by names such as SHADOWINGA.AVI, PURSUITA.AVI, or FOOTBALL.AVI and may be played via Windows Media Player. To play the files, insert the disk, and if a prompt does not appear, click on Windows Media Player, select File, and click on the drive in which you inserted the disk. The names of the files will appear and you can select to view the particular file you wish to view.

4. The words "structure" and "motif" are intended in the same fashion as Garfinkel intends the term "order" (Garfinkel, 2002, p. 118, n.45). They collect a lot in convenient glosses. The word "structure," taken as a description of actual instances of play, is misleading if understood in the Durkheimian sense of structure as a social fact, i.e., as social structure consisting of the achievement of everyday life through practices that are cohort-independent and constraining to societal members. The term "motif" is also misleading if understood via its musical meaning, wherein composers consciously utilize motifs and their elaboration in the composition of music. The use of "motif" in describing playing ball with Katie is much more akin to the musical metaphor of "jamming," in which musicians vary their play "around" or "with" a theme to new and unpredictable things within the music. Even here the musical metaphor is misleading with regard to actually trying to characterize the lived play with Katie, in that musicians are at least to some degree conscious of the motif with which they are "playing." Play with Katie was more often without self-consciousness, even to me while I was studying it, as it is virtually impossible to play ball with Katie at the same time one is reflecting on this activity (consider trying to drive your car while reflecting on the activities of driving). For

outsiders, the "structures" or "motifs" that Katie and I engage in during play may be
entirely unknown and even not observable (in the sense that they could be seen but not
recognized as such). For the outsider, these events cannot be seen or described in the way
that I can describe them. These events are not vulgar, i.e., are not available to be observed
and understood by just anyone. They require a certain knowledge of our play history in
order to be recognized. I mean to convey by these terms that for David and Katie there is
just a certain orderliness of play's bodily doings. They are not constraining so much as they
are doable repeatedly, vulgarly so for members, again for each yet another next time. Our
playing is done without specific training for the task. Our playing is not independent of
cohort or staffing. It is not doable by other cohorts or staffings. If there were a substitute
for either of us, our form of play would not be embodied in the play of the new dyad of
players. The most intricate ones described in the data belong only to Katie and me, or we
to them. In my view you can have it either way. This is what I am saying about us as the
cohort of these motifs' staffing. We are involved in "the concerted vulgar and uniquely
adequate competencies of order production" (Garfinkel, 2002, p. 176). Our play is done
in a way that is practically unconcerned with anything or anyone extrinsic to its circumstance.

5.   What I mean by this is that I can throw the ball very far or less far, making Katie's capture
of it difficult, or not. I can throw it so far that it is impossible for her to capture it (i.e.,
get to the ball before it stops rolling) at all. Katie accepts this without objection.
Whatever the case, she pursues the ball as fast as she can.

6.   Several readers commented on the difference between writing "Katie was proud" versus
"Katie appears proud," implying that the latter was all that I could legitimately claim. The
issue of whether, in what ways, and to what degree human or animals have access to each
other's inner states is not a simple one and will be discussed in subsequent chapters.

7.   This can be observed in Katie's reactions to successive "poor" kicks, which usually
resulted in her stopping play and staring at me with an expression and demeanor that say,
"Come on, get your act together."

8.   It is noteworthy that dogs vary considerably in their capacity to throw balls. There are
dogs without any capacity to do so, while others can literally shoot a basketball. There
are various television shows that feature pet sports, which is where I first observed
television-worthy dogs disproving the rule. Because each dog varies in its abilities, I label
the research object as (DPBWK). There is no general phenomenon of playing ball with
dogs that can be observed, only particular instances of it. Most dogs do not throw balls;
certainly not Katie. Depending upon individual capabilities, this provides for certain
asymmetrical bodily possibilities during play together.

9.   The choice of playing sticks is mentioned by Clint Sanders and discussed briefly in
chapter 6.

10. The difference between Katie retrieving from the water and Jack, the Labrador retriever who lives with us, is remarkable. Labs love water and Jack thoroughly enjoys
water retrieving.

11. Another victim of the editing process was an extensive appendix dealing with Johan
Huizinga's seminal study of play, *Homo Ludens* (1950 [1966]). Again reviewers felt that
the material was highly technical and for some readers would be a distraction from the
main arguments of the book. I have summarized some of the main issues in this admittedly lengthy note.

Because of the centrality of play in my work with the deaf and blind, Garfinkel recommended that I read *Homo Ludens,* calling it a seminal work in the study of play. I did so at the time and rediscovered the text while writing up my research on playing with Katie. Huizinga is concerned with the defining characteristics of play. He is a philosopher, not an empirical social scientist, and relies primarily on historical sources. His enterprise, generally speaking, is not usually part of EM studies. Those studies proceed on the basis that one does not need to know the history of play (conversation, queuing or what have you) in order to study the orderliness of playing (conversation, queuing) phenomena. Further, and in a slightly anti-Wittgensteinian bent, you don't need to study the history of the word "play," how it got to be, how it was used in the past and how it is used in twenty-first-century American English. In EM studies these matters are taken as givens (Garfinkel and Sacks's paper on formal structures is a theoretical exception). The appendix on Huizanga was devoted exclusively to these concerns.

Predictably, there were both similarities and divergences when comparing the formal, reasoned definition of play presented by Huizinga with that version of play with Katie that emerged through the research process. In the main, however, much of what Huizinga writes about play is surprisingly resonant with the findings of this current inquiry. The epigraph to this book describes how play is something that is natural to other animals, such as dogs, and that humans probably have not invented or added much to its natural expression. Huizinga is sympathetic to an evolutionary model that includes play, as I am, but he is not sympathetic with analyses that account for play by the existence of a play "instinct," as I am not. He characterizes explanations of play via the device of play instinct as "makeshift, an admission of helplessness before the problem of reality" (Huizinga, 1950, p. 8). Such explanations attribute to play survival or adaptive purpose and avoid play in its primary quality, i.e., as a nonrational totality in which participants have/make or experience fun (Huizinga, 1950, p. 3). His conception of play is very similar to ideas found in this text, for example that play is autotelic (needs to be understood in its own right), or that it needs to be studied locally, from the perspectives of the players as they play (as we do in EM). "We shall consider play in its manifold concrete forms as itself a social construction. We shall try to take play as the player himself takes it on, in its primary significance" (Huizinga, 1950, p. 4). For Huizinga, and in my view, play for dogs is no more or less a matter of hunting and herding than basketball is for humans.

Much of Huizinga's writing in the beginning of the book identifies defining characteristics of play. He was not afraid of making up definitions, as Garfinkel might say. Some of the key elements Huizinga identified in play clearly are reflected in the data about playing with Katie. The idea that play has an aesthetic quality—that it has a tendency to be beautiful but also possibly can get ugly—was certainly something stressed in the written data. Play has, loosely speaking, "rules." I call them "motifs" and do not identify these with the classical conception of rules in sociology, but we are talking about the same things from different perspectives. (I believe Huizinga is weak here in his treatment of the rule-governed character of play, which does not consist of simply following rules.) The idea that play is moral, that players understand what is right and wrong, is also a part of Huizinga's discussion, and my data. Huizinga also considers the idea that play can be fun while being serious. This is because play is ultimately a test of prowess, of one player bringing something off that the other is trying to prevent, i.e., of who is better. This was certainly true of Katie, who was very serious about her play. One very significant difference between the way play occurred between Katie and me and how it was defined by Huizinga was that play for Katie and me was a ubiquitous theme of life, spread all over our interactions whenever Katie could convince me to play. This was not consistent with Huizinga's observation that play is a time that is cut off from everyday (I take him to mean "instrumental") life. I would not characterize play with Katie in these terms.

Because definitions of play such as that provided by Huizinga are attempts at general solutions to the problem of play, there are likely to be ways in which such a definition either misses, or even essentially misconstrues, any instance of the phenomenon. This is basically Garfinkel's criticism of what he calls formal analytic theorizing, and the deficiency of that form of theorizing to explain any particular instance of the phenomenon. So Huizinga's fine formal analytic work is only partially helpful in understanding play with Katie.

A final part of the appendix dealt with the etymological derivation of the word "play" and how the various languages' senses of the term seem to have both common and divergent connotations. This seemed sensible for me to do, even before I read Vicki Hearne's remarks about how studying animals is necessarily studying language (see my discussion of Hearne's work in chapter 4). While this analysis did not lead to any concrete insights about play with Katie, the culturally relative differences embodied in the term and its normal usage could well be the basis for praxiological ones. It may be that different mother tongues structure play for their speakers, writers or signers in observably divergent ways. Those interested in reading the appendix on Huizinga in full can request a copy (David Goode, Deputy Chair, SAS Department, 4S236, 2800 Victory Boulevard, Staten Island, New York 10314).

12. Generally speaking there is a lack of interchangeability of perception and experience between dogs and humans. One cannot assume that dogs hear, see, smell, taste or feel as humans do. As far as we can tell by observation, they do not. However, this observation does not question that people and dogs can, for all practical purposes, cooperatively produce action and understand one another during that production. These perceptual and experiential differences did not come up as such during our play, only in my thinking about it. Sensory differences, as Vicki Hearne notes, can be used to point to the problematic of using human language to describe dog-human interaction.

13. Dogs' jealousy over the possession of play objects is common and takes many forms. Katie is usually expressive about other dogs' taking her ball or stick from her. In situations where the dogs are her friends she may bark or growl in displeasure, especially if the other dog tries to take the object from her mouth. She objects less when dogs are able to outrun her and fetch the ball or stick before she can get to it; she won't bark or growl at that. But with an unfamiliar dog the situation can be more dangerous. The worst dog bite I ever received was from trying to break up a fight about a ball between Katie and another small dog whom we had not met before. Two dogs who do not know one another and one ball lead to a dangerous situation.

14. From the descriptions of Katie's and my stick play in the park, it is clear that a geographically stable field of play is not a requirement or defining feature of that form of play. In those practices, play with the stick follows whatever path we might take, including off-trail areas such as streams, fields, embankments, or underbrush. The playing field is

mobile. This is true of some human games as well. And with the advent of the electronic videogame, neither a geographically stable field nor the co-presence of players is a requirement of play. Today games can be "played" without biological players.

15. See Appendix C: Ethnomethodology for a discussion of this concept.

16. Biological reductionist, evolutionary analogy and other ways of describing dog play sometimes refer to truncated hunting behaviors as its building blocks. Play is seen to consist of these hunting behaviors and further considered to be practice for the real thing (i.e., hunting). This view will be criticized. For now, the gnawing and general oral destruction this note refers to would be called under this kind of framework "dissect," referring to that part of the hunting sequence that occurs after the kill.

17. These remarks refer to time that is provided for by play and experienced by players. It is making time, not marking time, a distinction described in the works of both Sudnow and Garfinkel. The difference here would be between "clock time," which can be measured by a device such a clock or chronometer, versus "play time," which is made and felt by players during playing. In the above we have lazy time and intense time during play, which is not something captured by clock time.

18. A major theme of this research is that dogs in their relations with humans appear to be intrinsically and observably moral creatures. That is, they appear to have a sense of what is right and wrong in these affairs. This was evident in the data about play with Katie. But also consider Vicki Hearne's description of a dog executing its work at a formal competition, indicating to her "responsibility of a high order" (Hearne, 1986, 79):

> In one race, just as Belle started out for her run, another dog, a somewhat absentminded Old English Sheepdog, meandered onto the course and stood lumpily between two jumps. Belle, without faltering in her stride, aimed her shoulder at the sheepdog's flank, knocking him out of the way, and went on as though the path had been clear, doing her job. This is responsibility of a high order, not the sort dependent upon approval of me, or anyone else. (Hearne, 1986, p. 89)

This sort of responsibility is built into the corgi, and Katie is certainly an exemplar. This same sense of responsibility was evident in the narrations of corgis at work cited above or in Katie's vain efforts to herd the local deer population. The idea that dogs and other animals have a sense of fair play and morality was not commonly found in academic writing about animals until the 1970s. Today, this belief is a part of popular culture as well as animal studies. A recent article in *Time* magazine titled "Honor Among Beasts" (Lemonick, 2005) describes evidence for altruism and fair play among several species: dogs, dolphins, birds, and monkeys.

Notes to Chapter 3

1. Robert Mitchell was one of the initial readers of the manuscript that eventually came to be this book, specifically commenting that I had not taken the time to read the relevant animal studies literature. His critique was similar to that I had received for *A World without Words* (WWW), which was sociologically sophisticated but was relatively uninformed about the literature in special education on persons born congenitally deaf-blind. An indirect indicator of the correctness of Mitchell's criticism was that WWW sold well

in sociology and disability studies, but poorly in the special education marketplace. As described in the acknowledgments Mitchell has been a staunch supporter of this work throughout its revisions. He has supplied numerous references and articles in animal studies that I have incorporated into this book. He has also engaged in a serious dialogue with me over issues raised in the study, this over a period of several years. Simply put, without his input this book would have been much less than it is.

2. Intentionality is discussed by Mitchell in a 1990 paper quoted below, in which he offers a theory of play. That paper describes how intentions are read in animal behavior, what he elsewhere refers to as "intentionality in action" (here echoing Searle), and how such reading of intentions leads us to an appreciation of the organism's own tacit conception of its movements. He also argues that the claim that an organism has intentions does not mean that it understands or controls these intentions. Related to this is the issue that organisms need to understand each other's intentions in order to have coordinated interaction, which will be discussed below. Suffice it to say here that Mitchell and his colleagues do not postulate that mutual understanding is a necessary or sufficient condition for play.

> To say that an animal has a particular intention is to say that the animal itself is organizing its movements in a particular way to achieve, in a reasonable manner, a particular effect. [This view places the emphasis on how the animal experiences and organizes the world, and] through this appeal to the organism's tacit conception of its movements, we see how to categorize animal movements: an intentional interpretation offers a way to parse the stream of movements.
>
> For most animals are intimately tied to action, such that they are "intentions in action" and not intentions planned prior to action (see Searle, 1983).
>
> Also, because an animal has an intention does not mean that the animal understands why it has that intention, Thus, there is no paradox in stating that an animal intended to do something, but did not understand why and could not stop itself from acting so. (Mitchell, 1990, p. 200)

3. To me this switch does not indicate a change in the basic motif of play. That motif is "I have what you want and you will have to get it from me." What changes here is how it is to be played, based upon the in situ unfolding of play events between the players, in this case and as a matter of fact, the futile attempts of the shepherd to gain access to the contested play object. With that motif of play the unsuccessful player does a game move, "let's see if I pick up the rag whether he will try and get it from me." The suggestion is really not a new project so much as it is a modification, a jamming around, of the original play theme. It is a continuation of that motif's modifying unfolding in the play situation.

4. "Talk to dogs and infants share a variety of features. These include prosodic features (high pitch, whispering, and extended word duration), lexical features (frequent attention getting devices and distinctive words), complexity features, and many one-word utterances, redundancy features (high repetition), and content features (most present tense verbs, most about action and infrequently about mental states), as well as coordination features. However, to talk to infants has a higher . . . mean length utterance, more phatics (one word greetings), questions, declaratives, and deictic utterances, and fewer

exact repetitions and imperatives than talk to dogs (probably because speech has even less of an impact on an infant than on a dog" (Mitchell, 2001, p. 202).

The author notes the difficulty in making the comparison because there is a lack of data on these aspects of speech in infant research.

Further, it would seem reasonable that the differences noted have to do with the kind of listener to which the speaker is directing his remarks. It is not the case that speech simply has less of an impact on infants than on dogs. In some ways, especially in terms of the development of the listener, the impact of speech on infants is far more profound than that on dogs. The infant hearer is transformed by the hearing of speech into an infant thinker and speaker, and that expectation would be built into the motherese as a matter of "recipient design." The dog, on the other hand, is not transformed by speech— at least not to the same degree by any reasonable comparison. For them the impact of speech, including understanding of words, is direct—having to do with immediate bodily actions and their relationship to practical and concrete circumstances understood by the speaker. The dog is expected to take his or her turn in the conversation, not through utterances, but through action, its meaningful bodily participation in the practical event.

5. The idea that linguistic and nonlinguistic expressions are understood "indexically" is a central ethnomethodological observation. Indexical expressions refer to expressions whose sense cannot be determined without knowledge of their biography and purposes, the circumstances of their expression, the biography and identity of the speaker, and the previous relationship existing between the speaker(s) and hearer(s). As opposed to understanding verbal expression through their lexical meaning, indexicality points to the essentially circumstantial or occasional way expressions are understood in everyday interaction. Indexical expressions are understood as parts of, and meaningful with respect to, the specific, observable, unfolding, in vivo course of events of which interactants are a part.

6. The dog project "avoid fakeout" is defined as "While attending strongly to the object, the dog attempts to inhibit itself from chasing it when the person is playing fakeout (Mitchell & Thompson, 1990, p. 27). The human project "fakeout" is defined as "The person attempts to get the dog to move where the person appeared to have thrown or kicked the object, or the person attempts to make the one object look a more preferred object to the dog" (Mitchell & Thompson, 1990, p. 28).

7. Deception was rarely employed by Katie during play, but often by me. Her only overt, regular act of deception that I can bring to mind was her use of the directional properties of gaze (see my discussion of Sanders in chapter 6) to distract and misdirect me. This is a tactic she also uses with Jack and other dogs. The move consists of stopping play, staring intensely in the direction usually not oriented to the field of play, sometimes barking, until I or the other dog joins in to see what she is looking at. This is almost always a successful strategy.

8. Deception in play appears to be a sum-sum game; that is, in deception during play the outcome often benefits both players by making the game more fun. This appears to be somewhat different from deception in a zero-sum game, where the deceiver benefits from the deception but the victim of the deception does not. It may that we need to distinguish between these two forms of deception in play.

9. The textual data are uncensored. They report what I saw and felt about play with

Katie. There is, as one reviewer put it, perhaps an irritating and too coy character to some of the text. All reviews noted that I made much too much over my embarrassment regarding vocal participation, and also that I fail to carry out the promised empirical analysis. I was aware of this quality and of this failure, but have left the data as they were written. One cannot alter qualitative data any more than one can quantitative data.

10. Infant and adult humans also do the same, but dogs participate in this way exclusively.

11. The reader will recall the introduction, in which I describe looking at a particular case through a microscope and thereby revealing features that otherwise would go unnoticed or unrecognized, even though these may be essential to understanding the case.

12. Another issue with regard to terminology: the analytic terminology that is used to theoretically organize observations of play can be contradictory to the fun of play. The way play can be portrayed as deceitful, controlling, manipulative, victimizing and futile can give the impression that play is no fun at all. And while there are clearly parts of play that are not fun in the sense of being ecstatic or joyous, the overall impression conveyed by academic writing is often a dry, eviscerated version of events. This seems unavoidable and is true of both Mitchell's work and my own. Despite conscious efforts to keep the account local and add nothing, EM's way of characterizing and writing about everyday life is often very dry and academic. Its drama and lushness are lost.

13. You can create many kinds of dopes: psychological, behavioral, cultural, sociological, neurological and so on. The point is not that writing about matters in these ways is wrong. The idea means to convey that often these frames are used to imply that the matter at hand consists in the first instance, mostly or primarily, of events that are psychological, behavioral, cultural, sociological, neurological, and so on. In EM, primacy is given to the social event as practically and naturally produced and experienced by those involved. There are many reasons to do this, including the fact that such descriptions are sorely lacking in the scientific corpus. More than this, EM maintains that the lived orders of everyday life are achieved without need of theory, science, specialized training or knowledge. These orders are what can be observed in everyday life, and nothing more than what is observable need to be added to understand them. At the same time, with such descriptions in hand there is no reason why any set of concerns—psychological, cultural, or sociological—cannot be entertained. Without naturalistic descriptions (I realize this is a bad shorthand but will allow it anyway) we lack a crucial element in understanding human or dog-human reality. The lived orders of everyday life are not dependent in any way upon these academic conceptualizations and would go on as they are with or without them.

14. See, for example, Fran Waksler's 1991 volume *Studying the Social Worlds of Children*, particularly those articles dealing with kids' culture.

15. Note that this is not an argument that dog-human players cannot be aware that they are playing to practice. Whether particular players are or are not so oriented to play is an empirical matter and to be determined via empirical observation and description of dog-human play. At the park where I walk my dogs, I have seen dogs who are in training, for example to hunt, and they engaged in a repetitive retrieval of object that appears very much to be like play. I spoke to the guardians of these dogs, Labradors, and they said that the dogs were aware that they were in training for hunting. While I did not follow up the inquiry with "How do you know that?" I have no reason to disbelieve their claim. In any

case, the point I am making is that playing to practice is something that is an empirical matter, and not a theoretical one.

Notes to Chapter 4

1. For an alternative view, see John Andrew Fisher's "Disambiguating Anthropomorphism: An Interdisciplinary Review" (1991), in which he presents similar criticisms to those I will make of dog ethnographers. In Fisher's view, anthropomorphism, if taken to mean that actors can understand each other's perspectives, intentions and meanings, is no less right or wrong than theories of human interaction that claim persons can understand one another during the course of interaction. Fisher's conclusion is that "Without plausible defense that ascriptions of mental states to non-animals is a categorical fallacy, the most basic assumption of the critics of anthropomorphism is shown to be untenable" (Fisher, 1991, p. 84).
2. See, for example, Steven Clark's (1987) discussion of the philosopher's view of animals versus humans. Also see chapters 5 and 6 on the socially constructed dog.
3. I include an additional humorous but also persuasive example taken from Temerlin's 1975 account of raising a chimpanzee in his home, *Lucy: Growing Up Human.*

    > Lucy left the living room and went to the kitchen cabinet and took from it a glass, opened a different cabinet, and brought out a bottle of gin. She poured two or three fingers of straight gin into the glass. She then came back to the living room couch bringing her drink back with her. From the coffee table she picked up a copy of National Geographic magazine, lay down on the couch, and sipped her gin while leafing through the magazine. About three to five minutes later she stopped suddenly as though a good idea had hit her. She sat straight up and paused, put the drink and National Geographic on the floor, jumped up and went to the utility closet at the end of the hall, exactly fifty-seven feet from where she'd been sitting. She opened the door, took out the vacuum cleaner, brought the vacuum cleaner into the living room, and plugged it in a wall socket. She then removed the brush end from the long aluminum tube to which it was connected, and applied the pipe to her genitals.
    >
    > She continued to masturbate with the suction from the machine until she had what I inferred to be an orgasm (she laughed, looked happy and stopped suddenly). She then turned off the machine, picked up her unfinished glass of gin and her magazine, lay back against the couch and continued to drink again, contemplating the pictures in the National Geographic (Temerlin, 1975, pp. 105–108)

    Had he been present Darwin could have written this passage. It employs the vernacular for objects and actions. It is unabashedly anthropomorphic. It assumes a continuity, parallelism and resonance between the actions of chimpanzees and humans.
4. A way to make this clearer is through the philosophical device of imaginative variation. Imagine a deaf person without any formal language training (oral or sign) watching Darwin's dog, or Lucy on the couch. There are actually many such people around the world (many in poor countries that do not have schools for the deaf), so actually not a lot of imagination is required here. While many of these persons invent a way of

communicating (usually native signs coupled with pantomimic gestures), it can be said that their experience of things is not directly informed by language in the first instance. Yet, such persons would have no problem interpreting the "hot house" face of Darwin's dog, or Lucy's activities leading to orgasm. For an interesting video about persons with deafness who have no formal sign language see Oliver Sacks's BBC production *In Search of Lucy Doe.*

5. Although uncited by the author it should be noted that Wieder's treatment of chimp-human interaction is similar to that described by Hebb (1946, 1949).

6. The reader will forgive this long note, which provides Wieder's summary of Husserl's treatment of the experience of the Other and intersubjectivity. The vocabulary and intellectual arguments of Husserl's work cannot be easily comprehended by just reading the bullets in this note.

    • What is real and objective implies the existence of other egos as cointending those affairs.

    • When I apprehend a living body, I find a subject who co-constitutes the world with me.

    • The intentions that grasp the other organism and objective world do so indirectly, through an indirect sign-like appresentation.

    • Knowledge of the other's mind (of his experience of the world) is only knowable indirectly, through events produced by or of one's body.

    • The Other is given in a complex of sense strata, all but one of which (the ego) is appresented. The following is a list of the hierarchically ordered sense strata:

        —The animate organism.

        —The Other's governing ego, especially as it controls the soma.

        —The harmonious behavior of the Other's bodily contact.

        —The Other's primordial world that is his Here and my There.

        —A reflective layer of Other's senses such that they constitute his/her self-same body for him and for me (all that is entailed in the apprehension of the other animate organism there. The origin of the coordination of the modes, Here and There.

        —The coordination of Here and There founds the stratum of the physical body as given sensuously, the commonness of Nature.

        —The appresentation of Nature from Here and There founds its common nature.

    • *This body obtains its sense of objective sense by being a body over there for the Other, while at the same time being the selfsame body as the lived body for me.*

    Upon these levels are founded "modifications" of the one identical world for us all, modifications captured by the experience inherent in abnormalities (blind, deaf) and brutes. While their experiences may be radically different from our own they are experiences of the same world, involving a transformation of what we experience.

    Further strata include the sense of community of men in which there is mutual being for one another, entailing an objectivating equalization of my existence with that of all others.

    Upon these layers are founded the more complex and social objects of language and communication.

Husserl's analytic framework for intersubjectivity resonates with the data presented in *A World without Words* and in this writing. These data and this frame forms the basis for the general model of intersubjectivity presented below.

7. There is a pop psychology version of this argument—people say much more with their body than they do with their words. Dr. Phil, the TV psychologist, stated on a recent show, "You communicate 68% of your message by body language, and 28% by verbal content."

8. Of course if we are after a natural account of the phenomenon of (DPBWK), Katie can not be thought of as a stand in for a human player.

9. Mitchell (personal communication, July 2005) cites the work of L.T. Houbhouse (1901, 1915) as making essentially this same argument, i.e., that resemblances of animal and human behaviors allow for proper naming of behaviors that serve analogous functions, but that we cannot thereby conclude their identity in experience or reality. In the 1915 edition of his book he stated: ". . . if the behaviour of another being corresponds precisely in all is outer relations to that which I know of in myself as carried out in consciousness and never without consciousness, it is clear that in that other being some process occurs which performs the same functions as consciousness in me" (Hobhouse, 1915, pp. 18–19). The limitation of Hobhouse's method is that the animal may have a state of consciousness that differs, but not with respect to the basic or essential function(s) of the behavior. Since the behavior performs essentially the same function(s) for both beings, it is impossible to know if consciousness of either differs in nonessential ways. The consciousness of the other, dogs or humans, is taken for all practical purposes to be "the same." The imputation is "corroborated by the ever-repeated test of daily intercourse with our fellows" (Hobhouse, 1915, p. 17).

10. Michell also discusses single case studies, whose major limitation appears to be the inability to generalize to others of the species (or breed). While this limitation is real, having specialized in in-depth, single case studies, in my experience there are both limitations and advantages to this form of research. Because single case studies examine praxis microscopically, through such a lens one comes upon sociological phenomena that could not be discovered otherwise, especially phenomena that require a long-term, detailed-oriented commitment. An example of this is in *A World without Words*, in which I observed the Smiths, a family with a child, Bianca, who was deaf and blind and had failed to develop formal language (rubella syndrome). Although the clinical assessment of this child indicated that she had only very rudimentary communication skills, and that the family did not appreciate the degree to which the child was disabled, by observing this family in their home for an extended period I was able to discover and document how they were able to communicate with Bianca. No other method would have been able to make observable such communication practices. Over the years I presented the results of this research to other families with members who lack formal language. Often they would comment that the Smith family sounded very similar to their own, highlighting both similarities and differences in communicational practices. In a way this should not be a surprise. Certain kinds of social arrangements can be made observable through microscopic, in-depth analysis. Such arrangements are "lived orders" and what is made observable are both the unique ways they are created (lived) and also the more general aspects of their production (order). This is what the other families recognized when I described the

Smiths. So, the issue of generalizability of single case research is not a simple one, as some researchers argue, and not limited to the obvious truth that each case differs in some ways from the others.

11. Therefore many scientists view psychological attributions based on evidence as fallible, and attempt to avoid using them. Of course the possibility of error exists and occurs regularly. Yet there are ways, observably the case, that allow for correction once the misinterpretation is discovered. This is true for interactions between humans or between dogs and humans. Further, the fact that any method can be demonstrated to be fallible does not question its empirical status as a practice that is regularly employed by persons in interaction with each other or with dogs. To evaluate scientifically the psychological description made of dogs or other species by a theory or theories, or to systematically collect data about different aspects of play to enhance our general understanding of it and of animals' experience of it, are worthwhile enterprises. Certainly researchers so engaged would not want to rely upon any naïve device. However, it is important to note, as Mitchell and his colleagues do, that there are conundrums and problems of interpretation that come up with any approach to understanding animal psychology. Species biological identities are not fixed, they change over time with advancing knowledge in the sciences, and researchers should not naively employ biological evidence any more than they should observational evidence.

Notes to Chapter 5

1. Kete points out that the creation of the dog breeds we know today, the standardized breeds described in American Kennel Club publications and other manuals, occurred at the end of the nineteenth century, along with the development of dog shows and competitions. This is not to say that dog breeding was not done in antiquity and that the origin of some of today's breeds is recent. But lack of archaeological and documentary evidence makes it difficult to trace most breeds back beyond a relatively recent point in history. What is generally known is that many popular breeds emerged in the nineteenth century. With corgis there is reason to suspect greater antiquity, although the exact history of the breed is not possible to determine (as discussed in the introduction).

2. It is interesting to speculate about whether this "golden age" will continue in the future. Aside from the horrible mismanagement of dog breeding in our country, resulting in the mass euthanasia of dogs, there are reasons to be wary about the immediate future of companion dogs, including the fact that there is a rash of books about the history of dogs now on the market. As Neil Postman put it, historians come to bury, not to praise. At the least, the entry of historians on the scene signifies that dogs may be entering a declining stage, that they have had their most robust phase. Postman makes the argument about the history of childhood literature, and I think one can make a similar case regarding dogs. Also note that Postman and others have discussed the commodification of children and how age categories are employed in marketplace dynamics, and similarly we see this regarding the various industries surrounding dogs.

3. The matching of working dogs with their human partners is a critical part of their relationship and must be take into consideration if that team is to be workable, i.e., successful, at what it is meant to do. Thus Michalko and Smokie were carefully matched in terms of personality, style, physical size, and strength, thereby enhancing their possi-

bility of success. There is no similar matching with companion dogs and their guardians, who are left by and large to find one another in some sort of haphazard, ungoverned process of purchase or rescue. I am continually amazed at the lack of fit between dogs and owners whom I meet on walks with my dogs in the local park. It's a lack of fit that can take many forms: size, temperament, look, number of animals, lack of control, and so on. The mismatch can be humorous, or not.

4.   Note here, Smokie as the Martian anthropologist observing human blindness. Not really. He's thoroughly terrestrial in origin. But he is indifferent to symbolic characterizations of blindness, as a Martian might also be.

5.   Aesthetic appreciation for the grace and efficiency of guide dog work is common in accounts of guide dog users. A particularly interesting and moving one is Morris Frank's account of his dog, Buddy, crossing New York's West Street in the early 1930s (today West Side Highway but back then a six-lane, two-direction nightmare of traffic). Morris Frank was one of the earliest guide dog users in the United States and was in New York to promote the idea of guide dogs and guide dog schools. Frank had offered to cross the busiest street in New York City, and West Street was it. In what he knew was a dangerous situation, he had no choice but to trust that Buddy was completely competent and up to the work. From his view he described the crossing as "utter chaos." Buddy would advance, then go back, then advance again, then retreat again, doing this same pattern over and over amidst the whir of traffic, the honking of horns, yelling and the rest. When finally Frank reached the other side, one reporter was right behind him. He told Frank that this was the most remarkable thing he had ever seen. All the reporters were still back on the other side of the street because they could not manage to get across. A blind man, with a dog's leadership, had. Perhaps this is why Frank was reported to call Buddy, who actually was a she, "that magnificent beast." This account is taken from Bill Mooney's one-man play about Morris Frank, *With a Dog's Eyes: Capturing the Life of Morris Frank*, produced by the Seeing Eye, Inc., Morristown, New Jersey.

6.   The nature of the training involved in guide dog work is hidden to most outside observers. Michalko relates several stories in which he plays with the ignorance and apparent social opacity of guide dog work. For example, he uses the ignorance of guide dog work to amaze onlookers with Smokie's ability to know when to cross the street. Of course it is Michalko who through the harness signals Smokie to cross. Michalko believes that the training required to be a good guide dog is the same as that required to be a good human:

> Human beings . . . are tied to nature but not determined by it. Dogs, on the other hand, are understood as nature, and as such they require training. As human beings, we understand the concept of training within the humanistic categories of education and socialization. This is why we are often amazed by the abilities of a guide dog, even its ability to distinguish left from right, when we are not amazed by the same ability in a person. (Michalko, 1999, p. 134)

The question I will pose at the end of chapter 6 is whether Katie and I could have been involved in the learning and elaboration of the ways of play (ethnomethods) between dogs and humans that are characteristic of late-twentieth-century, middle-class America. In the above excerpt from Michalko, the idea that socialization and training are essentially different sorts of processes is questioned. Another way to look at this is to acknowledge that dogs and humans learn practices related to recognizable social forms, play, work, feeding, fighting, etc. Dogs and humans share what Schutz would have called "recipe knowledge" (1974). This specific cultural form, though asymmetrically available to dogs and humans, is learned by both.

A somewhat similar view is expressed by Hearne (1986, pp. 55–57): "To learn to talk with a dog involves mutual participation in everyday activities." In fact, for Hearne talking means more than speaking, or at least different from mere speaking. Talking involves a shared sense of morality. Dogs learn everyday activities through obedience, initially mechanically but eventually with meaning. Hearne (and Michalko) liken this to the way babies learn to be human and to talk with adults. She writes about a dog she is training:

> What we surrender to matters of course. Salty appears to have no choice about surrendering to me, but to say that as though it distinguished her from us is to overlook the degree of choice any of us has about surrendering to our native tongues [or to primary socialization in general]. My training methods, like teaching method, depend on her willingness to cooperate. (Hearne, 1986, p. 57)

Without implying overall homogeneity or sameness, neither humans or dogs have volitional choice about surrendering to the ways society has taught them to produce everyday actions.

7. Hearne writes about the power of formal training to transform the dog: "The dog is a domestic animal, and the postures appropriate to his life with human beings come to transform him and the actions he performs, even it is done mechanically and reluctantly at first" (1986, p. 32).

8. I do not want to give the impression that I did not train Katie and Jack. Both were taught basic commands of "sit," "stay" and "come." These were practiced regularly and re-warded with food and other reinforcers. Training in these basic commands is part of a basic responsibility for all guardians and can be extremely useful in dangerous circum-stances.

Notes to Chapter 6

1. This is not to say that there are not a variety of scholars from various disciplines who continue to discuss mind and its relationship to other phenomena (see Searle, 1987).

2. Again I refer the reader to Coulter's seminal respecification of cognitive psychology. Note that it is typical of social scientists to write about standards before having a basic grasp of the actual matters of interest (see especially Garfinkel's 2002 discussion of Sacks's Gloss).

3. In his 1996 address, "Ethnomethodology's Program," Garfinkel said, "We learned in graduate school there is a free democracy of theories. You pick whatever you need" (p. 10, n.12). Another way to put this would be that while actions, for example playing with your dog, or teaching a deaf-blind child, are usually done in observably repetitive ways, they are analyzable from virtually an indefinite number of perspectives, limited only by human imagination and interest.

4. This discussion parallels that of Michael Lynch about the sociology of science, in which he notes that reflections about scientific knowledge are filled with insights about science

but are often not the result of detailed observation about the actual everyday practices of science or scientists.

5. Schutz is proposing that, applied to this instance, dogs are "socially constructed" via society's stock of practical knowledge about them. Members are taught this practical knowledge and use it in their dealings with dogs. Social construction is a gloss, like documentary method, that is perhaps too clear and far reaching, which is why we needed to give it flesh in this current analysis. The social member is not generally aware of the social machinery he or she uses and does not think of him or herself as in the midst of constructing objects and events in the everyday world. In fact, as Marx pointed out through his use of the term "reification" most people experience their constructions as given objectively or naturally. Yet, ethnomethodologists and other careful observers of everyday life can observe these constructive processes, for which the term "social construction of dogs" stand. We can see the ways in which dogs are routinely characterized and treated. We can observe the semantics of animal terms and how they get contextually employed. Such terms are part of the stock of practical knowledge or technical knowledge particular to that society (although globalization of culture is increasingly undermining this particularity). With regard to dogs, as discussed in the previous chapter, this involves recognition and production skills with regard to the various kinds or types of dogs—companion dogs, show dogs, police dogs, personal assistance dogs, attack dogs, celebrity dogs, and so forth. Because of their adaptability and malleability, dogs are particularly suited to this wide range of human definitions and practices. The culture's mother tongue provides the member with these powerful ways of producing and recognizing these animals. The cultural stock of knowledge becomes indirectly available to dogs, who learn them through the guardian's or trainer's behaviors towards them. This occurs as the dogs become good ballplayers, show dogs, companion dogs, etc. Knowledge about dogs is not distributed equally throughout society. Knowledge of dogs is dependent upon context, involvement or lack thereof, and the specific details and nature of that involvement. Distribution of ways of understanding dogs varies socioeconomically, reflecting the ways dogs are integrated into life in poorer versus richer neighborhoods. See Nash (1989) for an interesting study of the physical and interactional construction of the British bulldog.

6. Some subjects, deeply disturbed by the behaviors they had observed and recorded, felt it necessary to justify along with their observations that their families were nonetheless good families. Other students became aware of behavior that disturbed them to such a degree that they felt it necessary to make the results part of family life and to discuss what they had seen with family members. In several cases these discussions resulted in serious conflict, and in one case protracted conflict.

7. The *Barnhart Concise Dictionary of Etymology* describes the word *symbol*'s original sixteenth-century meaning which is consistent with its usage here—the capacity of actions, spoken words, gestures, signed language, written words, and images to stand on behalf of or refer to something other than itself.

8. For example, some who have watched Katie and I play have commented upon her holding the ball in her mouth as a form of social control. "She is trying to control you," is not an uncommon comment. While the behavior is clearly interpretable in this way, and while that reading may contain an element or slice of truth, it does not appreciate its biographical and game-specific nature. Acts of play together are open to indefinitely

various readings that transform the events into things that stand on behalf of something else. For players, however, these same actions are knowable objects of everyday practice that are not symbolic and "require" atheoretical, praktognosic understanding to actually be accomplished.

9. By understanding meanings I refer to that model of social order that sees shared meanings among actors as the basis for orderly interactions. By shared meanings among actors it is meant that actors have the same interpretations of utterances and events, and thereby coordinate their activities together.

10. As a matter of observation, symbols entered play on those occasions when, for example, I would use the phrase, "Do you want to play bally with me?" which was taken by Katie, depending on exactly where we were, to refer to a next series of pre-game events— getting the ball from the ball stash, going to the back door, etc. These Quinean, indexical readings of my phrases fit the definition of symbol as employed in this text.

Hearne (1986) also appears to appreciate that shared meaning cannot be used to explain the orderliness of relationships between dogs and people:

> With horses as with dogs, the handler must learn to believe, to "read" a language s/he hasn't sufficient neurological apparatus to test or judge, because the handler must become comprehensible to the horse, and to be understood is to be open to understanding, much more than it is to have shared mental phenomena. It is as odd as Wittgenstein suggested to suppose that intersubjectivity depends on shared mental phenomena—he likes to talk about color patches— since we are primarily talking to someone, which pretty much guarantees little area of phenomenological overlap, even when I say just what you would say. So we are still poking at the edges of the biggest mystery of all about language—that it exists. (Hearne, 1986, p. 107)

11. When speaking, writing or signing, one always uses a language in a way that selects out of a whole of experience or event certain elements, and then treats those elements as standing on behalf of the entire event or experience. This linguistic "snapshot" and its equation with the thing itself is one of the tricks of language Wittgenstein wrote about. A physician once asked me, "How is it that your work with Christina (the deaf and blind child I knew at the State Hospital) any different than working with a chimpanzee?" I was taken aback but responded, "If a chimpanzee were a deaf and blind child there would be no difference." This is not to say there might not be some things similar, actually I don't know enough about working with chimpanzees to say, but to extract these, as a snapshot of the whole situation and treat them as the same, or the subjects within them as identical, is a serous error in scientific reasoning.

12. As advanced in the previous chapter, all ways of describing dogs are socially inscribed, emphasizing certain features or aspects of dogs and not others, reflecting the interests and position of the person(s) doing the description. In the following case, Michalko offers a description of his guide dog that emphasizes the dog's nonhuman, as opposed to person-like, features:

> Remember that your dog is still just a dog. You have to give him time to be that. Not just relieving him and feeding him, that's obvious. You have to let him be a dog once in a while. Actually, you should let him be that every day. He needs play time. Your dog has to have a chance to be a dog, just to play. (1999, p. 134)

Note here that playing and being just a dog are equated. The intent is to make the reader aware that dogs have a unique set of needs separate from those of humans. In the descriptions in the text it is not play in the sense of the kind of play I describe with Katie that Smokie is allowed to do. It is peeing, sniffing, exploring, etc., dog-style. The point here is that constructions of dogs can choose to emphasize their human-like features or non-human features.

13. One reader commented that Sanders emphasizes the dog as person theme because of his ethical commitment to animal rights. If that is indeed what is occurring in this case, the extension of the ethical into the scientific, then I would say this is a dangerous practice scientifically. I have the same commitment to the ethical treatment of dogs and other animals, but I do not believe these values should structure how I observe and analyze dog-human interaction at the level of basic description.

14. The exceptions here are those few species—birds and primates—that have been taught humanly authored communication systems (sign, speech, symbol systems). While these animals tell us something about the malleability of their vocal structures and processes and about their intelligence, due to the highly contrived circumstances of such experiments, they tell us little about naturally occurring communication systems between animals and humans. Hearne also raises some serious ethical concerns about these experiments and the validity of their findings, especially with regard to primates (1986, pp. 39–41). With regard to dogs, some dogs have been claimed to be able to recognize as many as several hundred words. While singing dogs are not uncommon, very few dogs, mostly television rarities, actually can speak, and even those can actually "enunciate" only very few words or names. These speaking dogs have a rare ability for verbal mimicking.

15. As mentioned elsewhere, animal researchers have attempted to "talk" to animals, from primates to lions to cows, in their own terms. An interesting account appears in Trivers's (1990) account of introducing his friend to birds in his garden by singing to them. After describing the strategies he uses to make up bird songs, he adds a new section to introduce his friend:

> The assumption behind this, of course, is that birds are sensitive to this [i.e., his strategies of producing song], that they will come to understand things and perhaps say something novel back. My son and I even acted out sequences in which he will agree to answer to his whistled name so that the birds can connect my whistling of my son's name not only with hand gestures toward him but with his whistling back toward me . . . (Trivers, 1990, p. 187)

Such "experiments" are based upon the assumption that understanding between humans and other species is possible because, to use an old language, they share aspects of the *Umwelt*—in this case the abilities to perceive and respond similarly to visual and aural aspects of the situation. Using the general model of intersubjectivity presented in chapter 3, birds and humans share intersubjectivities that are antecedent to communication or formulation into language. They can apparently hear sounds similarly enough. It is through this that the whistling communication becomes possible. One can explain this through Darwinian logic (that animals and humans share an evolutionary past and therefore a common biological inheritance) or phenomenological one (wherein intersubjectivity in the everyday world would be the same for "all possibly imagined monads").

16. For a discussion of directed gaze in humans and cats see Goodwin and Bradshaw (1997). Also see Garfinkel (2002, p. 209).

17. As described in the text at several points, members can and do have radically divergent interpretations of "intent behind" particular conversational utterances, as well as of what is going on generally. While all utterances and expressions are indexical, requiring knowledge of the speaker and circumstances in order to be interpretable, it would be entirely mistaken to interpret indexicality to mean that hearers of an utterance therefore hear it in the same way, and as the intended meaning of the speaker or signer.

18. The study of deceit in dog-human play has been given some attention. Trivers remarks "your act of fooling me is not a morally neutral act (1990, p. 184)." Vicki Hearne's writing is filled with examples of dogs (and other animals) deceiving or tricking their guardians and trainers, as are the writings of other dog observers. Mitchell and his colleagues acknowledge the importance of this topic. My own observation, based upon watching Katie and Jack at home, is that dog play has a definite moral dimension to it, as well as a power dimension. It is moral in the sense that one or more of the players can either adhere to or violate (play with) some trusted state of affairs. What and how this is done can constitute either acceptable or unacceptable alterations and may produce verbal (human) and gestural (dog) expressions thereof. When such actions are observable in dog-human or human-human play, they are indications of a moral dimension of play for players. See Mitchell & Thompson (1993) for an extended discussion of deception in dog-human play.

19. One would think (following Schutz here) that various types of temporal structures would be part of Sabaka's experience, without any way implying that these would be qualitatively comparable to human experience of temporality. Importantly in this regard, whatever their subjective experience, human and dog time(s) are at least similar enough to provide for the possibility of every day coordinated action, in the here and now and in longer terms. Further, play transforms players in its creation of played time, the temporalities of the play actions themselves. These temporalities were not the same as clock time or marked time. Similar to this argument, there is some arbitrariness to asserting that an animal with various senses should be understood through its dominant sense, relegating the others into the background. It would be akin to saying human beings should be understood primarily through their vision. Dogs have sight, hearing, touch, smell, and sense time and if this is what Shapiro intends by the phrase "bodily experience" then what he is writing makes more sense than a narrower interpretation. The idea that dogs are primarily olfactory creatures, as opposed to "bodily" is common in the literature. An interesting fictional example may be found in Olaf Stapleton's science-fiction novelette *Sirius*.

Notes to Chapter 7

1. As a member of a listserv on which there are ethnomethodologists and other sociologists, nicknamed the "Ethno Hotline," I announced my study of playing with Katie in hope that others with similar interests would respond. What I actually received in response was a barrage of e-mails, some supporting what I had announced and some that were absolutely incredulous about the idea of studying playing with a dog. My announcement and a couple of examples of each type of response will indicate how ambivalent these responses were.

Without sharing the entirety of my posting about studying playing with Katie, the following is the end of that text.

> I am currently conducting research on playing ball with my dog. I have collected several hours of videotape and some ethnographic materials related to this topic. The analysis is motivated by the activity's ordinariness, unremarkability (seen but unnoticed), apparent unanalyzability, massive social presence, regularity, recurrence, i.e., its social facticity in the contingently, just here, just now, first time through again, sense of social facticity employed by contemporary EM. The purpose of the analysis is to achieve a praxiological account and natural history of our playing ball together. It is not concerned primarily with addressing issues related to animal mindedness, human-animal relations generally speaking, animal human communication, and various other formal analytic foundational treatments of such issues, I would like to try and understand what Katie . . . and my ball playing together consists of in this instance.

I thought this was stated clearly and would be unproblematic, especially to a community of ethnomethodologically sympathetic readers. I requested persons with similar interests respond. I received postings that even doubted the seriousness of my announcement. The fact that the reaction to this study by other ethnomethodologists, and ethnomethodological sympathizers, was so ambivalent indicated that it was unclear, at least to others in the community to which these data were intended to be meaningful, that they were socially meaningful representations serving the social purposes of some specific group. Responses to the announcement of this study indicated ambivalence to the very idea of the project, let alone meaningfulness of the data collected. On the one hand there were those who apparently understood the idea fully, and without any reservation endorsed it and even offered help. On the other, there were those who did not even take the project seriously, even in one instance questioning whether the posting was a joke on the members of the listserv! (I must admit how much I enjoyed reading that particular posting.) Here are a few incredulous reactions, questioning the location of this inquiry and its data in the research community to which they were intended.

> At first I thought it is a joke. But maybe it isn't. So consider your final utterance
> . . .
>
> And, I second [the above person's] inquiry. I just didn't bother to respond, I'm glad someone else did. Any answers out there?

And,

> If your posting was a joke, you should learn to be clearer in your cues. If your posting was not a joke, you should realize that dogs are much better at interpreting these cues than humans are—so much better that it's difficult to see if you would learn anything about humans', rather than dogs', skills. It might be very depressing to see how strong a bond is formed by skill at interpreting cues, completely independent of intelligence, social responsibility, physical appearance, publications and presentations, and all those things we spend our lives on.

These incredulous comments were met on the Ethno Hotline with many "defenses" of my project and its rationality, ethnomethodological merit, relevance to previous discussions in social science and so on. But through these ambivalent reactions I was led more acutely to the question, for what purpose and to whom is this document, these videotapes, the rendered images from the videos, intended? What is their work and to whom is that work directed?

First and foremost the text and audiovisual data are things constructed in use and intended-to-be-used, by me. Their production and my own interest in their analysis reflects my training as an ethnomethodologist, and my own particular understanding of the ethnomethodological project. While their comments were not specifically methodological or directed to matters of videography, because of the response I was forced to think more clearly about how and why I used the video technologies available to me as I did. The inquiry was motivated by those "in order to" motives that were presented in the biographical introduction, and in these senses reflects years of thought about the analysis of everyday social orders and its epistemology and methodology. The data bear the stamp, even if not always clearly visible, of that motive. The work of constructing these data, visual and textual, is primarily to allow me to build an "adequate" description and analysis of my play with Katie—of an instance of ordinary society. While I am building for myself, it is in a way that intends as an audience other ethnomethodologists and other social scientists studying dog-human interaction. I believe it was G. K. Chesterson who wrote, "I don't write for those who don't get it." That is true of this research. The researcher's conception of who these persons are and what we share in common are built into the way the data are constructed-in-use and employed-in-analysis.

That the videotape data were "constructed in use" is meant descriptively, not as a principled or theoretical statement. Similarly, the video-captured sequences were carefully chosen and produced in order to illustrate textually labeled features of play to which they "corresponded." Both forms of visual data were intended to provide visual details of the events described in the written data by utilizing the various devices and assumptions described by Braun and Green (1986). Because of the careful editing and selection of taped materials and the detailed instruction contained within the text as to how to see them, images and tape were transformed into documentary evidences of the textually constructed "underlying patterns." They are so thoroughly documentary in nature and that there is little way for them to serve the author as data in the traditional sense (i.e., as ways of deconstructing investigating features of naturally available play). This is the method, the analytic device, that gave life to the version of play presented in this book.

As I pursued publication and engaged in exchanges with various reviewers I came to understand that there is another audience, those who have a genuine interest in the mundane practices witnessed in dog-human relationships, and who have first hand knowledge of "these objects in themselves." In spite of the ethnomethodological terminology and discussions, it will be those who know dogs best who will most likely appreciate what is in the autoethnography and the visual data. Once, after showing a tape of me playing with Katie at a faculty seminar, I was interrupted by a colleague just as I began to explain it. She owns three dogs and remarked, "you don't have to explain it to me, I see it every morning," and then began her own exposition. (The "it" to which she referred is the "order" part of the "lived order" of playing with dogs.) Because of the vulgar availability of many forms of retrieve play, general and even "idiosyncratic" features can be known to the population that staffs it.

For the readership familiar with dogs, the videographic data will serve to remind them, as it did my colleague, of details of well-known practices. Unlike Marey and other early scientists using photography, their interest, as my own in the current research, will not be in videotape's capacity to reveal what they cannot ordinarily see. Instead, it is the ability of the video data to display the details of the "already familiar," to make these details more easily inspectable and appreciable, that will interest the dog trainer and pet guardian. Neither would look to such data to discover the essence or essentials of human-dog play.

References

Adell-Bath, M., Krook, A., Sandqvist, G. & Skantz, K. 1979. *Do we need dogs? A study of dogs' social significance to man.* Gothenburg: Gothenburg University Press.

Angus, personal communication, no date as cited by Hart (1995).

Aries, P. 1962. *Centuries of childhood: A social history of family life.* New York: Knopf.

Aristotle. 1962. *Nichomachean ethics,* Book II. Indianapolis: Library of Liberal Arts, pp. 15–25.

Arluke, A. & Sanders, C. 1996. *Regarding animals.* Philadelphia: Temple University Press.

The Barnhart concise dictionary of etymology: The origins of American English Words. 1995. Edited by Robert K. Barnhart. New York: The H. W. Wilson Company.

Bekoff, M. & Allen, C. 1998. Intentional communication and social play: How and why animals negotiate and agree to play. In M. Bekoff & J. Beyers (Eds.), *Animal play: Evolutionary, comparative and ecological perspectives.* Cambridge: Cambridge University Press.

Bogdan, R. & Taylor, S. 1989. Relationships with severely disabled people: The social construction of humanness. *Social Problems* 36, no. 2: 135–148.

Braun, M. 1992. *Picturing time: The work of Etienne-Jules Marey (1830–1904).* Chicago: University of Chicago Press.

Button, G. 1991. *Ethnomethodology and the human sciences.* Cambridge: Cambridge University Press.

Castenada, C. 1972. *Journey to Ixtlan: The lessons of Don Juan.* New York: Simon & Schuster.

———. 1971. *A separate reality: Further conversations with Don Juan.* New York: Simon & Schuster.

Cicourel, A. 1964. *Methods and measurement in sociology.* New York: Free Press

———. 1974. *Cognitive sociology: Language and meaning in the social sciences.* New York: Free Press.

Clark, S. 1987. The description and evaluation of animal emotion. In C. Blakemore & S. Greenfield (Eds.) 1999. *Mindwaves: Thoughts on intelligence, identity and consciousness.* Oxford: Basil Blackwell Ltd.

Coulter, J. 1983. *Rethinking cognitive theory.* New York: St. Martin's Press.

Crist, E. 1996. Darwin's anthropomorphism: An argument for animal-human continuity. *Advances in Human Ecology* 5: 33–83.

Darwin, C. 1872 (1998). *The expression of emotions in man and animals,* third edition. Oxford: Oxford University Press.

Durkheim, E. 1938. *The rules of sociological method.* Chicago: University of Chicago Press.

Fisher, J.A. 1991. Disambiguating anthropomorphism: An interdisciplinary review. In P. P. G. Bateson & P. H. Klopfer (Eds.), *Human understanding and animal awareness.* Perspectives in Ethology, vol. 9. New York: Plenum.

Garfinkel, H.G. 1967. *Studies in ethnomethodology.* Englewood Cliffs, NJ: Prentice Hall.

Garfinkel, H.G. 1996. Ethnomethodology's program. *Social Psychology Quarterly* 59, no. 1: 5–21.

———. 2002. *Ethnomethodology's program: Working out Durkheim's aphorism.* Ann W. Rawls (Ed.). Lanham, Maryland: Rowman & Littlefield Publishers, Inc.

Garfinkel, H.G. & Sacks, H. 1969. On formal structures of practical action. In *Theoretical sociology*, J.C. McKinney & E. Tiryakan (Eds.). New York: Appleton-Century and Crofts.

Garfinkel, H.G. & Wieder, D.L. 1992. Two incommensurable, asymmetrically alternate technologies of social analysis. In G.W. Watson & R.M. Seiler (Eds.), *Text in context.* Newbury Park, NJ: Sage.

Goode, D. 1983. Who is Bobby? In G. Kielhofner (Ed.), *Health through occupation.* Philadelphia: F.A. Davis.

———. 1994a. *A world without words: The social construction of children born deaf-blind.* Philadelphia: Temple University Press.

———, ed. 1994b. *Quality of life for persons with disabilities: International perspectives and issues.* Cambridge, MA: Brookline Books.

———. 1996. A general phenomenology of intersubjectivity with children born deaf-blind and who fail to develop formal language: Further reflections on *A World without Words.* In *The development of communication: What is new?* Suresnes, France: Editions du Centre national de Suresnes.

Goode, D. & Waksler, F.C. 1990. The "missing who": Situational identity and fault finding with an alingual deaf-blind child. *Sociological Studies of Child Development* 3: 203–223.

Goodwin, D. & Bradshaw, J. 1997 (n.p). Gaze and mutual gaze: Its importance in cat/human and cat/cat interaction. Paper presented at the meeting of the International Society of Anthrozoology. Boston, July 24–25.

Green, D. 1986. Veins of resemblance: Photography and eugenics. In Patricia Holland, Jo Spence and Simon Watney, *Photography and politics—Two.* London: Comedia Publishing Group.

Grünwald, E. 1934 (1970). Systematic analysis. In J.E. Curtis & J.W. Petras (Eds.), *The sociology of knowledge: A reader.* New York: Praeger, p. 222.

Harper, D. 1994. *The new complete Welsh corgi.* New York: Howell Book House.

Hart, L.A. 1995. Dogs as human companions: A review of the relationship. In J. Serpell (Ed.), *The domestic dog: Its evolution, behaviour and interactions with people.* Cambridge: Cambridge University Press.

Hearne, V. 1986. *Adam's task: Calling animals by name.* New York: Vintage Books.

———. 1994. *Animal happiness.* New York: Harper Collins Publishers, Inc.

Hebb, D.O. 1946. Emotion in man and animal: An analysis of the intuitive processes of recognition. *Psychological Review* 53, pp: 88–106.

———. 1949. Temperament in chimpanzees: I. Method of analysis. *Journal of Comparative Psychology* 42: 192–206.

Hempel, C. 1966. *The philosophy of natural science.* New York: Prentice Hall.

Hobhouse, L.T. 1901. *Mind in evolution.* London: Macmillan & Co.

———. 1915. *Mind in evolution,* 2nd edition. London: Macmillan & Co.

Huizinga, J. 1966 (1950). *Homo ludens: A study of the play element in culture.* London: Routledge & Kegan Paul.

Humane Society of the United States, 2004, www.hsus.org/ace/11831, June 24.

Kete, K. 1994. *The beast in the boudoir: Petkeeping in 19th century Paris.* Berkeley: University of California Press.

Latour, B. 1988. Mixing humans and nonhumans together: the sociology of the door closer. *Social Problems* 35, no. 3.

Lemonick, M.E. 2005. Honor among beasts. *Time,* July 11.

Lynch, M. 1997. Ethnomethodology without indifference. *Human Studies* 20: 371–376.

———. 1993. *Scientific practice and ordinary action: Ethnomethodology and the social study of science.* New York: Cambridge University Press.

Mackay, R. 1973. Conceptions of children and models of socialization. In H.P. Dreitzel (Ed.) *Recent Sociology,* No. 5: 27–43, New York: Macmillan.

Mandel, N. 1991. The least-adult role.... In F.C. Waksler (Ed.), *Studying the social worlds of children.* London: Falmer Press.

Mannheim, K. 1936. *Ideology and utopia.* New York: International Library of Psychology, Philosophy and Scientific Method.

Merleau-Ponty, M. 1962. *The phenomenology of perception.* London: Routledge & Kegan Paul.

Messent, P. R. 1983. Social facilitation of contact with other people by companion dogs. In A.H. Katcher & A.M. Beck (Eds.), *New perspectives on our lives with companion animals.* Philadelphia: Temple University Press, pp. 37–46.

Michalko, R. 1999. *The two in one: Walking with Smokie, walking with blindness.* Philadelphia: Temple University Press.

Mitchell, R.W. 1990. A theory of play. In M. Bekoff and D. Jamieson (Eds.), *Interpretation and explanation in the study of animal behavior.* Boulder, Co.: Westview Press, pp. 197–225.

Mitchell, R.W. 1997a. Anthropomorphic anecdotalism as method. In R.W. Mitchell, N.S. Thompson, & H. Lyn Miles (Eds.), *Anthropomorphism, anecdotes and animals,* pp. 151–169. Albany, NY: SUNY Press.

———. 1997b. Anthropomorphism and anecdotes: A guide for the perplexed. In R.W. Mitchell, N.S. Thompson, & H. Lyn Miles (Eds.), *Anthropomorphism, anecdotes and animals,* pp. 407-427. Albany, NY: SUNY Press.

Mitchell, R.W. & Hamm, M. 1997. The interpretation of animal psychology: Anthropomorphism or behavior reading? *Behaviour* 134: 173–204.

Mitchell, R.W. & Thompson, N.S. 1986. Deception in play between dogs and people. In R.W. Mitchell & N.S. Thompson (Eds.), *Deception: Perspectives on human and nonhuman deceit.* Albany, NY: State University of New York Press.

Mitchell, R.W. & Thompson, N.S. 1990. The effects of familiarity on dog-human play. *Anthrozoös* 4, no. 1: 24–43.

Mitchell, R.W. & Thompson, N.S. 1991. Projects, routines, and enticements in dog-human play. In P.P.G. Bateson & P.H. Klopfer (Eds.), *Perspectives in human ethology* New York: Plenum Press, pp. 189–216.

Mitchell, R.W. & Thompson, N.S. 1993. Familiarity and the rarity of deception: Two theories and their relevance to play between dogs *(Canis familiaris)* and humans *(Homo sapiens). Journal of Comparative Psychology* 7, no. 3: 291–300.

Mitchell. R.W., Thompson, N.S., & Miles, H.L. (Eds.) 1997. *Anthropomorphism, anecdotes and animals.* Albany, NY: SUNY Press.

Nash, J.E. 1989. What's in a face? The social character of the English bulldog. *Qualitative Sociology* 12, no. 4: 357–370.

Picard, M. 1961 (1948). *The world of silence.* Chicago: Henry Regnery Co.

Pollner, M. 1987. *Mundane reason: Reality in everyday and sociological discourse.* Cambridge: Cambridge University Press.

Pollner, M. & Goode, D., 1990. EM and person-centering practices. *Person-Centered Review* 5, no. 2: 203–220.

Postman, N. 1982 (1994). *The disappearance of childhood*. New York: Vintage Books.

Sacks, H. n.d., n.p. A foundation for sociology. Manuscript, Department of Sociology, University of California Los Angeles.

Sacks, H. 1967. Lecture, introduction.

Sacks, O. 1996. *In search of Lucy Doe*. British Broadcasting Company II, Arte TV France, Rosetta Pictures. Produced by Christopher Rawlence.

Sanders, C. R. 1999. *Understanding dogs: Living and working with canine companions*. Philadelphia: Temple University Press.

Schutz, A. 1974. *Collected papers I: The problem of social reality*. The Hague: Martinus Nijhoff.

Searle, J. 1983. *Intentionality*. Cambridge: Cambridge University Press.

Serpell, J. (Ed.) 1995. *The domestic dog: Its evolution, behaviour and interactions with people*. Cambridge: Cambridge University Press.

Shapiro, Kenneth J. 1990. Understanding dogs through kinesthetic empathy, social construction and history. *Anthrozoös* 3, No. 3: pp. 184–195.

Sigman, S. 1983. Pets and their owners: A pilot ethnography. *Final Report to the Gerontology Center, Institute for Human Development*, Pennsylvania State University, and the Green Island Foundation (June).

Stallones, L., Marx, M., Garritty, T.F., & Johnson, T.P. 1988. Attachment to companion animals among older pet guardians. *Anthrozoos* 2, 118–124.

Temerlin, M.K., 1975. *Lucy: Growing up human: A chimpanzee in a psychoanalyst's family*. New York: Souvenir Press.

Trivers, R. 1990. Deceit and self-deception. In J.K. Eisenberg (Ed.), *Man and beast*.

Turner, D.C., 1985. The human-cat relationship: Methods analysis. In *The human pet relationship*. Vienna: IEMT, 147–152.

von Uexkull, J. 1934. A stroll through the worlds of animals and men. In K. Lashley & C. Schiller, *Instinctive behavior*. New York: International Press.

Wieder, D.L. 1980. Behavioristic Operationalism and the Life-World: Chimpanzees and Chimpanzee Researchers in Face-to-Face Interaction, *Sociological Inquiry* 50, Nos. 3–4: pp. 75–103.

Wittgenstein, L. 1953 (1958). *Philosophical Investigations, Third Edition*. Trans. G.E.M. Anscombe. New York: Macmillan Publishing Company, Inc.

Index

www.ingramcontent.com/pod-product-compliance
Lightning Source LLC
Chambersburg PA
CBHW071855270326
41929CB00013B/2237